Praying with One Eye Open

PRAYING WITH ONE EYE OPEN

MORMONS *and* MURDER *in* NINETEENTH-CENTURY APPALACHIAN GEORGIA

MARY ELLA ENGEL

The University of Georgia Press
Athens

© 2019 by the University of Georgia Press
Athens, Georgia 30602
www.ugapress.org
All rights reserved
Designed by Erin Kirk New
Set in 10 on 14 Walbaum

Most University of Georgia Press titles are
available from popular e-book vendors.

Printed digitally

Library of Congress Cataloging-in-Publication Data

Names: Engel, Mary Ella, 1953- author.
Title: Praying with one eye open : Mormons and murder in
nineteenth-century Appalachian Georgia / Mary Ella Engel.
Description: Athens : University of Georgia Press, [2019] | Includes
bibliographical references and index. | Appendix 1. North George
converts organized by Branch; Appendix 2. Members of mob accused
of Elder Joseph Standing's murder.
Identifiers: LCCN 2019008098| ISBN 9780820355610 (pbk. : alk. paper) |
ISBN 9780820355252 (hardback : alk. paper) |
ISBN 9780820355245 (e-book)
Subjects: LCSH: Church of Jesus Christ of Latter-day Saints—
Georgia—History—19th century. | Mormon Church—Georgia—
History—19th century. | Mormon missionaries—Georgia—History—
19th century. | Standing, Joseph, 1854-1879.
Classification: LCC BX8615.G46 E54 2019 2019 |
DDC 289.3/75809034—dc23
LC record available at https://lccn.loc.gov/2019008098

For Emily, Laney, and Sophie

And when he said, Amen, we looked back, and there were four men . . . with guns on their shoulders. I said to my companion, "that is another lesson, from this time on in the South, I shall pray with one eye open."

—J. Golden Kimball, LDS Southern States missionary, 1883

Contents

Acknowledgments xi

List of Illustrations xv

Introduction 1

CHAPTER 1.
"I Find My Dream Literally Fulfilled":
John Morgan in Georgia 8

CHAPTER 2.
"There Is Something Terrible Coming": Establishment
of the North Georgia Mission Field 23

CHAPTER 3.
"One by One They Leave Us": The First Expedition
of Georgians to the West 43

CHAPTER 4.
"Women Is the Only Subject to Be Talked On":
Threats of Violence in North Georgia 66

CHAPTER 5.
"The Day of Grace Is Gone": The Murder of
Joseph Standing 101

CHAPTER 6.
"Think Not When You Gather to Zion,
Your Troubles and Trials Are Through":
Georgia and the Mormon Question   128

Conclusion   150

APPENDIX 1.
North Georgia Converts Organized by Branch   155

APPENDIX 2.
Members of Mob Accused of
Elder Joseph Standing's Murder   181

Notes   187

Index   221

Acknowledgments

It was 1998 when I first learned of Elder Joseph Standing's murder. An undergraduate history major at Kennesaw State University, I had been granted the honor of cataloguing the Bowling C. Yates Papers, now featured in the Georgia History Collection of the KSU Archives. As Yates was the first superintendent of Kennesaw Mountain National Battlefield Park and the man chiefly responsible for the park's early development, his papers deserved organization, and that became my responsibility. So between classes, I huddled in one corner of a library storage room and attempted to make sense of a lifetime's worth of documents. During breaks, I entertained myself by reading his field notes, recorded in small, cramped handwriting in compact, pocket-sized journals. A keen student of Georgia history, Yates enjoyed a good story, and his journals contained dozens of them, conveyed to him by informants he met as he traveled the state. One of those stories drew my attention, becoming the topic of my dissertation and claiming—so far—a good twenty years of my life. The storyteller, an old man from north Georgia, confided to Yates that he had once participated in a "Mormon massacre." Yates did not afford the claim serious consideration; in fact, he dismissed the account as the product of a "damn liar." I, on the other hand, was captivated. Mormons? Massacre? In north Georgia?

It was at Kennesaw State University that I first learned to do historical research. I am eternally grateful to Thomas A. Scott, who introduced me to the challenges and pleasures of archival research and taught me the importance of local history. I could not have asked for a more generous mentor. I was similarly blessed at the University of Georgia, where I benefitted from the wisdom and encouragement of the history faculty. I am especially grateful for the thoughtful consideration of my dissertation committee: John Inscoe, Kathleen Clark, Jim Cobb, and Diane Batts Morrow. With typical humor, Jim Cobb challenged me when I first told him about this study: "If this is just about Georgians behaving badly, there's nothing new about that." I appreciate his tolerance and hope I've convinced him that this is a story worth telling. Kathleen Clark and Diane Batts Morrow provided sound advice and feedback, and I am forever grateful to them. I am singularly indebted to John Inscoe, who shepherded me through the doctoral program, guided my dissertation, and continues to play a central role in my life as advisor, mentor, and friend. My admiration of and appreciation for him are unparalleled. I once told him that he was my role model in all things, understanding full well that I could never achieve his scholarly expertise but hoping that I might manage to emulate his extraordinary kindness. I continue to work toward that goal.

Many others helped me as I researched and wrote this book. I appreciate my friends in the Society of Appalachian Historians who valued and informed this work, especially the late Durwood Dunn, Gordon McKinney, Bruce Stewart, Steve Nash, and Andy Slap. Thanks to Ron Butchart and Amy Rolleri, whose extraordinary work on the Freedmen's Teachers Project set the standard for historical research.

I benefitted greatly from the generous support I received from the Joseph Fielding Smith Institute for LDS History at Brigham Young University. It was in Provo that I first met Richard L. Jensen, then a research historian at the institute and now coeditor on the Joseph Smith Papers Project. Thank you, Richard, for making me welcome during my many research trips to Provo and Salt Lake City. I am indebted as well to the archivists, librarians, and staff members at Brigham Young University and the University of Utah.

It was a great privilege to work at the LDS Church History Library in Salt Lake City. Though I am not a member of the church, the very knowledgeable scholars, librarians, and staff welcomed me and patiently endured endless questions and requests for archival materials. In Georgia, I relied upon the expertise of the archivists at the Georgia Department of Archives and History who provided vast collections of court, military, and tax records that inform this book. The public historians at the Whitfield-Murray Historical Society generously shared their knowledge with me, and I am especially grateful to Marcelle Coker, who volunteered to drive me to the site of Joseph Standing's murder in the early days of this project.

Numerous individuals have contacted me over the years—from Utah and Georgia—to share their own family histories and memories. Patricia Dockery, Karen B. Keeley, Vera Edna Browning Kimball, and Janet Stoddard all reached out and provided me with information that helped me re-create nineteenth-century families, neighbors, and communities. Any mistakes in the genealogies produced are mine and not theirs.

I am fortunate to have found a home at Western Carolina University, where I am surrounded by caring and supportive colleagues. Thanks to Saheed Aderinto, Rob Clines, Andy Denson, David Dorondo, Rob Ferguson, Ben Francis-Fallon, Gael Graham, Alex Macaulay, Libby McRae, Scott Philyaw, Jessie Swigger, and Vicki Szabo. As I tell them all the time, I am so proud to be a member of this faculty. I learn from them and I am inspired by them. Richard Starnes is my dean, my colleague, and my friend, and merits a special thank-you for championing me throughout my professional journey. I am also grateful for the encouragement and support of Jim Lewis, Honor Sachs, Kathy Orr, Rebecca Scheidt, Sue Abram, and Sam McGuire. Former WCU graduate student Beverly Ellis spent long hours transcribing handwritten census records from microfilm and assembling the data that are foundational to this study. I cannot properly express my appreciation for her hard work.

How fortunate I also am to be working with the good people at the University of Georgia Press who have guided me through this process. My editor, Mick Gusinde-Duffy, has supported me from the very beginning, and I am profoundly grateful for both his insight and patience. Thanks to Thomas Roche and Beth Snead and everyone involved in the process of copyediting, design, and production. I appreciate Joseph Dahm's careful attention to the manuscript (which involved reining in my extravagant use of commas, among other things). I am grateful for the assistance of Don Larson and Rob McCaleb of Mapping Specialists, Ltd., who took my notes gleaned from census reports, tax records, and missionary diaries and managed to create an extraordinary map of the nineteenth-century mission field in north Georgia.

As I wrote this book about families, I thought often of my own family. My mother did not live long enough to see this book published, but I think she would be so pleased. My father has encouraged me every step of the way, reading endless drafts, offering sage advice, and urging me on when my energy flagged. From him, I have learned what it means to be persistent, resilient, and loyal. In many ways, this is his book, too. My children, Scott and Sarah, are still the best gift I will ever give the world. I hope they realize that my primary goal in life is to make them proud. Through Sarah I gained Kevin, and I am so grateful for him. My sister, Susan, who loves ferociously and unconditionally, always cheers me on. She and her husband, Jay, seem to have forgiven me for not always paying adequate attention to their lives, and I hope they know how much I appreciate that they take better care of me than I do of them. To Lu and Jim Mottley, thank you for the love and laughter, and your sometimes-irrational belief that I would finally finish this book. Your confidence gave me confidence. I am grateful to my cousin Melanie Hall, whose Appalachian journey mirrors my own, and with whom I share a love of these ancient mountains. Thank you, Melanie and Bill, for keeping me grounded.

I am especially blessed to have three granddaughters who are an endless source of joy. To Emily, Laney, and Sophie—who affectionately (and apparently without irony) call their grandmother "Dodo"—this book is for you.

Illustrations

FIGURE 1. John Hamilton Morgan, president of Southern States Mission   9

FIGURE 2. Warning to the Mormon elders   72

FIGURE 3. Elders Joseph Standing and Rudger Clawson   92

FIGURE 4. Joseph Standing's grave in Salt Lake City, Utah   124

FIGURE 5. Face of Standing Monument naming members of the Georgia mob   125

FIGURE 6. Face of Standing Monument declaring, "There is no law in Georgia for the Mormons"   125

FIGURE 7. Mary (Molly) Hamblin in Colorado   145

FIGURE 8. Group portrait from the LDS Sunday School in Colorado   146

FIGURE 9. Stone that marks the spot in Whitfield County where Joseph Standing fell   151

MAP 1. North Georgia Mission Field, 1876–1879   24

Praying with One Eye Open

Introduction

In 1879, Samuel Street and William P. Schultz cooperated to produce a survey map of Whitfield County, Georgia. Though Street surveyed the land, Schultz drew the map, assigning property owners to individual squares on a carefully drawn grid and marking the locations of important social and industrial landmarks: stores, schools, mills, and churches. He identified topographical features as well as the routes of two railroads that intersected in the county seat of Dalton. And in the northwest portion of the county, where Whitfield hugs the border of Catoosa County, the mapmakers chose to commemorate a place of such local significance that it merited a designation on the map—a location unique as the only one linked specifically to an *event*. Schultz's precise lettering identified a small black dot as the "spot where Mormon Standing was killed, July 1879."[1]

Sixteen months after he first carried his message into north Georgia, Mormon elder Joseph Standing was dead, murdered by a mob of twelve men. To the Church of Jesus Christ of Latter-day Saints (LDS Church), Standing's murder represented only the latest in a series of religious persecutions, dating back to the church's emergence out of the "burned-over" district of western New York State during the period of intense revivalism known as the Second Great Awakening. Founded by Joseph Smith Jr. in 1830—the same year that Smith produced the Book of Mormon—the LDS Church attracted both derision and devotion. Critics questioned Smith's claim that the Book of Mormon was revealed to him and that its translation was divinely inspired, while church members accepted Smith as prophet and embraced his vision of a restored Christian church. Similar to other restorationist movements of the time, Latter-day Saints believed in a return to the primitive church, Hebrew ideals, and Old Testament practices. Accordingly, Latter-day Saints rejected all existing religions, believing them to be apostate versions of Christ's church.[2]

Missionaries from the LDS Church first traveled south in the 1830s, but it was 1843 before the first Mormon elder reached Georgia, and then only to pass through the state on his way from Alabama to North Carolina. The church did assign four missionaries to Georgia in 1844 to preach the gospel and campaign on behalf of Joseph Smith's bid for the presidency; however, that endeavor proved of short duration, cut short by the assassination of the candidate. Still, Mormon historian Leonard Arrington estimated that in the church's antebellum efforts in the South, as many as two hundred thirty Mormon elders baptized at least thirteen hundred southern converts. Of that number, at least a thousand "and probably many more" converts left the South to join Mormon settlements, including the "cotton missionaries" sent to southern Utah's "Dixie" to cultivate the staple. In the years just prior to the Civil War, missionary activity in the South virtually ceased. With the abatement of sectional warfare, missionaries ventured from Utah again—and back to the South. The area served by the Southern States Mission of the 1870s quickly earned a reputation for violence and persecution.[3]

The 1879 murder of Southern States missionary Joseph Standing in Georgia confirmed the region's notoriety. Despite that, there have been few modern examinations of Elder Standing's death. Most link his murder to the virulent nineteenth-century anti-Mormonism that also cost the church its first prophet as well as an enduring southern tradition of extralegal violence; thus, Standing's death resulted from Georgians' religious intolerance coupled with an abiding martial spirit that encouraged mob violence. Historians also point to southern concerns with maintaining status, reputation, and order, which often dictated a violent response to those perceived as disrupting social norms. Or, it has been suggested, perhaps the frustrations and dislocations of the postbellum South encouraged a violent reaction against "spiritual carpetbaggers." Scholars who noticed that Elder Standing met his death in Georgia's mountains also refer to a distinctive highland culture, isolated and fearful of outsiders, characterized by feuding, whitecapping, and collective violence of moonshiners against local informers and federal agents.[4]

In the quest to explain the persecution of Mormons as part of a larger pattern of southern extralegal violence, all these explanations ring at least partially true. An acknowledgment of Georgia's violent past, however, does not mean that anti-Mormon violence, particularly Standing's murder, should be attributed to a general regional proclivity toward violence, as such treatments lack explanatory power. This book offers a different view, arguing that the mob violence against Standing was a *local* event, best understood at the *local* level. As the evidence confirms, the men who erupted in violent opposition to LDS missionaries were motivated by what they perceived as the negative impact of Mormon proselytizing on families and community. In this examination, Standing's murder becomes a tool to uncover the complex social relationships that linked north Georgians—families, kin, neighbors, and coreligionists—and to illuminate the ways in which mob violence attempted to resolve the psychological dissonance created by Mormon missionaries.[5]

In laying bare the bonds linking Georgia converts to the mob, this book reveals Standing's murder as more than simply mountain lawlessness or religious persecution; rather, it is a consequence of tensions resulting from separating converts from loved ones and dependents from heads of household. Initially, southern Saints fashioned a new Georgia community of likeminded believers. Ultimately, they transferred that community to Manassa, Colorado, answering the church's call to "gather" in the new western Zion. It can be no coincidence that the men accused of Standing's murder were connected to converts who had left, or were preparing to leave, for the West. If this was, as it seems, a *private* mob, is it possible that family—or, more precisely, the preservation of family—prompted the violent behavior of the mobbers? In 1879, Georgia newspapers suggested just such a motive. According to published reports, the people of north Georgia "were determined not to submit to see Christians led astray and families broken up" by Mormon missionaries. Another local newspaper justified the attack on Standing as a defense of household and womanhood, explaining that the "good citizens" of north Georgia "could not stand any longer the bad influence that his preaching had upon the female portion of the neighborhood."[6]

It is true that conversion to the LDS Church in the nineteenth century often created distance, both religious and geographic, between neighbors and kin. The Mormon practice of plural marriage, or polygamy, also convinced unconverted Georgians that neighbors and loved ones had been seduced into a corrupt and licentious religion and invited suspicions that missionaries focused their efforts on north Georgia's women. Later, the *Atlanta Constitution* would attempt to reassure readers that only undesirable women left Georgia for the Mormon colony in the West. Readers should not be concerned about the losses, a reporter wrote, as the converts "were mostly poor and shiftless folks, and generally past middle age. One or two pretty girls are known to have gone, but most of the women were old and ugly." While the loss of poor, old, and ugly women did not concern Atlanta residents overmuch, especially as they felt safely removed from the intensity of Mormon proselytizing, the writer correctly identified the gender anxiety that would cost Elder Standing his life. When north Georgia's women conspicuously violated dominant gender orthodoxies in their defiant support for, and defense of, Mormon missionaries, they invited the intervention of male members of the community. Fearing the loss of mountain women to the West and angry at their own inability to control female religion and sexuality, mountain men first attempted to discipline unruly females, then rose up in opposition against the Mormon elders. Had Standing's message been less persuasive, he may have escaped harm; the success of his conversion efforts all but guaranteed retaliation from those intent on enforcing cultural norms and defending their own households.[7]

Such tensions can be revealed only by studies of family and kin, locality and community. Appalachian scholars have frequently employed such concentrated studies in order to counter persistent theories about Appalachian exceptionalism, yielding important insights into mountain race relations and class distinctions and challenging stereotypical notions about Appalachian isolation, backwardness, and sectional loyalty. Such community-wide studies provide useful models for this study of social life in northwest Georgia. An examination at this level reveals the attendant loyalties and stresses that accompanied community relationships and thus challenges descriptions of community as a mechanism that encourages unity and order; instead, community is revealed as a location where disagreement, as well as agreement, takes place.

Though the murderers' motivations can be traced to local disruptions, the implications of this study go far beyond the local. The animus against Standing and other LDS missionaries was certainly informed and reinforced by anti-Mormon rhetoric that regularly flowed from southern pulpits and newspapers. Further, the murder itself thrust local actors and Georgia's mountain region into a national debate regarding the Church of Jesus Christ of Latter-day Saints. The Standing murder served as a convenient case in point for critics who employed it to advocate and rally public support for the continued repression of Mormonism at both the state and national levels. The debate would be only partially resolved in 1890 when the church officially abandoned plural marriage. The "Mormon Question" asked Americans to consider the limits of religious freedom, but also raised important questions about the proper role of government in defining marriage and family. These questions remain unresolved today.[8]

This religious mission to the Georgia mountains also tells us something about Appalachia. Because it places Mormon missionaries within the contested religious terrain that was Appalachia in the last decades of the nineteenth century, and prior to the Appalachian missions of mainstream Protestant denominations, this book changes the region's religious history. Also significant is the fact that the arrival of Mormon elders in northwest Georgia coincided with the social and economic dislocations that marked the transition from Reconstruction to the New South. The success of the missionaries and the lure of the western church reveal much of the postwar uncertainties and anxieties that characterized the period. Georgia converts responded to the familiar push-pull of migratory forces, and we can use their experiences in the postwar mountain South to better understand late nineteenth-century Georgia. Under the influence of the Latter-day Saints, hundreds of Georgia Saints left the state for a better life in the new Mormon Zion, an experience that transcends regional boundaries and places nineteenth-century Appalachian Georgians within broader national movements to the West.

Standing's death and the trials that followed occupy a central dramatic position in this narrative, but that tragic event represents neither the beginning nor the ending of the story. The beginning, in fact, dates back to 1864 and the man who organized and presided over the establishment of the LDS Church in Georgia, and ultimately the entire Southern States Mission—John Hamilton Morgan. Morgan left behind an extraordinary collection of documents. Mission reports (often published in Salt Lake City's *Deseret News*, which served as the mouthpiece for the church) document the establishment of the Georgia branches and the colony in Colorado, but Morgan's correspondence with supportive Saints in Utah and fellow Southern States missionaries as well as his private mission journal offer more intimate accounts of both the challenges and successes in the state. Morgan's papers also provide a unique window into the lives of his Georgia converts—ordinary mountain folks who found themselves at the center of local, state, and national efforts to restrict or eliminate the church.

As this book focuses on the lives of common folks, its importance may also reside in the attempt to restore ordinary Georgians to the historical record. A prominent Georgia historian once referred to the state's poor farmers as the "little" men, the "forgotten" men, of the late nineteenth century. In their own time, mountain farmers merited more derisive descriptions. In an 1873 article for *Lippincott's Magazine*, titled "A Strange Land and Peculiar People," Will Wallace Harney emphasized the physical and cultural isolation of southern mountaineers. Historian Henry D. Shapiro credits Harney with "discovering" Appalachia, a region at once "in but not of America." By the 1890s, mainstream Americans, especially those representing the nation's Protestant denominations, would mount missions to the mountains, dedicated to the material, spiritual, and cultural uplift of those for whom "peculiar" meant deprived, depraved, degraded, and degenerate.[9]

Coincidentally, Mormon apostle Orson Hyde addressed Salt Lake City's Mormons in 1873. "I will make a few remarks upon the idea of our being a peculiar people," he said. "You know that we are regarded as such, and if we look upon ourselves from a proper point of view, we shall readily admit that in this respect outsiders have given us an appropriate name; for we are a peculiar people whom God has chosen to serve and honor him." By "peculiar," Hyde meant, of course, that the Saints were a people set aside by God, chosen by God, though Americans beyond Utah might have applied Webster's conventional definition of *strange*, or *odd*, instead. This, then, is the history of an encounter between two "peculiar" peoples—Georgia's mountaineers and the Latter-day Saints—both perceived as requiring America's intervention.[10]

CHAPTER ONE

"I Find My Dream Literally Fulfilled"

John Morgan in Georgia

As 1876 drew to a close, Mormon missionary John Morgan penned a letter to the faithful in Salt Lake City. He had left his previous mission post, he reported, to travel to Georgia "in fulfillment of a desire to visit this country" and "in answer to a call to preach." A letter from Georgia prompted his relocation. He did not reveal the name or address of the southern correspondent, just the message, which was a request for "some one to come here and preach." Morgan responded immediately, borrowing money for train fare to Chattanooga, where he disembarked and set off on foot into the northwest corner of Georgia. It is not clear whether his arrival satisfied the needs of the letter writer, but the letter may have influenced his first decision, which was to carry his message to Rome in Floyd County. There he hoped to hold his first meeting, perhaps win his first converts. As he walked toward Rome, he found his mind wandering, so when he suddenly encountered a fork in the road, it startled him from his quiet meditation. He studied his two options, momentarily confused, "uncertain as to which road . . . would lead him to Rome." As he puzzled over the problem, he realized that he had once dreamed of just such a situation.[1]

In his dream, Brigham Young stood at the very fork in the road where Morgan now vacillated. The prophet addressed Morgan's indecision, explaining that the fork to the right would lead to Rome, his original destination; however, if Morgan took the road to the left, it would lead him to a profound spiritual

FIGURE 1. John Hamilton Morgan, president of the Southern States Mission. John H. Morgan Photograph Collection (P0605), box 1, folder 1, Special Collections, J. Willard Marriott Library, the University of Utah.

discovery. At the time the dream occurred, Morgan found it confusing, as he had not yet joined the LDS Church. So when he shared the strange dream with his Utah landlady over breakfast, it was "more in a spirit of joking and humor than anything else." His hostess understood Morgan's mental perambulations to be something more than amusing. She interpreted the dream, explaining that in the future he would be sent on a mission for the Mormon Church: "You will be going over the same road you saw in your dream and will come to that identical fork in the road. Brigham Young will not be there, but don't forget what he told you." A decade later, John Morgan remembered her advice. He faced the fork in the road and then turned left, away from Rome and toward the small settlement of Haywood Valley, where he would establish the first branch of the church in Georgia. He was, in fact, in Chattooga County, much closer to Dirt Town than Rome.[2]

"I find my dream literally fulfilled," Elder Morgan reported. In his letter, which was directed to the editor of the *Deseret*

News but intended to communicate mission news to supportive Saints as well as church authorities, he described the success of his Georgia labors. Though "the opposition has been bitter, as it usually is," his ten-week endeavor had produced satisfying results. "We have a good church building," he wrote, "controlled entirely by the Saints," and each Sabbath day he carried his message to new members and their families, an audience of about fifty Georgians. Further, he could report that most of that number intended to leave Georgia for the West, in order to gather with the Saints in Zion. John Morgan claimed no credit for his remarkable achievement; instead, he suggested that a greater force directed his movements. It may have been divine intervention that guided Morgan to Haywood Valley in 1876, but the road he traveled in northwest Georgia was a familiar one. As he neared that momentous and symbolic fork in the road, Morgan had been preoccupied, his mind reflecting back to his last passage down that same road—as a Union soldier in 1864.[3]

The Civil War carried Morgan far away from his farm home in Illinois, a distance measured in miles and maturity. John Morgan was born to parents Garrard and Eliza Morgan in Indiana but relocated with his family to Illinois in 1852 when he was ten years old. There the family of eight settled on a small farm in Coles County. Thomas and Sarah Bush Lincoln, the future president's father and stepmother, lived nearby, and the Morgan family followed Abraham Lincoln's political ascendency with great interest. Certainly devotion to the new president influenced John Hamilton Morgan's decision to enlist in the Union Army in 1862. Citizens of Illinois also perceived a real menace in Confederate movements toward Kentucky at that time. John Morgan believed, as many did, that if Confederates gained control of Kentucky, an invasion of Illinois would surely follow.[4]

Morgan was twenty years old and filled with enthusiasm for the Union cause when he mustered into service on September 6, 1862, as a private in Company I of the 123rd Illinois Infantry. Private Morgan found himself among thousands of new recruits sent to assist the Army of the Ohio as it addressed Confederate efforts in Kentucky. He had only a month's worth of soldiering to his credit when he prepared to engage the enemy for the first time at Perryville. Though Morgan survived, fully a quarter of the green troops of the 123rd Illinois fell at Perryville, most in a mad, unorganized downhill attack against approaching Confederates. Those who survived the initial attack quickly scrambled up the hill to safety, gained the crest, and then continued to run toward the rear. In the engagement at Perryville, an inglorious commencement to Morgan's military career, the 123rd Illinois paid a terrible price: a fourth of the regiment fell there, while the remainder broke and fled.[5]

Winter of 1863 found young Morgan languishing in camp in Murfreesboro, Tennessee, the 123rd Illinois now assigned to William S. Rosecrans's Army of the Cumberland. But his correspondence suggested no waning of enthusiasm for the war, even after Lincoln's Emancipation Proclamation of January 1 turned federal forces into "armies of liberation," a shift that discomfited countless folks back home. Newspapers passed among Union soldiers in the field, many containing editorials that decried an antislavery war. Morgan confided to his parents that he was feeling "a little riley" on hearing criticism of Lincoln, especially from Illinois citizens. "What in the name of all that is good and bad at once do the people of Illinois mean," he wrote, "every mail brings intelligence of dissatisfaction with the Administration; people cursing Lincoln for an abolitionist and everything else that can be thought of!" In the missive, he railed against both southern rebels and northern traitors: "Were it possible I would wish that Lincoln could assume the power of a dictator for 12 months and would hang every man that dared utter one word in favor of rebellion or peace." Lest his family should somehow misunderstand, he restated his resolve, writing, "We of the army are in for nothing but the subjugation or annihilation of the South."[6]

Morgan's ability to annihilate southern combatants ratcheted up sharply in the spring of 1863 when his regiment was assigned to Colonel John T. Wilder's mounted infantry brigade and equipped with Spencer repeating rifles. It was with spurs on his boots and new rifle at hand that Morgan mounted up in June 1863 and moved out in advance of the Army of the Cumberland toward Bragg's Confederates and Chattanooga. The city was the prize, and it seemed easily won, but the maneuvers of both armies carried the war, and Morgan, to the rough terrain of northwest Georgia. One imagines that Morgan eyed his surroundings with interest. Perhaps he considered the likelihood of encountering the enemy within the intimidating woods; he undoubtedly did not imagine a future in which he would tramp through the same terrain on behalf of the LDS Church.[7]

The Armuchee Ridges of northwest Georgia lie to the west of the Blue Ridge divide, at the southern end of the Appalachian Mountains. In 1863 dense forests of chestnuts, oaks, and hickories sheltered secluded mountain coves; between the ridges ran wide valleys, irrigated by numerous creeks, rivers, and mineral springs. The names assigned the waters provided Union troops with clues to the region's original inhabitants—Chattooga, Etowah, Coosa, Oostanaula, Conasauga, Coosawattee, Coahulla, Oothcalooga, and Chickamauga. Federals observed the remains of the Cherokee Nation with fascination and struggled with unfamiliar names assigned to the region's physical features, names that defied easy spelling or pronunciation. "This is the former home of the red man," Morgan would later write, noting that "many evidences still exist of the former owners of the soil, in the names given to the rivers, mountains, valleys, and prominent points."[8]

White settlers moved onto the lands from which Cherokees had been forcibly removed in the 1830s, but the lack of access to outside markets discouraged large-scale commercial agriculture in antebellum northwest Georgia. The arrival of the railroad proved to be the region's greatest economic catalyst, attracting travelers to the region and opening mountain communities to regional networks of exchange. Favorable locations along the Western and Atlantic line prompted the founding of towns like Ringgold in Catoosa County and Dalton in Whitfield County, which quickly assumed importance as the region's economic hub. Once the Civil War began, the Western and Atlantic Railroad played a critical role in the Confederate war effort, supplying southern forces from a major production center in Atlanta. Thus the rail line became a magnet for Union forces, though the first attack on the Western and Atlantic produced little more than local excitement when, on April 12, 1862, James J. Andrews and a small group of Union raiders stole the locomotive *General* at Big Shanty and ran it north. Their plan—which was to destroy track, burn bridges, and wreck telegraph communications as they raced toward Chattanooga—failed when southerners aboard the locomotive *Texas* set out in pursuit. Andrews's men were pursued through Dalton to Tunnel Hill and were finally captured just past Ringgold after a ninety-mile chase.[9]

The 1863 invasion of northwest Georgia created greater anxiety. After abandoning Chattanooga, Bragg drew his Confederates back into Georgia. Believing the Confederates to be on the run, Morgan and the men of Wilder's Lightning Brigade rushed into Georgia and toward the bloody confrontation that was Chickamauga. Prior to the great battle, Wilder's men engaged Confederate cavalry several times—in Catoosa, Whitfield, and Walker counties—and by September 17 only Chickamauga Creek separated the combatants. The Battle of Chickamauga began the following day for Morgan and Wilder's Brigade when they could only slow a Confederate advance across the creek and toward Rosecrans's main army. In the two days of fighting that followed, Wilder's men displayed enormous courage, especially when called upon to make a bold counterattack that temporarily halted the rebels in their rout of federal forces. Chickamauga was, to borrow Morgan's own wartime phrase, "all that was good and bad at once." Redeemed from their panic at Perryville, the 123rd Illinois performed nobly at Chickamauga, though both sides suffered tremendous losses, those of the federal forces in a losing cause. The 123rd Illinois reported only twenty-four men killed, wounded, or missing. John Morgan recognized one of the deceased, a comrade with whom he had exchanged jackets before the battle. He left his fallen friend in northwest Georgia and joined the rest of Rosecrans's federals as they limped slowly back to Chattanooga.[10]

By the time John Morgan prepared to reenter northwest Georgia in the spring of 1864, Union prospects seemed brighter.

The Confederates had been swept from their strong positions on Lookout Mountain and Missionary Ridge. Now Ulysses S. Grant intended several offensives to pressure Confederate forces, and he charged William T. Sherman with one of them: the capture of Atlanta. For that purpose, John Morgan and the men of Wilder's Brigade remounted and moved to join the main body of the Army of the Cumberland near Dalton in northwest Georgia. From Tennessee, they advanced into Alabama and over Sand Mountain, then over Lookout Mountain to Chickamauga Creek, where reminders of the disastrous battle lingered. Union soldier Oscar Osburn Winther described the scene: "It was a full moon so I could see well . . . thousands of dead, hastily buried, were around me. The winter rains had, in many places, washed off part of the thin covering and arms and legs protruded from the ground. It was a ghastly, ghostly sight, and I should not have been surprised if I had seen ghostly forms around me, but nothing disturbed the stillness of the night but the hoot of an owl or the distant firing." From Chickamauga Creek, Wilder's Brigade moved over Pigeon Mountain and Taylor's Ridge, then halted to forage for supplies.[11]

Thomas Barbour's Chattooga County farm lay along Armuchee Creek, just east of Taylor's Ridge and Summerville, and only a sixteen-mile journey southeast to Rome. For two days in mid-May, Barbour remembered, Wilder's men made a temporary residence there. On the first day, they emptied his barn, removed four mules from the corral, and fed two hundred bushels of wheat to their horses before turning to the contents of Barbour's house. As evening fell, the federals tore through the farmhouse floor to gain easier access to the cellar, which Barbour claimed housed hundreds of pounds of bacon. The next morning, after a night that saw the partial destruction of his home, Barbour's seven head of cattle joined a small drove of confiscated livestock. But the Georgian observed the federal efforts with something approaching equanimity; he was, after all, "a Union man."[12]

Certainly north Georgia's mountaineers rallied only slowly to the Confederate cause. Thomas Barbour remembered that he cast his ballot for Stephen Douglas in the presidential election of 1860. When Lincoln triumphed in the national election, Georgia secessionists worried that the areas of the state with few slaves—the mountain counties to the north and the wiregrass/pine barrens of south Georgia—would resist secession, and they were largely correct. Barbour recalled that he "exerted all my influence against secession," predicting that "if the Union was broken up we were ruined." When the war began, he turned his energies against the Confederacy. "From the very beginning of the rebellion," he wrote, "I sympathized with the Union cause. I thought the Union was worth more to the people than all their property, negroes, & everything else." Presumably, he included his own substantial property in that calculation, a total estate that exceeded forty-two thousand dollars in value and included sixteen slaves.[13]

Barbour believed that he enjoyed some influence in his northwest Georgia community, as he had once served as a captain of the local militia and held the elected office of justice of the peace. Neighbors confirmed Barbour as "bitterly opposed to the war," urging all who would listen to "stay out of the war" and "have nothing to do with it." William L. Marshal, who lived nearby, even credited Barbour with assisting his escape from Confederate service. Unsurprisingly, Barbour also did all he could to extricate his own sons from the Confederate Army. When son Thomas J. Barbour deserted after two months' service to the Confederacy, his father assisted an escape to the North, where young Barbour served out the rest of the war in service to the Union. Like his brother, John J. Barbour initially embraced the Confederate cause, only to be rescued when his father paid a substitute three thousand dollars to take his son's place. Three thousand dollars richer, the substitute soon deserted, slipping away into the countryside as quickly as possible. "I wanted the rebels whipped," Barbour wrote, so when he encountered Confederates, he did all he could "to get them out of the army . . . to weaken the rebel cause."[14]

While his Unionist friends supported him, Barbour's other neighbors denounced him as an enemy to the Confederacy. Family and friends, including Barbour's Confederate son-in-law, feared that the old man faced potential harm if he fell into the hands of rebels. Though Barbour claimed he was often cursed as "a damned old Union son of a bitch," he escaped injury, despite the fact that on at least one occasion the family was plagued by the Gatewood Scouts, a band of Confederate sympathizers who demanded money under threat of death. Residents reported the deaths of at least nineteen Unionists at their hands, but northwest Georgia was home to pro-Union guerrillas as well, and innocent civilians occasionally found themselves in the crossfire of rival guerrilla bands.[15]

When Wilder's men arrived on his Chattooga County farm in May 1864, Barbour watched impassively as the federals collected foodstuffs and livestock, extending willingly to Union troops what he had denied the Confederacy, complaining only when soldiers damaged his property in their enthusiasm. Most of the damage occurred when the soldiers broke open barrels of whiskey they had confiscated earlier. "They were nearly all drunk," Barbour noted sourly, "and tore up nearly everything." The federals lingered on Barbour's farm for two days then departed, with full bellies and aching heads. Perhaps John Morgan eschewed the contraband whiskey, as he prided himself on his abstemious habits, or so he claimed in a letter written to his mother in late 1863: "As regards my habits," he wrote, "I neither smoke, drink liquor or play cards. I have plenty of reading matter and duty to keep me busy." In 1864, he possessed clarity enough to commit his surroundings to memory, for he would eventually locate Thomas Barbour, the Georgia Unionist, again.[16]

In the campaign for Atlanta, in which Union troops forced Johnston's army steadily south toward Atlanta, Sherman employed Wilder's Brigade to secure bridges, threaten Confederate rail lines, and harass the Confederate rear guard as the federals moved south. In May the Lightning Brigade met the enemy at Dallas; in June Wilder's men confronted rebels at the base of Kennesaw Mountain. In July they waded the Chattahoochee River under Confederate fire and then destroyed the King textile mills at Roswell. As Sherman slowly strangled Confederate resistance in Atlanta, the Lightning Brigade moved east and engaged in a frenzy of destruction at Stone Mountain, Oxford,

Covington, and Conyers. Then, as August drew to a close, they advanced with Sherman's forces toward the last Confederate supply line at Jonesboro, and by September, Confederates evacuated the city of Atlanta. While Sherman pursued his march to Savannah and beyond, Wilder's Brigade joined General James H. Wilson's raid on the Confederacy's productive capabilities in Alabama. By the time they finished their mission, the Confederacy lay in ruins.[17]

The Civil War over and the obligation to his country satisfied, John Morgan mustered out of service in June 1865. He returned to Illinois for a brief visit with his parents before departing for New York, where he enrolled for the fall term at Eastman's Commercial College. He anticipated a career in accounting after completing the one-year curriculum, even considered returning to the South to establish a business in Murfreesboro, Tennessee. His life took an unexpected turn when a Utah cattle rancher hired him to drive a herd of Texas longhorns from Missouri to Salt Lake City. Perhaps his desire for adventure remained unsatisfied, for Morgan accepted the challenge and reached Brigham Young's new Zion in time to celebrate Christmas 1866. Salt Lake City held promise for an ambitious young man, Morgan believed. He studied the growing population and bustling commercialism and noted that the territory lacked an educational institution to provide business training to the city's young men and women. After being in Salt Lake City only a month, he opened Morgan Commercial College to the city's students. The enterprise appealed to his entrepreneurial spirit, but he was also, according to his family, "subconsciously becoming enamoured with the city and its people."[18]

Morgan was not yet a member of the LDS Church, but church leaders supported his educational endeavor. Students quickly filled his classrooms, including the children of Nicholas Groesbeck, a Latter-day Saint and one of the wealthiest men in the territory. Sixteen-year-old Mellie Groesbeck captured the twenty-five-year-old headmaster's attention at once. By the time they married in 1868, John Morgan's conversion to Mormonism was complete. The college expanded rapidly, as did Morgan's young family. Mellie gave birth to a daughter in 1870, the same year the college outgrew its original building, as Morgan then offered business classes to six hundred students.[19]

His call to mission service came in the fall of 1875 when the church formally established the Southern States Mission, a new effort to win converts for the Church of Jesus Christ of Latter-day Saints. Elder Henry G. Boyle, already at work in Hickman County, Tennessee, assumed the leadership duties of mission president, and church authorities called seven men—among them John Morgan—to join Boyle in Tennessee to receive mission assignments. Boyle selected John D. H. McCallister to serve with him in Arkansas; David P. Rainey and Joseph Standing were to continue the mission in Tennessee. George Teasdale and John R. Winder accepted a mission to North Carolina but intended to pass through Georgia on the way. Boyle sent David H. Peery to Virginia alone, perhaps because Morgan requested and received permission to delay his trip south. Instead, he planned to visit his parents in Illinois and attempt to convince them to accept the Mormon message. Such diversions were not unusual and reflected the hopeful belief that if one family member responded to the LDS gospel, others might as well. To Morgan's abject disappointment, his Illinois ministry produced no conversions within his family; still he considered his time in Illinois well spent as "traveling around through the country has given me the experience that I need." He resolved to continue his mission in Illinois.[20]

In an 1830 revelation, Joseph Smith decreed that Mormon elders would travel "without purse or scrip," their needs to be met by those among whom they labored. So as Morgan moved beyond his parents' community, he learned to rely on the kindness of strangers for meals and housing. Though locals frequently denied him food and shelter, he repaid hospitality when he found it, by plowing fields, picking potatoes, and planting melons. On occasion, meals carried a near intolerable price, as he learned when he was subjected to a "terrible storm of poetry that was poured out upon me by the author." Better to labor in the fields, he discovered, than be forced to serve as after-dinner audience to farmer-poets. As he had once done in Georgia,

Morgan followed railroad tracks in Illinois, moving from one small rural settlement to another. In each new community, he called upon residents, making appointments for private meetings with all interested parties. To accommodate larger public gatherings, he secured local schoolhouses or meeting halls, though he occasionally showed up at the scheduled hour to find the doors locked. Experience taught him that he was most successful when he remained in one locality for an extended period, and he publicly endorsed the recommendation of Elder Miles Romney, missionary in Wisconsin, who suggested that elders "would do better to concentrate their labors" in one area. Morgan agreed, having discovered that people attended their first LDS meeting as they would "attend a circus, or panorama, merely out of curiosity," and it often required two or three meetings to overcome the initial prejudices of potential converts.[21]

Morgan, in turn, offered practical advice to prospective missionaries not yet called to service. Weeks of endless walking convinced him of the need for sturdy footwear, so he advised each missionary to purchase heavy, double-soled boots or shoes of good quality. Clothing must be similarly stout to withstand the rigors of missionary service, and he recommended that new elders pack at least three sets of underclothing and three colored shirts. Collars required more frequent changes, so he suggested at least a half dozen linen collars and a pair of "old-fashioned saddle pockets to carry the complement in." More burdensome were the reference books the missionary should carry—a copy of the Bible, the Book of Mormon, a Latter-day Saint hymnbook, and assorted publications. Of all the texts they carried, missionaries considered the Bible to be paramount in importance. As historians of nineteenth-century LDS missions have noted, Mormon elders preached *about* the Book of Mormon but *from* the Bible. As members of a lay priesthood, they enjoyed considerable autonomy in preparing their sermons, though church authorities instructed missionaries to focus on the "first principles," the major points of the Latter-day Saints' restored gospel—faith, repentance, baptism by immersion for the remission of sins, and the gifts of the Holy Spirit. When prospective converts questioned or challenged what they heard, elders turned to the Bible as proof. The call to gather with fellow Saints in the West came only after conversion, as the church believed that the lost should be brought "first to the Church and secondly to Zion." Despite injunctions to that effect, John Morgan advised missionaries to assist potential converts in imagining life in Utah by carrying images of Salt Lake City, "a few of Brother C. R. Savage's fine views of our public buildings and leading men." But those images could also soothe a homesick missionary, and Morgan may have pulled them from his pack occasionally as a reminder of what he had left behind.[22]

Proselytizing was lonely work made more tolerable by the assignment of a missionary companion. Latter-day Saints attempted to emulate Christ's example by sending disciples "by twos," though that New Testament ideal often went unrealized. Morgan labored alone in Illinois for nearly four months prior to the arrival of twenty-one-year-old Joseph Standing in mid-February 1876. Elder Standing was the son of British converts who had made the arduous journey to the valley of the Great Salt Lake. There, Standing's father made a good living as a stonecutter and supported his wife and ten children comfortably in Salt Lake City's Twelfth Ward, a neighborhood that demonstrated the scope and diversity of nineteenth-century mission efforts. Among their Utah neighbors were a lawyer from Iowa, a surveyor from New York, a shoemaker from Pennsylvania, an artist from England, and a bookbinder from Norway. Prior to his Southern States Mission call, Joseph Standing served the city as a fireman with the Wasatch Engine Company. Cheered by Elder Standing's company, Morgan ventured from Illinois into Indiana, and within a short period the two developed a close friendship. But when summer came, Standing decided to travel to Canada to visit relatives and Morgan found himself alone again. He confided to his journal that he keenly missed the missionary companion who had helped him "cope successfully with the darkness and prejudice that I have to contend with." Standing rejoined him in August 1876, in time to celebrate the arrival of a letter from Brigham Young containing Morgan's honorable release from his first mission. But Morgan had in his possession another letter, too—requesting a missionary in Georgia—so he advised church authorities of his intention to travel there. Standing also intended to relocate to a new mission field, in Purdy, Tennessee.[23]

As Morgan moved south, he studied the terrain with interest, noting that the physical devastation left by opposing armies "had not entirely disappeared." Forests, he observed, "yet retain the evidence of cruel war in broken limbs and shattered trunks," but the scarred landscape seemed appropriate to a broken people. Towns that had once been bustling and lively, he wrote, "now lie dead and lifeless, with only lone chimneys, that seem to stand sentinel over the desolation around them, a people not yet recovered from the terrible scourge of war, and looking forward with dread to the future." Perhaps he should not have been surprised by broken landscapes; he had, after all, participated in the devastation. Walker and Catoosa counties still bore the scars from the mighty battle at Chickamauga in 1863. General Sherman also used Catoosa County as the assembling point for his 1864 Atlanta Campaign, gathering more than a hundred thousand Union soldiers there before marching on Atlanta. When Union soldiers moved on the city, they laid waste to the towns in their path. Chattooga County residents remembered that federals spared only Unionist-owned Trion Cotton Factory from destruction; similarly, those who experienced Sherman's march through Catoosa County recalled that he spared only that county's courthouse because he valued the Masonic meeting hall on its third floor. The Atlanta Campaign opened with a skirmish at Tunnel Hill in Whitfield County, the first of several battles there, and Union troops actually moved through Floyd County twice: first in the movement from Chattanooga toward Atlanta and a second time after the fall of Atlanta when they pursued Hood's army back toward Tennessee.[24]

When Elder Morgan disembarked from his train in Chattanooga, he decided to walk the distance to Rome, his original destination, and "along the way to visit historic battlefields and shrines which he knew years before." He felt especially anxious to visit the grave of the fallen comrade with whom he had exchanged jackets prior to the battle at Chickamauga. After his death, and based upon identification in the jacket, the young man had been laid to rest as "John Morgan," so Morgan now searched for his own name among memorials to the dead. As he walked, "his mind wandered back continuously" to his Civil War experience "among those very mountains and valleys." In fact, he believed "he had been over every mile of the country through which he was walking." Days later he found himself at that significant fork in the road, reliving the past and remembering his dream. Obedient to the prophet's advice, he turned left and away from Rome.[25]

Elder Morgan's turn to the left and away from Rome in 1876 carried him back to the Chattooga County farm of Thomas Barbour, on whose property he had foraged in May 1864, as the Lightning Brigade moved toward Atlanta. Barbour's memory of Wilder's visit assisted him in successfully claiming recompense from the federal government after the war. Morgan's recollection of his Chattooga County sojourn proved equally vivid, guiding him back some twelve years later, armed only with a Bible and the Book of Mormon. Perhaps the Union veteran and the southern Unionist recalled that time; if so, Morgan did not record the shared memory in his journal or correspondence, but a relationship surely blossomed. In November 1876, Morgan and Barbour waded into Armuchee Creek, where Barbour was baptized into the Church of Jesus Christ of Latter-day Saints. An examination of Morgan's record of baptisms reveals that the family and community network that once sustained political loyalties still survived to foster religious loyalties, for waiting their turns in the cold waters were Barbour's two sons and his neighbor, William L. Marshal.[26]

CHAPTER TWO

"There Is Something Terrible Coming"
Establishment of the North Georgia Mission Field

The bulk of Morgan's combat experience occurred in Georgia, mostly in and around the northwest counties he selected as his postwar mission field, and his determination to seek converts in the area, more than a decade later, surely reflected his familiarity with the region and its inhabitants and his own belief that the Latter-day Saints would receive a receptive audience there. His optimism proved well founded. After establishing a branch of the church in Chattooga County's Haywood Valley as a base of operations, Morgan negotiated kin connections and neighborhood associations to expand his mission field. For instance, Haywood Valley's Gabriel Barbour created a link to brother-in-law William Manning of Floyd County's Beech Creek Branch. Similarly, Price and Nathaniel Connally of Walker County's Cassandra Branch provided missionaries an introduction to niece Elizabeth Nations Elledge in Catoosa County. In time, Morgan's efforts produced branches in Chattooga, Floyd, Walker, Catoosa, and Whitfield counties, and in the months just prior to Joseph Standing's death, elders also established branches in Polk and Fannin counties. Only one branch of the church existed in Georgia outside the Appalachian counties. Mormon elder Thomas E. Murphy, who proselytized among kinfolk in Georgia and Alabama, apparently created the Jonesborough Branch in Clayton County specifically to meet the needs of his family, and when Elder Murphy returned to Utah in 1877, he took with him a nephew and niece from that branch.

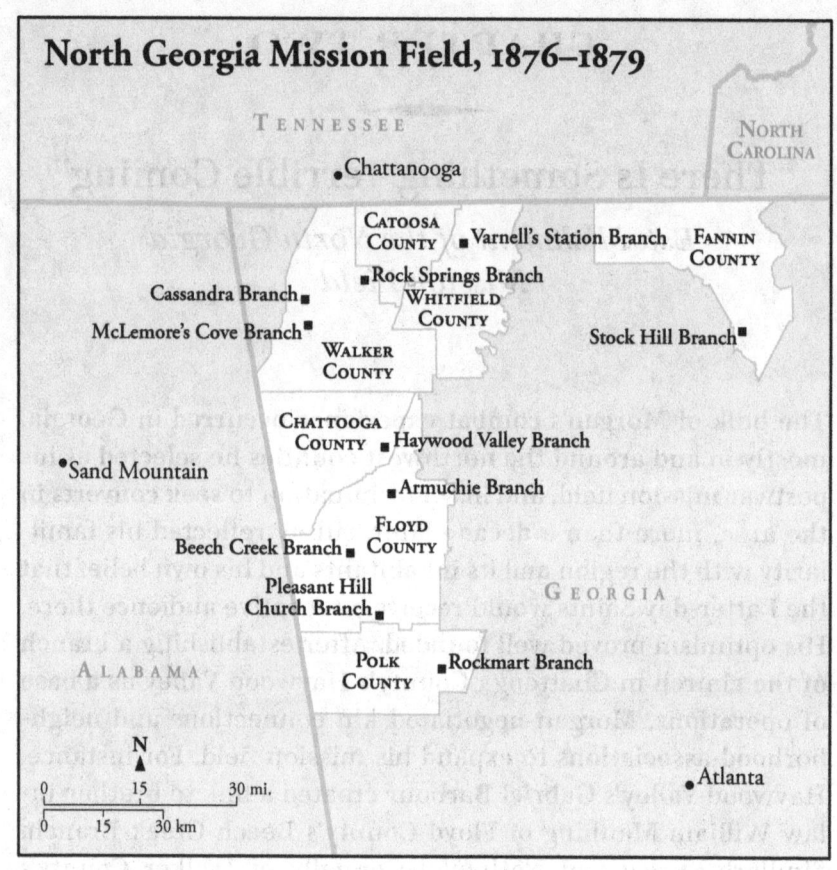

MAP 1. **North Georgia Mission Field, 1876–1879.**

Map created by Mapping Specialists, Ltd., Fitchburg, Wisconsin.

Sources used to establish the locations of branches in North Georgia include Report of Branches of the Church in Georgia, John Hamilton Morgan Papers, J. Willard Marriott Library, the University of Utah; Conferences Established by John Morgan in the Organization of the Southern States Mission, JHM Papers; Converts of Elder John Morgan in North Georgia during His First Mission in 1876, JHM Papers; and typescript of John Morgan's Journal, November 1875–November 1892, JHM Papers. Locations were further verified by examining records for branch members in federal manuscript census population schedules and county tax digests and record books.

Elder Murphy rarely coordinated his efforts with John Morgan; instead, Morgan reached out to James Lisonbee, a fellow Southern States Missionary laboring in northeast Alabama. A native southerner, Lisonbee had returned to the state of his birth seeking converts, and in early 1877, he established the Grove Oak Branch of the church on Alabama's Sand Mountain. This, too, was familiar territory for John Morgan. In spring 1864, Wilder's Brigade had moved from Tennessee into Georgia, crossing over Sand Mountain in a terrific thunderstorm. Shortly after their initial meeting, Morgan convinced Lisonbee to leave his established Alabama branch in the care of others, and from April to July 1877, the elders traveled together in northwest Georgia. They shared the "first principles" with potential converts, working together to baptize, then confirm, new believers, but Lisonbee also advanced an economic model that Morgan believed would benefit poor mountaineers. In 1874 Brigham Young had reinstituted the United Order, a program intended to return Utah's Saints to a more communal way of life, restore economic self-sufficiency, and resist integration into the national economy. Inspired by Joseph Smith's communitarian vision for economic and social life, the United Order stressed economic cooperation and the elimination of poverty. According to this model, Mormon settlements often organized into voluntary producer cooperatives, allowing members to contribute money and property to the order, receiving a return according to the amount of capital and labor invested. In other cases, the orders reflected a more complete commitment to communal life, with members relinquishing all of their property and sharing equally in the product. Either way, Young intended the order to replicate a supportive family, and as president of the United Order of Monroe, Utah, Lisonbee could speak to the value of a communitarian response to individual needs.[1]

Mormon successes in the Appalachian counties of Alabama and Georgia apparently convinced Morgan to restrict his own missionary efforts to the Georgia mountains; in fact, his letters suggest that he envisioned a region that stretched across the northernmost counties of Alabama and Georgia and into North Carolina. Later, bemused newspapers reporters in Atlanta would report that Mormon elders "stick to the mountainous districts," though they could not explain the phenomenon. One correspondent admitted that "no one can tell why the Mormons have devoted so much time" to the region "in which they have been working so long. They are not to be found elsewhere, but they seem to be determined upon captivating the section spoken of" in northwest Georgia.[2]

Morgan's determination to focus on the Georgia highlands requires explanation. A simple justification for his self-defined field of labor rests in the assumption that residents of the mountain South espoused Union sympathies, so would prove more receptive to the former federal. His return to the self-proclaimed Unionists of Chattooga County certainly proved congenial, but Morgan did not limit his proselytizing to those opposed to the Confederacy. The irony of the current situation did not escape him, and he noted that "he was now laboring to bring into the fold of the church . . . the very men and women with whom he and the boys in blue were then contending." His mission journal revealed the extent to which memories of the Civil War dogged his footsteps as he traveled again the ridges and valleys of northwest Georgia. He enthusiastically shared his wartime exploits with Elder Lisonbee and conducted battlefield tours whenever Mormon elders passed through Georgia. He visited with former federal soldiers in Chattanooga, and in more solitary moments, he escaped his missionary labors to wade Chickamauga Creek. Perhaps the intensity of his past mission informed his current one, for Morgan embraced his work as a soldier would, and before the first year of his Georgia mission had passed, he could report to Salt Lake City that "a general spirit of inquiry has sprung up throughout all this mountain country."[3]

By the time John Morgan arrived in the South, Georgia had been readmitted to the Union and Democrats had effectively "redeemed" the state from Republicans. Surprisingly, given his wartime desire for "nothing but the subjugation or annihilation of the South," the former federal soldier expressed little interest in the political machinations that restored Georgia to the Union. He did, however, view with foreboding the Compromise of 1877 or "corrupt bargain" struck following the contested presidential election of 1876 that ended Reconstruction in the South and withdrew federal troops from the region. "The Southern States are torn and rent by political and religious strife from centre to circumference," he reported in a January 1877 letter to the *Deseret News*. Georgians, he wrote, seemed "like animals caught in the snare," standing "in momentary expectation of mighty events that seem to them to be in the near future," fearful of a renewal of regional hostilities and with no desire for war. He encouraged those he encountered to flee the region, its politicians, and their religious beliefs, but he confronted reluctance: "The very air seems filled with the shadows of coming events, and the people feel and see it, but it seems impossible to convince them of the feasibility of the plan of escape."[4]

North Georgia promoters were not so pessimistic. In the immediate aftermath of the war, Georgia boosters predicted that the region would play a prominent role in the state's recovery and argued that the Armuchee Ridges of northwest Georgia showed special promise. As early as 1869, an *Atlanta Constitution* correspondent reported from Dalton that "the mountains are awake, and the busy rustle of an increasing activity warns you that North Georgia is crowding to the front." He noted the fertile hills and valleys but also pointed out that "the country is matchless for manufacturing." Residents of the region were "throwing off [their] Rip Van Winkle stupor" and "enterprise is buoyant," he enthused. Reports from an 1869 press excursion to north Georgia encouraged exploitation of the valuable mineral region northwest of Atlanta. "All that the people of North Georgia have to do is to awake from their lethargy and grasp the rich prize that is slumbering beneath their feet," Atlanta newspapers enthused. In 1873, a Ringgold citizen suggested that *all* Georgia residents were asleep as they were "really not aware of the mountains of wealth we have here for them." And he sounded a cautionary note: if Georgians failed to act, he warned, the state's mountain resources would fall into the hands of outsiders as "northern and foreign capitalists have their agents reconnoitering among our mountains."[5]

In fact, it was the Civil War that introduced many of Appalachia's future entrepreneurs and industrialists to the abundance of natural resources in the region. Northern soldiers who fought in and around Chattanooga—among them John T. Wilder of the Lightning Brigade—were the first to notice the evidence of coal and iron ore in that area. Only two years after his release from military service, Wilder relocated his family from Indiana to Chattanooga, Tennessee. With two associates he organized the Roane Iron Company, then dedicated the next half century to extracting east Tennessee's natural resources. Like his former commanding officer, John Morgan also cast an acquisitive eye across enemy country; however, when Morgan returned to the South, it would be to exploit only the untapped *human* resources of the area.[6]

Morgan preferred to labor in north Georgia because he believed the mountain region to be healthier than counties in the southern part of the state. In reports to LDS Church authorities, he noted that "there is an abundance of mountain country that promises very fair indeed, and is in my opinion one of the healthiest sections of the Union . . . [this] portion of the South being cool and well watered as well as very healthy." Georgians also believed in the healthfulness of the region's climate and boasted that "no country under the sun has been so munificently blessed as North Georgia . . . she has been looked to as the land of health and vigor, of mild and genial skies." In fact, one booster doubted "whether there is a section of country in the United States more desirable to live in than North Georgia." More temperate climate aside, the perceived healthfulness of northwest Georgia's mineral springs, believed to possess unique medicinal properties, drew tourists from both the North and the South. Young women, local newspapers reported, seemed especially drawn to a spring that promised "Beauty."[7]

The mountain South also offered refuge from the yellow fever or "Yellow Jack" that cruelly visited the South each summer, especially coastal cities like New Orleans and Mobile. The wealthiest southerners fled desperately north at the first sign of the scourge, with a frenzy that Morgan likened to wartime. They are "fleeing before it," he wrote of an unusually virulent outbreak in 1878, "as they would from an army of invasion, while those who are overtaken are perishing miserably in its track." Even residents of Chattanooga evacuated in that year, leaving the city nearly deserted and under quarantine to deter visitors from farther south. But Morgan reassured the Saints in Utah that they need not fear for Georgia missionaries as "out in this mountain country we do not apprehend any trouble, as the pure mountain air will counteract the influences of our malarial districts."[8]

Concern about deadly disease aside, it is also possible that Morgan preferred Georgia's mountain districts because fewer black Georgians lived there. During the nineteenth century, LDS Church authorities excluded blacks from the priesthood, although Southern States missionaries occasionally carried their gospel to black Americans. Elder Henry Boyle reported that he baptized three black Virginians in 1868, for example, and in 1883 missionary Joseph Morrell visited a black woman in South Carolina in order to administer to her ailing son. Morgan's decision to proselytize in northwest Georgia effectively eliminated blacks from potential conversion. Overall, black Georgians represented nearly half of the state's total population, but the northernmost counties claimed a disproportionately small number of them. Of the seven counties that made up Morgan's northwest Georgia mission field—Catoosa, Chattooga, Fannin, Floyd, Polk, Walker, and Whitfield—census takers designated 79 percent of the total population as white. Blacks represented only 18 percent of the population, and individuals identified as "mulatto" made up the remaining 3 percent. Indeed, Fannin County claimed only sixteen black heads of household, a number that represented a mere 2 percent of the total population. In the southernmost part of Morgan's mission field (the counties in closest proximity to Georgia's Black Belt or Cotton Belt) the African American population was highest. In both Floyd and Polk counties, for instance, census takers estimated the black population at 27 percent.[9]

Floyd County's black residents dampened Morgan's enthusiasm for Rome, a city he often praised: "The negroes are generally idle and vicious, congregating in towns and cities, where great swarms of them can be seen sunning themselves on the street corners, having become corrupted to the lowest degree, physically and morally." Eventually, Rome's favorable location overcame Morgan's prejudices, and in 1878 he located his headquarters in that city. There is no record suggesting that Morgan proselytized among northwest Georgia's black population, however, and no reason to believe that northwest Georgia's whites would have welcomed or approved of a biracial church.[10]

Though he limited his attention to mountain whites, Morgan saw ample fuel for his proselytizing zeal. Based upon his observation, the South was a vast region of lost souls, and when he examined the state of Georgia from his Chattooga County vantage point, the task ahead of him seemed daunting. In a letter to Utah, Morgan stressed the enormity of his task and the potential richness of his new mission field: "I look around and realize that, here in this State of Georgia, there are two millions and more of people only a small portion of which ever heard the gospel." Nevertheless, with all two million to choose from, Morgan deliberately selected those in the mountain counties of northwest Georgia to receive his message. Clearly his description of the state, though it implies an unchurched population, referred only to those who had not yet received the message of the Latter-day Saints. It was certainly not the case that northwest Georgians lacked the opportunity to practice religious devotion.[11]

Just as the Second Great Awakening swept across the "burned-over" district of western New York in the first decades of the nineteenth century, revivals transformed the mountain South too, and Baptists and Methodists soon dominated the southern mountains. In general, the harshest doctrines of Calvinism—the emphasis on original sin and Calvin's bleak predestinarianism, in which only a select few achieve salvation—gave way to a more gentle Arminianism, which acknowledged the human role in salvation and an individual's ability to make a decision to accept God's saving grace. Yet keen observers of Appalachian religion have argued that the persistence of Calvinism distinguished mountain churches and separated them from the Protestant mainstream. Calvinism, which emphasized a merciful but all-powerful God and the innate powerlessness and sinfulness of humans, survived in the mountains. The result was often perceived by outsiders as a dour and fatalistic belief system that produced a dark and passive worldview, a "latter-day mentality" as one scholar put it. Religious scholars identify other regional characteristics: a strongly individualistic, emotional, and evangelical faith that produced numerous independent and nondenominational churches, a stress on the importance of baptism, and a deep and abiding faith in the authority of the Scriptures.[12]

Elder Morgan most often encountered Baptists and Methodists in the mountains, not surprising given that those denominations dominated the state's religious landscape. In 1877, the *Atlanta Constitution* estimated that one out of every six Georgians belonged to the Baptist church (although it did not distinguish among Baptist subdenominations), while Methodists ranked second in popularity. "At the cross roads a church stands, generally Baptist or Methodist," Morgan wrote in 1877. Churches were quite primitive, he observed, "simply a shell of a building, without any ceiling or sides or overhead, devoid of paint and destitute of any means of warming the attendants." The shelters accommodated revivals, which were held "as soon as the corn is laid by, so as not to interfere with the work, and at the same time secure a comfortable season of the year to serve the Lord in." Such gatherings often prompted admonishments against Mormons, Elder Morgan believed: "The ministers who hold forth at these houses almost invariably warn their members of the sin and wickedness of going to hear a 'Mormon' Elder preach, and do not hesitate to stoop to any misrepresentation to accomplish their object."[13]

Despite condemnations from local pulpits, Morgan maintained that the beliefs and practices advanced by Mormon missionaries felt familiar to mountain folks—the emphasis on faith and repentance, the importance of baptism (often in living waters), and the laying on of hands for the reception of the

Holy Spirit and the gifts that followed. He also noted a general receptivity to the restorationist desire to return Christianity to the New Testament church, a distrust of denominations, and a preference for lay preachers rather than trained clerics. Nineteenth-century mountain preachers, like Mormon elders, often lacked formal training, received no pay, and relied on revelation from above. For both mountain preachers and Mormon elders, the Bible, both the Old Testament and the New, was an essential text.

Elder Morgan's northwest Georgia mission field provided a rich menu of religious choices from which to choose. In addition to Methodist, Baptist, and Presbyterian churches, there were Episcopalian, Catholic, Congregationalist, Disciples of Christ, and African Methodist Episcopal congregations. Walker County, which boasted forty-four churches, even claimed one Universalist congregation.[14]

As a result of this denominational diversity, northwest Georgians were "torn to pieces religiously," Elder Morgan reported. He believed that Georgians suffered under the influence of an evil and powerful apostate church that ruled "Babylon" and corrupted the gospel of Jesus Christ through the false teachings of its "hireling priests." Thus, he accepted as his responsibility the wrestling of lost souls from the evil and greedy influence of north Georgia's spiritual representatives. The LDS Church, which rejected a paid ministry, saw corruption in the salaries paid to ministers, believing it to be money better spent in behalf of the poor. North Georgian Benjamin Echols, whose conversion to Mormonism likely shaped his memories and fostered a criticism of mountain religious life, remembered attending many different churches but being drawn to none in particular. "I couldn't get interested enough to join any one of the churches. Each one claimed that their church was the only right one to join but I could not see where any one of them was better than the others." He recalled that attending church meant traveling approximately four miles to meetings that were held on a sporadic basis, as one circuit preacher was paid to service four churches. On Sundays when no sermon or Sunday School meeting was available, Benjamin and his friends congregated at swimming ponds or visited with neighbors, but they respected the Sabbath, which meant "no work no hunting no fishing." Echols remembered that paying the minister proved a burden too, even for one as celebrated as Methodist circuit rider Sam Jones, who "did his first preaching in our cirket [sic] and was paid five hundred dollars a year by the four churches." Eventually, he noted, Sam Jones "could get five hundred in one day," an amount that would have enraged John Morgan.[15]

In addition to the perceived greediness of Georgia's preachers, Morgan saw proof of ministerial indifference all around him. Northwest Georgia's poverty convinced the elder that the state's ministers cared little for their flocks. Rex Thomas Price, a historian of nineteenth-century Mormon missions, observed that LDS elders often preferred to labor in the poorest of districts and "may not have made a real effort to reach the rich and powerful," based on a belief that "God's people could be found among the humble and poor, not the rich and proud." Northwest Georgia yielded an abundance of humble and poor. According to his missionary journal and mission reports, Morgan expected to find northwest Georgia only partially healed from the devastation of the recent war—he had, after all, participated in causing that devastation. He anticipated that Georgia's citizens still suffered, fiscally and emotionally.[16]

Arriving as he did, after the national panic of 1873 and during the severe economic depression that followed, Morgan made frequent references to the financial insecurity that plagued north Georgians. Still, he expressed shock at the discovery that northwest Georgians faced "poverty of the most pinching character." As he made his way across the ridges and valleys of his new mission field, he recorded his impressions and sent them back to Utah, where they were reproduced in newspapers and delivered to Salt Lake City readers. He described in near-ethnographic detail his visits to two-room homes constructed entirely of logs that were "daubed with clay, red or yellow . . . the stoop and portico slowly rotting away," window glass gone and replaced by "various articles of wearing apparel too numerous to mention."

Families, he reported, subsisted on an unhealthy diet of bacon and corn bread, but dulled their hunger with the "constant use of tobacco." When questioned about the deplorable state of affairs, Morgan continued, the "man of the house" said it seemed as though "a curse was devouring the earth," as "his wheat won't head out, his oats won't grow high enough to cut, his corn does not produce anything, his fruit is blasted and the earth refuses to yield its increase." Asked to speculate further, most north Georgians traced their current troubles back to the war. "You hear it on all sides," Morgan wrote, "*'since the war.' 'Since the war'* appears to be the explanation for all the evils they are subject to." Perhaps they intended only to date their troubles to the postbellum period, but they may have been affixing blame to the conflict itself. More introspective or perhaps more melancholic farmers interpreted their postwar difficulties as indicators of divine punishment, explaining that "there is something wrong, that the people are not right, that God is displeased with them, and that there is something terrible coming."[17]

The poverty of Georgia's highland residents undoubtedly influenced Morgan's decision to labor in the mountains of northwest Georgia. In the counties that made up Morgan's chosen mission field, African Americans and those identified by census takers as "mulatto" clearly suffered the most. In none of the counties under consideration did black heads of household possess more than one percent of the total wealth. White heads of household fared much better, of course, with an average combined real and personal estate valued at eleven hundred dollars, but such an average was deceptive. In fact, the distribution of wealth in each county was highly uneven, with wealth concentrated in the hands of only a few. A sampling of the ten wealthiest heads of household in each county, for example, revealed that, on average, ten individuals claimed a disproportionate 18 percent of the total wealth. In fact, in Morgan's north Georgia mission field, only a third of household heads owned total estates valued at greater than five hundred dollars. Another third claimed a real and personal estate valued from one dollar to five hundred dollars, and a third owned nothing at all. If one accepts the definition of a "poor man's" household advanced by the *Atlanta Constitution* in 1877, "a little farm worth $500, stock and provisions to carry it on with, the house furniture to do a poor family," most northwest Georgians would have understood themselves to be very poor indeed.[18]

Poorer still were Morgan's northwest Georgia converts. By comparing mission reports, correspondence, and missionary journals to the 1870 U.S. Federal Census population schedules, sixty-three male and female convert heads of household have been identified. Although Thomas Barbour, the wealthiest of the Georgia converts, claimed real estate and personal property valued at $5,300, that figure represented a much greater economic resource than most new Saints enjoyed. The average total wealth per convert was $469, considerably less than the northwest Georgia average of $1,100. There were carpenters, brick masons, cabinetmakers, grocers, teachers, and a Methodist minister among the converts, but the majority of the heads of household (86 percent) were engaged in farming. As their fellow northwest Georgia farmers did, convert households produced Indian corn, winter wheat, oats, and livestock, although sheep often outnumbered swine. Only convert households in the southernmost counties of Morgan's mission field produced any cotton: James Allen, William R. Manning, and William Marshal of Floyd County each produced one bale, while Caleb Jennings managed to produce two bales of the staple on his Chattooga County farm. Women also played a significant role in household economies. Convert Thomas A. Lawrence, whose marriage apparently produced no sons but eight daughters, cultivated winter wheat and Indian corn, but also significant quantities of wool, butter, molasses, and honey, as well as home manufactures valued at one hundred dollars. It is significant, however, that of the 86 percent of converts considered farmers, only a third owned land of their own, roughly the same number deemed worthy of inclusion on county agricultural schedules in 1870, which suggests that the majority were engaged in some form of tenancy or farm labor. The rest were landless, relying on either extended family or some form of tenancy for survival or hiring themselves out as farm laborers for wages of twenty-five to seventy-five cents per day. Such individuals worked merely to survive, with few hopes of upward mobility. For them, the lure of western lands may have proved irresistible.[19]

At least two landowning Walker County converts brought their farm laborers to the LDS Church. Farm laborer C. Frank Payne and wife Jane began attending branch meetings with employer James M. Faucett. Similarly, William C. Kilgore of McLemore's Cove reported in 1870 that he paid $175 in wages for that year, and part of it, at least, compensated farm laborer John Smalley, who likely resided in one of Kilgore's two houses. County tax assessors reported that Smalley owned nothing of value himself—no land, no livestock, no tools, no furniture, no household goods, and no money. Overwhelming in their repetitive misery, identical reports were filed for Smalley in every year from 1874 to 1883. Smalley's decision to join the McLemore's Cove Branch invites speculation that the young laborer faced both religious and economic pressures, and that certainly may have been the case, for branch membership sometimes afforded economic security to a young man possessing no land and an uncertain future. By 1880 McLemore's Cove Branch member Andrew J. Holland employed Smalley.[20]

Some converts had suffered an impressive postwar decline of economic power. William R. Manning of Haywood Valley had amassed a considerable fortune prior to the Civil War. After moving from a small farm in south Georgia's Dooly County, the Mannings discovered real prosperity in Floyd County. In 1855, in partnership with D. J. Sanders of Rome, Manning established a dry goods and grocery store. Though unfamiliar with Manning personally, an agent for the R. G. Dun Company reported that Manning "is thot [thought] to be a clever man"—clearly an understatement—and predicted success. Initially Manning could contribute no more than three thousand dollars to the firm, but the agent expressed confidence in his abilities and honesty. Reports through 1856 and 1857 indicated that D. J. Sanders & Co. was "doing well" and had accumulated a value in excess of fifty thousand dollars, but by January 1858 William Manning was "out of the firm," selling his share in time to avoid a February fire that completely destroyed the business. Manning appeared on the 1860 manuscript census twice, suggesting that he maintained a home in Rome and a farm in the Floyd County countryside, and was listed on the county's slave schedule as the owner of seven slaves. The aggregate value of his estate, real and personal, exceeded eighty-five thousand dollars prior to the war; in 1870, the census taker recorded an aggregate value of twenty-three hundred, which reflects a near-crippling economic loss of 97 percent in a decade's time.[21]

Elder Morgan may have had men like Manning in mind when he wrote that "some of the largest planters cannot raise enough to supply their families with the bare necessaries of life, but are forced to annually dispose of small tracts of their land to enable them to live from year to year." But the "poverty-stricken condition of the poor," he wrote, "is terrible to contemplate, and day by day it grows steadily worse. The taxes are high and the people dispirited." Missionaries speculated that high taxes necessitated the switch to cotton agriculture—cotton provided cash for taxes—but northwest Georgians also stripped their homes of valuables, selling luxury items to satisfy tax collectors. In 1878, Price Connally of Walker County proudly listed among his possessions watches and jewelry valued at ten dollars. A year later, those items had disappeared from his household.[22]

Unhappy witnesses to visits from Georgia tax assessors, Mormon elders reported back to Utah that "taxes here in the country are 90 cents on the $100, and everything that can be used, and much that cannot, is assessed. Just think of the house-wives bringing out their crockery, tin plates, china ware, wooden ware, pots, kittles, skillets, smoothing-irons, clothing, etc., placing value on the same and taking an oath to its worth!" A two-hundred-dollar exemption of personal property from taxation sheltered those with the poorest households from taxation; however, a one-dollar poll tax established by Georgia's Democratic Redeemers effectively disenfranchised poor whites and blacks from voting. As a result, those who defaulted on their taxes suffered both economically and politically. At least three Georgia converts to Mormonism appear on county tax digests as defaulters, indicating a degree of desperation, defiance, or apathy.[23]

Even those with small landholdings often confronted diminishing land values, as did Thomas A. Littlejohn of Floyd County. He owned nothing at all in 1870, no real or personal estate, but in 1871 he married the daughter of convert John B. Daniel, who gave over fifty acres of land, valued at two hundred dollars, to his new son-in-law. By 1874 Littlejohn claimed an estate worth four hundred seventy dollars. But the land's value steadily diminished over time, to one hundred fifty in 1875, then to a hundred and finally to fifty dollars by 1879. The good fortune and heady financial ascent of 1871–74 evaporated by the end of the decade, and by 1880 the total value of Littlejohn's household, which now included four small children, sank to only a hundred fifteen dollars. Efforts to trace Georgia converts over time and place reveal that the poorest moved frequently, with mobility serving as an economic strategy. In certain cases, like the Haynie family of Floyd County, who moved on a near-yearly basis, changes of address must be tracked by observing the birthplaces of their children: the first two children were born in Georgia, the third and fourth in South Carolina. By the time the fifth and sixth children appeared, the Haynies had returned to Georgia, but the seventh and eighth children were born in Alabama. The ninth child, Fannie, claimed Georgia as her place of birth. For the Haynie family, the concepts of home and community must have been remarkably fluid, and this may explain their willingness to consider new religious and economic opportunities in the West.[24]

Or perhaps economic concerns would override religious considerations entirely. Church authorities acknowledged this possibility and worried that some would come to Zion for purely temporal reasons. Even Brigham Young once speculated that the willingness of converts to migrate to the new Zion could have been motivated by economic rather than religious reasons; he conjectured that "many embrace the Gospel actuated by no other motive than to have the privilege of being removed from their oppressed condition to where they will not suffer. They will embrace any doctrine under the heavens, if you will only take them from their present condition." Certainly critics of Mormonism believed this to be the case and suggested that the church's appeal was more economic than theological. In 1879 an Atlanta reporter unknowingly echoed Young's conclusion in an article that explained the appeal of the Mormons' communitarian message: They "talk about the fertile valleys of Utah, the lavish fruits and the luxurious crops, the fine city of Salt Lake, in which every Mormon had part ownership—in short the pretty pastoral life wherein the richest valley of earth, with little work and a powerful and contented life, was offered to all comers. This picture won the fancy of many a poor farmer who had scratched for years in the scanty soil of our hills at home, and could hardly keep body and soul together, and of many a woman, young and old."[25]

The Mormon message *should* appeal especially to north Georgia's women and children, John Morgan said, as those "deprived of their natural protectors" suffered the most. He expressed surprise to see northwest Georgia's females, white and black, married or unmarried, laboring with hoes in fields of corn, cotton, and cane, reporting that "women work in the field indiscriminately with the men." Field labor prompted a relaxation of race and gender boundaries that Morgan found distasteful, such as when he witnessed a black man cradling wheat while a white woman followed closely behind in order to bind the crop. Georgia's women suffered for lack of men, Morgan believed, and Georgians believed this as well. The *Atlanta Constitution* suggested that the Civil War had robbed Georgia of the "flower of her manhood," estimating that females exceeded males by over sixty thousand. John Morgan calculated more precisely, concluding that the state possessed "26,199 more females of a marriageable age than males." They could find husbands in Zion.[26]

Census data confirm that nearly 16 percent of the total households in the northwest Georgia mission field—over eighteen hundred households—were headed by females, and it is possible that Elder Morgan would have considered the women to be "of marriageable age," although he did not define the phrase. Further, female heads of household, who represented 16 percent of the total number of households, possessed only 7 percent of the total wealth, supporting Morgan's supposition that single or widowed women and children suffered most severely. Sarah Fullbright of Catoosa County, the only convert female head of household to appear on the 1870 agricultural schedules, maintained a fifty-acre farm that supported daughters and grandchildren. On thirty improved acres, she raised a small quantity of winter wheat and oats; twenty acres of woodland supported three pigs and two cows, livestock with a combined estimated value of only thirty-two dollars, yet invaluable as a source of meat and milk for the family. In her nineties when she converted to the LDS Church, "Granny" Fullbright anticipated no husband in her future. She did likely yearn for the spiritual and temporal security promised in the western Zion.[27]

John Morgan's rediscovery of north Georgia coincided with America's new awareness of Appalachia as a distinct and unusual place. It was in the decades immediately following the Civil War that local color writers began to describe the region as a "strange land" populated by "peculiar people," convincing many Americans that Appalachian society had developed in very different ways than had the rest of the country. Their articles emphasized the poverty and ignorance of southern mountaineers and portrayed a way of life culturally out of step with America's new industrialization and urbanization. Over time public fascination with tales of feuding and moonshining gave way to a new perception that the rugged geography of the southern mountains hindered the development of a people likely to be the last representatives of the American frontier. Intellectuals like William Goodell Frost, president of Berea College in Kentucky, successfully framed the destitution and backwardness of Appalachian Americans as a product of their geographic isolation and argued forcefully for intervention. As the initial enthusiasm for educating southern blacks faded after Reconstruction, idealistic Americans turned their attention to mountain whites, a group perceived to be as needy and backward as the freedmen but possessing the pure Anglo-Saxon blood of America's ancestors. Though America's development had passed them by thus far, residents of the southern highlands, it was believed, needed only "education, religion, and civilization" in order to "advance with the rest of the nation." Protestant churches rushed to offer relief in the form of home mission societies and settlement houses; in fact, as Loyal Jones has pointed out, "no group in the country" prompted more concern among Christians than did the unchurched souls of Appalachia. "Never have so many missionaries been sent to save so many," he argues, "as has been the case in Appalachia." By the mid-1880s, in the spirit of competitive Christianity that characterized those years, the Presbyterians, Methodists, Baptists, and Episcopalians all turned their attention to the mountains.[28]

The LDS mission to Appalachian Georgia thus predates the establishment of mission efforts undertaken by mainstream Protestant denominations. As Henry David Shapiro observed about Appalachia in the 1890s, Protestant missions to Appalachia were "regularly represented as a defense against the encroachments of low-church Protestant missionaries, Roman Catholics, and especially Mormons, whose active proselytizing in Appalachia during the nineties worried everyone, and whose presence in the mountains seemed a thrust at the very heartland of America and a potent basis upon which to launch an appeal for funds well into the twentieth century."[29]

Considered within the context of this powerful religious impulse into the mountains, John Morgan's mission to north Georgia seems to fit neatly within a larger movement dedicated to cultural uplift and determined to propel mountain folks back into American society. The Mormon Church, however, did not intend a mission to Appalachia and would not—at this particular time—have supported a program that encouraged cultural assimilation. At midcentury, the church firmly set itself apart from America's dominant culture when church officials acknowledged the practice of plural marriage, or polygamy. Morgan likewise had little interest in preparing the inhabitants of his mission field to join the nation's march into the twentieth century. Elder Morgan believed that a world of sinfulness and corruption existed beyond the boundaries of the Mormon Zion. He understood that his goal was to warn Americans of their danger and to gather believers to the West. He had already given up on America, finding "the spirit of adultery and sin everywhere." Instead, he argued *for* isolation, explaining to potential converts the importance of "gathering to Zion," a physical separation that symbolized spiritual separation. According to this millennial doctrine, Mormons were to remove themselves as much as possible from the sinful world and gather together with fellow church members to prepare for the return of Christ. Under the influence of the Gathering, most new Latter-day Saints left their homes to resettle in Mormon centers in the West. In the 1880s and beyond, Protestant home missions would promote programs intended to ameliorate sinfulness, poverty, and ignorance in Georgia; Morgan offered simply to transport Georgians out of their current conditions.[30]

CHAPTER THREE

"One by One They Leave Us"

The First Expedition of Georgians to the West

On February 15, 1874, the *Atlanta Constitution* introduced Sunday readers to a new and thrilling feature. Written by an unnamed author expressly for the use of the newspaper and published in serial form over the course of several weeks, *Minnie Moreland; or, Love's Desperation* promised subscribers a "Story of Frontier Life in the Far West, a Part of the Country Prolific of Frightful Adventure, Wild Romance and Terrific Drama, Based upon Actual Experience." Set in 1870, the first installment in the series introduced John Moreland of north Georgia. Moreland, a former Confederate officer, had returned from noble service to the southern cause to find his home and property "greatly depreciated in value, and his affairs, by reason of absence, in great disorder." His native state suffered similarly. According to the story, it required only a cursory examination to confirm for Major Moreland "the dismal state of society in Georgia, the general impoverishment, and the utter demoralization of the laboring class." It was clear, he realized, that in postwar Georgia "he would be compelled to commence life anew almost from the lowest rung of the ladder." Instead, he resolved to abandon his home for the economic promise of the West.[1]

Friends importuned him to reconsider, reminding him of the danger and difficulty of frontier life, but he would not be dissuaded. So he turned his face westward and, on a cold and crisp winter day, began his exodus from the state. Accompanying him were his wife, son, former slave John—whose alleged devotion to the family was so strong "that he asked the privilege of emigrating with them"—and eighteen-year-old Minnie, Major Moreland's daughter and the heroine of the story. Described as a blue-eyed, golden-haired beauty, Minnie attracted numerous admirers in north Georgia, some suitors traveling great distances to meet her, and her popularity would persist in the West. Still, it was with a heavy heart that the Morelands left Georgia behind. According to the author, Major Moreland's "emotional nature was deeply stirred" as he moved his small family toward the train that would bear them away, and he looked back one last time before crossing the border from Georgia. "Lookout Mountain loomed behind him in the distance," reminding him of the land he held dear, but he remained resolute in his westward migration.[2]

At this point, the author interrupted the narrative to remind readers of the Georgians who had mirrored Major Moreland's behavior. The emigrant trains bearing people from the state had become a common and "painful" sight, he wrote, the "effects of the war causing the abandonment of old associations and the dear Georgia homestead." He continued, "It is fresh in the minds of all how many thousands of our people emigrated from Georgia . . . with the hope of bettering their condition." But, he warned ominously, "we shall see if the journey of Major Moreland proves as disastrous as it did to so many who emigrated . . . only to sicken and die, or return to the old homestead after a brief absence of suffering, privation, and disappointment." Suffer the Moreland family did. As the novel's plot developed for Atlanta readers over the course of the spring, they were likely enthralled by the fictional Georgia family's western exploits. In their first winter in the West, young Willie Moreland died. The family also faced animal attacks, natural disasters, murderous white raiders, and marauding Indians who burned the family's little log cottage to the ground and abducted Minnie. Taken at face value, the story fulfilled its promise to deliver to readers "frightful adventure, wild romance, and terrific drama." Conversely, the story could be read as a cautionary tale, warning Georgians of the perils accompanying emigration to the West.[3]

Almost as quickly as Confederate guns were silenced, Georgians moved to abandon the state, a fact that did not escape the notice of those interested in rebuilding. North Georgians seemed particularly eager to leave. In 1871 members of the Georgia legislature addressed the issue in a letter published in the *Atlanta Constitution* that noted that "a very considerable number" of north Georgians "are discontented and unsettled, and hundreds of them are removing to the great West," even though "Georgia cannot well afford to spare her own native manhood at this time."[4]

Only weeks before Minnie Moreland's story appeared in the *Atlanta Constitution*, a columnist for that paper opined that "perhaps no subject is attracting more attention in the South" than that of immigration and emigration. The southern states required labor—black and white—and this writer urged the Georgia legislature to move aggressively to attract workers to the state. The northern sections of the state were especially suited to white labor, he wrote, as it was "neither hot nor malarious, pleasant in all seasons, without a climate fever or disease of any kind, well-wooded and well-watered—a country which white labor ruled even in the old days, and one which only lacks an additional supply of it to blossom like the rose. In this upland country white labor has for a long time predominated." But the exodus *from* Georgia threatened to negate any successful recruitment. In the same week, another article described the "unwelcome spectacle" of five hundred emigrants, black and white, on their way out of the state. "Truly we cannot stand this sort of thing ... just think of the labor and benefit of five hundred stout energetic workingmen," each representing a family of four or five, with an aggregate loss to the state of perhaps two thousand laborers. The writer argued that "it is a dead loss to break up homes and a heavy expense to settle in new places. The chances are against the emigrant. He has to encounter sickness. He has to build up new associations and make new friends. If he fails he is bad off indeed—a stranger in a strange land. The thing must be stopped. As we urged yesterday in an article, the railroads must afford no facilities to such emigration, while the agents who are tempting our labor away by false promises must be restrained in their nefarious work."[5]

The *Atlanta Constitution* persisted in documenting the defection of north Georgians in small columns dedicated to local news, as it did in May 1877 when writers reported on a marriage between Mr. F. M. Puryear and Walker County's Miss Anna Brown, "one of McLemore's Cove's most beautiful daughters." Mr. Puryear, who had left the state for Texas seven years prior, traveled to Georgia for the wedding but intended to return to Texas with his bride immediately afterward. The columnist penned a dolorous postscript to the wedding announcement: "*One by one they leave us.*"[6]

In that same month, Elder John Morgan's thoughts also concerned emigration. A diary entry on the seventh day of that month contains his first reference to "gathering" the southern Saints to the West. "The spirit of emigration is taking hold upon the Brethren generally," he wrote, "and I am much in hopes that all will try and emigrate this Fall." Not only were Morgan's Georgia Saints resolved to go west; so were James Lisonbee's northeastern Alabama converts. Both missionaries apparently felt that a successful conclusion to their missions necessitated the relocation of southern converts to the western Zion. In April 1877 the elders announced a joint Georgia-Alabama conference in Chattooga County's Haywood Valley "to prepare the Alabama and Georgia Saints to gather West." Of the considerable obstacles they faced, perhaps the most pressing problem was the fact that the LDS Church specified no western destination for migrating southern converts. It seems that Morgan first intended to deliver his converts to Arizona, and in this he may have been influenced by the news that then–Southern States Mission president Henry Boyle planned to organize a company of Arkansas Saints to travel to Arizona. So at the end of May, Morgan wrote a letter to Elder Lot Smith, responsible for new Mormon settlements on the Little Colorado River in Arizona, and requested help. He proposed moving the southern converts by rail to the end of the Texas and Pacific line; at that point, they would travel by wagon to their final destinations in Arizona, if Smith could provide wagons and draft animals for transportation.[7]

Instead of replying directly, Elder Smith forwarded Morgan's letter to church president Brigham Young, who replied to

Morgan a month later. Young counseled against taking the southern converts to Arizona as the Saints there "were not in a position to render the aid asked," and he suggested an alternate plan: "As Zion is constantly growing so must we extend our settlements, and we are of the opinion that it would be well for the Saints gathering from Georgia and other Southern States . . . to locate in some favorable spot in the western portion of Texas, or in New Mexico." Morgan must make the final decision, he wrote, but "the spot selected should be a healthy one, with an abundant supply of water" for irrigation purposes. Further, Young encouraged Morgan to locate the southern Saints in the vicinity of the "Lamanites," Native Americans "over whom our brethren and sisters could wield an influence for good." Though Mormon racial theories discouraged proselytizing among black Americans, Latter-day Saints exhibited a particular interest in Indians. Believing American Indians to be descended from Hebrews who had migrated to America and were thus "part of God's chosen people," Mormon missionaries labored zealously to bring Native Americans to the church, believing that exposure to the gospel would produce a physical and spiritual renewal. President Young felt that both Indians and converts would benefit from a close association, as the Lamanites possessed an invaluable understanding of the land and its agricultural potential.[8]

The advice likely disconcerted Morgan and Lisonbee as neither missionary possessed any knowledge of Texas or New Mexico or the region's resident American Indians. Uncertainty about their eventual destination aside, the issue of funding the company also challenged the success of the mission, as the church in Utah offered no financial assistance to the emigrants. Despite their poverty, southern converts would bear the financial burden of expedition costs. Arranging favorable railroad rates assumed primary importance, and Morgan accepted that responsibility himself. He traveled from northwest Georgia to Chattanooga repeatedly, negotiating with railroad agents there for the best possible ticket prices, a task complicated by government efforts in Georgia and Tennessee to discourage emigration. The *Atlanta Constitution* repeatedly called on Georgia's railroads to discourage those who wished to leave the state. The railroad companies "were feeling the pressure so strongly," Morgan realized, that they had raised emigrant rates by a third.[9]

By August's end, Morgan reported to Brigham Young that the southern Saints planned to depart from Chattanooga for Memphis, then St. Louis, and finally Pueblo, Colorado. From Pueblo, he said, they would travel by wagon to their final destination, as yet undetermined, though he asked the church president if Taos, New Mexico, might offer a suitable site for settlement. Railroad officials agreed to charge $41.11 per person for travel from Chattanooga to Pueblo, but offered a 25 percent discount if Morgan assembled a traveling group of more than one hundred, a number he hoped to achieve before departure in November. Morgan finally convinced railroad officials to reduce the transportation costs to $29.80 per adult—children under the age of twelve traveled at half fare—but the lower cost required the expedition to depart from Scottsboro, Alabama, rather than Chattanooga. Lisonbee's Alabama Saints would travel only forty miles to the departure point, it was estimated, but Morgan asked Georgia Saints to negotiate three times that distance across difficult and mountainous terrain. Once all parties assembled in Scottsboro, the entire company intended to begin the journey by train to Pueblo, about one hundred miles south of Denver.[10]

Upon reaching the end of the line at Pueblo, the terminus of the Atchison, Topeka and Santa Fe Railroad, Morgan hoped to either purchase or rent wagons to complete the journey to New Mexico, but he admitted that he possessed very little information regarding either Colorado or New Mexico. He expressed reservations about travel during the winter months in Colorado and speculated that the company would winter at Pueblo then move on to a permanent settlement in the spring. Surviving a season in Pueblo necessitated employment for the southern converts, and again Morgan sought advice from Brigham Young, asking "could men find work at the end of the railroad in Colorado?" Sadly, Morgan's query never reached its intended recipient. Morgan posted his correspondence in was "endeavoring to pick out the strongest of the saints" to join the first company of emigrants, a journey intended to open the way for future expeditions. He pointed out that the expedition company included "carpenters, a blacksmith, a brick and stone mason, a shoemaker, and some farmers, all generally skilled in the use of tools and some specifically so in the pursuit of their trades." Additionally, he wrote, "We shall be able to take tools of almost all kinds and workmen to use them . . . also seed of every description."[13]

Morgan chose members of the first expedition from the Chattooga and Floyd County branches. Felix B. Moyers, who had publicly urged members to commit to gathering, prepared to join the first company, as did Moyers's friend and neighbor Elias Dennington. In anticipation of Moyers's absence, Morgan named young Joseph Haynie as the new president of Floyd County's Armuchee Branch. The recent birth of a daughter likely prevented Joseph Haynie from relocating, but his younger brother Patrick "Pack" Calhoun Haynie agreed to make the trip and Joseph Haynie's father-in-law, Francis Marion Weldon, committed to the expedition as well, preparing the way for family members to follow. Indeed, Joseph Haynie joined the second expedition in the spring of 1878, and his second child would be born in Colorado. From the Haywood Valley branch, Morgan selected William L. Marshal, Thomas Barbour's Unionist friend. Marshal's neighbor George W. Wilson also prepared to leave Georgia for the West, and Confederate widow Caroline Matilda Cosby Bagwell agreed to accompany her children, Tobe and Henrietta, to Colorado. Daniel Rice Sellers of Alabama also prepared for the journey along with his wife, son, and daughter-in-law. Several friends and neighbors joined the Alabama contingent, along with Daniel's younger brother and sister, their spouses, and their children. Morgan estimated that a total of fifty or sixty southern Mormons intended to depart for the West in mid-November. The rest, he said, planned to follow in the second expedition in the spring.[14]

How fully the southern converts understood Morgan's plans for them is not clear. Daniel Sellers later recalled that they expectation of a speedy response, but when the reply came two weeks later, the message proved unexpected and unwelcome. Brigham Young was dead.[11]

Despite Young's death, or perhaps in response to it, Elders Morgan and Lisonbee redoubled their efforts to lead their southern Saints toward the western Zion and organized another Haywood Valley conference for the first week of October in order to discuss the arrangements for emigration. Men who presided over local branches assembled: John J. Barbour of Haywood Valley, Felix B. Moyers of Armuchee, John B. Daniel of Beech Creek, and William C. Kilgore of McLemore's Cove. Representing the Alabama Saints, Daniel R. Sellers traveled to Georgia from the Grove Oak Branch on Sand Mountain. Both Morgan and Lisonbee addressed the Saints on the importance of the move west, urging "the necessity of a united effort on the part of the Southern Saints in regard to emigration." One by one, converts rose to express their commitment and urge a community response. Felix Moyers of Floyd County turned to the assemblage and reminded them of the religious imperative to leave Georgia, to "gather out of Babylon." His friend, Elias Dennington, went further, offering financial assistance to poorer Saints, publicly pledging "all that he possessed" to help the poorest Saints to emigrate "that we might all gather up to Zion together." Brother Sellers of Alabama endorsed Dennington's suggestion and went even further, arguing on behalf of a "general use of property" to enable all the Saints to emigrate. "As long as he had a dollar surplus, over and above the amount to carry him and his family to Zion," Sellers said, "it could be used to emigrate the poor Saints." The cooperative effort assisted poorer converts, but Georgians apparently cooperated to provide for a poor missionary too. Elder Lisonbee, who had reached the end of his mission but lacked the money to travel home, received loans totaling seventy-five dollars from Haywood Valley Branch members George Wilson and Thomas A. Lawrence.[12]

By late October 1877, John Morgan reported to new church president John Taylor that plans had been finalized and that he believed themselves bound for New Mexico. Perhaps they considered the details of their ultimate destination in the western Zion unimportant. Possibly their lives in the South had become so precarious, so unpredictable, that they were willing to tolerate further uncertainty in their lives. Or they may have simply trusted that God would make the way clear for this company of religious pilgrims. In this instance, their thoughts must be ascertained from their actions.[15]

In the days following the October conference and prior to November 12, the date set for departure from Georgia, Morgan's converts struggled to convert crops and what few assets they possessed to currency in order to accumulate cash sufficient to cover the cost of transportation. On October 18, Elders Morgan and Lisonbee assembled with Pack Haynie's family and friends for a corn shucking, Lisonbee reporting that "we helped shuck corn and stayed all night," pausing in their efforts long enough to baptize the baby born to Joseph Haynie. They then moved to the home of the new grandfather, Francis Weldon, who also hosted a corn shucking. They returned to Pack Haynie's in time to accompany the young man to market at Rome where he hoped to sell a wagonload of freshly ground cornmeal. After converting his crop to cash, Haynie offered up for sale all his possessions, save those things that might prove essential to a colonist. Felix Moyers employed a similar tactic. The train fare Morgan negotiated required Moyers, with a family of six adults and two children, to produce over two hundred dollars, a tidy sum for a landless cabinetmaker. So when Elder Lisonbee stopped at Moyer's Floyd County home, he found the Georgian "hard at work making ready" for the move, having already sold most of his belongings. The missionary accepted the family's invitation to supper, which fifteen-year-old Sallie Moyers prepared "in a brass kettle and on an old stove cake griddle with the handle broken off," but Lisonbee found all to be in good spirits. Of the visit, he wrote, "we had a fine time generally."[16]

John Morgan asked the Georgia Saints to begin the journey on November 12, and on that date wagons carrying the Marshals, Wilsons, and Bagwells departed Haywood Valley for Scottsboro,

Alabama. Felix Moyers's party left Floyd County two days later. Elder Lisonbee left on Thursday, traveling with the third and last group of Georgia Mormons, as did Elder Thomas Murphy, who had completed his missionary service and was returning to Utah accompanied by S. Murphy McKinney and Delila Murphy, his niece and nephew from Clayton County, Georgia. Pack Haynie traveled with them, as did a non-Mormon teamster hired to transport the party's goods first to the city of Summerville, then to Alpine, on the Georgia-Alabama border.[17]

Weather proved an almost insurmountable obstacle. Elder Lisonbee recorded in his diary that "it rained very hard most of the day and we had to foot through the rain and mud . . . the water just ran down the road." They made only seventeen miles that first day, as the poor weather slowed their progress and finally forced them to stop at an abandoned house for the night. They fared better on Friday and managed to catch the heavily loaded Moyers party who had, in desperation, hired a local man to help pull their wagon. With his assistance, the Moyers family crossed the Little River, but the wagon had only begun the climb up Lookout Mountain when one of the wheels broke, necessitating a two-mile retreat to have it mended. Aware that they all labored under a deadline, Haynie's party continued to the crest of Lookout Mountain, where they camped for the night. Early the next morning, they broke camp and prepared to move down the western slope. One wonders if the Georgians, like the fictional Major Moreland, took a moment to cast a longing look back as Lookout Mountain receded into the distance. If so, it did not slow their departure from the state. Emergency repairs did, for as they proceeded toward a mountain gap at Fort Payne, they ground to a halt again when one of Pack Haynie's wagon axles came apart.[18]

While his Georgia converts strained to reach Scottsboro, John Morgan finalized travel plans in Chattanooga, but by November 17 he was also en route to Scottsboro, where he expected to find emigrants assembled. Though he found only some of his Georgians gathered there, he circulated among them, offering encouragement to those already weary and experiencing doubts.

That evening he preached to the campers and announced that they should be prepared to depart from Scottsboro on November 19. Privately, he was worried. Haynie's party, forced to stop for repairs, still had not arrived, and neither had Lisonbee's Sand Mountain converts. The departure date came and passed. In fact, the Sellers party, which included several ox-drawn wagons, departed from home only in the early morning hours of November 20. By late afternoon of that day, a concerned Morgan borrowed a horse and left camp in a heavy rain to search for them, locating the party in the process of ferrying the last wagon across the Tennessee River on a large raft, a precarious crossing as the river was high and turbulent due to the heavy rains. The sun had already set when the Sand Mountain contingent rumbled into camp at Scottsboro, but it would be November 21 before Lisonbee and Haynie finally joined the assembled company.[19]

Though Morgan did not achieve the number he initially hoped for, he counted seventy-two emigrants from Georgia and Alabama as they boarded a Memphis and Charleston Railroad train bound for Corinth, Mississippi. At Corinth, they transferred to the Ohio and Mississippi Railroad for travel to Columbus, Kentucky, where the cars were transported across the Mississippi River by boat. At St. Louis, they transferred to the Missouri Pacific Railroad for Kansas City, where Elders Lisonbee and Murphy, as well as Murphy's two young relatives from Georgia, left the company to board a train that would carry them home to Utah. Finally, the weary Colorado-bound travelers transferred to the Atchison, Topeka and Santa Fe Railroad for the final leg of their trip.[20]

For four days they rode, often sleeping in their chair cars overnight. As they traveled, the southern folk gazed curiously at the vista spread before them, especially Daniel Sellers of Alabama, who said he had never before traveled more than a hundred miles from the place of his birth. The train chugged into Pueblo's depot late Saturday, but it was Sunday morning before the exhausted southerners finally disembarked into the cold and windy Colorado winter with, as yet, no certainty of their ultimate destination. The group of men, women, and children, likely clutching coats intended for milder Georgia winters, looked to John Morgan for direction. He found temporary shelter for the company in an abandoned theater with several stoves to provide warmth; still, when he paused to record the day's events in his diary, he noted tersely that it was "very cold."[21]

Morgan hoped that Pueblo's reputation as "the warmest place in Colorado, as well as one of the healthiest" would hold true. A bustling railroad town of about six thousand inhabitants, Pueblo also boasted new foundries and rolling mills that could offer winter employment to southern converts. The Arkansas River divided Pueblo, north and south, and his desire to maintain the company in a more secluded setting—a place that would offer privacy and isolate the Saints from corruptive influences—led Morgan to South Pueblo, where he found an appropriate settlement site on an island where the Arkansas River curved below the Santa Fe Avenue bridge. The heavily wooded location offered a natural windbreak and a good source of water, but there were other advantages to the location. A Pennsylvania company, located just north of Santa Fe Avenue, produced railroad rails in a new rolling mill, and its manager promised winter employment to the southerners, who apparently viewed the assumption of wage labor as a necessary expedient to accomplishing their goal.[22]

John Morgan shared his plans in a letter written to President John Taylor. The company intended to remain in Pueblo for the winter months, he wrote, in barracks they would construct on the South Pueblo site. As the company included carpenters, a brick and stone mason, and others familiar with tools, he believed they could manage the construction without additional assistance. The southerners intended to work through the winter, Morgan reported, as the mill's manager agreed to furnish jobs "as fast as the necessity of his business demands workmen." In Pueblo, common day labor yielded wages that ranged from a dollar fifty to two dollars per day, much higher than the twenty-five to fifty cents per day that laborers earned in northwest Georgia. If the transition from independent, albeit poor, farmers to wage earners troubled the southern converts, Elder Morgan did not mention it. Instead, he stressed their unity of purpose and the collective nature of the endeavor. "We think of buying beef and food and doing our own slaughtering, our flour by the 1/2 ton, our potatoes by the wagon load," he wrote, though he suspected that the information he shared with Taylor might be old news, as he knew that Elder Lisonbee should have already reached Utah to provide President Taylor with details of the expedition. In fact, Elder Lisonbee barely made it home. Suffering from pneumonia, Lisonbee died on December 10, 1877.[23]

After the southerners broke ground on the Pueblo barracks, Morgan called the company's men together to discuss the establishment of a United Order. He shared his conviction that a communal lifestyle best ensured the colony's material survival and emphasized its collective purpose. He advised the company to pool their meager funds in order to buy food and building supplies for the barracks, then to elect a president to make decisions regarding purchases and expenditures. They would pray together, labor for the benefit of all, pay the wages they earned into the common treasury, share a common domicile, and break bread at a common table. They would, in fact, live as one large family. Family was the model John Morgan imagined for the southern company, but his Georgia converts surprised and disappointed him. Both Felix Moyers and Elias Dennington rejected the United Order, refusing to join the organization. The dispute appeared to have been triggered when Georgian William Marshal nominated Daniel Sellers of Alabama as president and treasurer of the United Order of Pueblo. Though the company "unanimously" elected Sellers to the position, Moyers and Dennington subsequently announced that they intended to abandon the communal barracks for rental homes in Pueblo.[24]

According to Mormon historians, Brigham Young imagined the United Order as "a society in which the people would make and raise all they needed to eat, drink, or wear and still realize a surplus for sale to outsiders," and that vision coincided neatly with the economic goals of many Appalachian Georgians. Despite that, some of Morgan's converts thwarted the plan. They may have balked at contributing funds to a common treasury over which they would have no control or laboring on behalf of people not related by blood, even though Morgan, like Brigham Young, consistently emphasized the familial ideal to Mormon cobelievers. Or if dreams of economic advantage informed the decision to go west, perhaps their dedication to private property and profit overwhelmed utopian visions of religious cooperation. John Morgan noted but never explained the nature of the Georgians' objections, but he clearly recalled Moyers's enthusiastic public address in October when he urged the Georgia Saints to gather in the West, as well as Dennington's pledge to contribute "all he had" to the cause. When the men rejected the United Order, Morgan shared his disgust in a diary entry, revealing that both Felix Moyers and Elias Dennington had "kicked out of the traces and showed a bad spirit."[25]

The Sand Mountain converts, likely more secure in their relationship with Sellers, willingly contributed their money to the common treasury and provided most of the $400.00 taken into the fund. Daniel Sellers, the new president and treasurer, himself contributed $161.15, the largest amount from a single contributor. Georgians Pack Haynie and Tobe Bagwell, who both intended to live in the barracks, joined the order and donated $13.36 and $1.00, respectively. Three Georgians contributed monies but did not join the United Order: Francis M. Weldon contributed $4.33, William Marshal donated $7.65, and George Wilson added $50.00 to the total, but they, like Moyers and Dennington, rejected life in the barracks, choosing instead to rent houses in Pueblo. Felix Moyers, true to his sudden reversal of opinion, neither joined the order nor provided money for its support. When Elias Dennington offered John Morgan a grudging two-dollar donation, the missionary angrily refused to accept it. So in his report to President Taylor, Morgan reluctantly admitted that "two heads of families"—presumably Moyers and Dennington— "may not be able to meet the subject of" the United Order. He attempted reassurances, pointing out that "they are small families and possibly it is all for the best," and confided that he hoped to retain the rebellious Georgians in close proximity to the winter quarters "where they will be under our influence and control."

Of the others, he reported, "The brothers and sisters are all in good spirits, and the spirit of union has been with us."[26]

On November 28, despite dissension within the small company, the southerners put aside their differences to begin construction of the barracks, a welcome shelter from the Colorado weather, which Morgan described as "cold and blowing a perfect hurricane." Completed in four days' time, the wooden building measured fifteen hundred square feet, the interior space partitioned to provide a room for each family measuring ten by fifteen feet. Communal kitchens and dining areas occupied each end of the rectangular space. As the majority of the Georgians abandoned the communal building for rental homes, Alabama Saints occupied most of the rooms, although Caroline, Tobe, and Henrietta Bagwell, as well as young Pack Haynie, also settled into rooms there. Still, Elder Morgan maintained his public optimism about the familial ideal, writing that "the spirit of union has been with us . . . we are at present all eating at the same table and one man is purchasing all we use."[27]

The Colorado climate taxed both the spirits and health of the converts—locals reported nighttime temperatures of ten degrees below zero—and by the time they set up housekeeping in their new living space, many in the company suffered illness. Elder Morgan dutifully ministered to their needs but announced on December 3 that he planned to return home to Utah. Morgan's hope that "the company will hold together all right and be ready to move in the spring" apparently justified his decision to abandon the Saints in Pueblo for the winter. Duty done, he anticipated a release from his missionary service and a reunion with his wife and two children after an absence, he calculated, "of 2 years, one month and ten days." So only two weeks after reaching Pueblo, and despite fearful apprehension and objections from the southern company, Morgan boarded a train for Salt Lake City.[28]

In his conversations with Taylor and other authorities, Morgan seemed justifiably proud of his mission success. Though the permanent settlement site for the southern converts remained unclear, Morgan continued to promote the idea of establishing the colony in New Mexico. He publicly advanced the New Mexico plan in the *Deseret News* and, in anticipation of such a move, explored possibilities for employment. In mid-December he met with officials of the Denver and Rio Grande Railroad who were promoting extensions of the railroad into adjacent territory and expressed a need for labor. They accompanied him to meetings with President Taylor and, according to Morgan, "offered to assist our emigration materially in opening up New Mexico and Arizona" by agreeing to hire southern laborers. A successful resolution to the issue of the new Mormon colony consumed most of Morgan's attention in December and became more critical in January 1878 when he was called to replace Henry Boyle as president of the Southern States Mission.[29]

Anticipating the elder's return to the South, and with as yet no resolution for the southerners wintering in Pueblo, President Taylor requested that Morgan relinquish the decision of a permanent settlement site to another, asking instead that Morgan recommend someone capable of guiding the Georgia and Alabama converts to a new home. To that end, Elder Morgan made recruiting trips to Utah settlements and obligingly produced names of several men he felt competent to do the job, but each individual advanced by Morgan was rejected by President Taylor. Finally, Taylor offered a recommendation of his own, asking Morgan to call upon James Z. Stewart of Draper, Utah, only recently returned from a second mission to Mexico, to inquire about his willingness to undertake a third, shorter mission.[30]

Elder Stewart recalled that in his meeting with Taylor he was directed to "go to Pueblo and visit the Saints at the Barracks and then go and find a suitable place to locate them ... then to transfer them and locate them on the place I would select." While he was experienced at establishing Mormon colonies, proficient in Spanish, and willing to perform the task, Stewart understood the obstacles facing the southern company. "Knowing from what Elder Morgan had told me that these people were poor, and had none of the necessary equipments for locating and making a living in a new and unimproved section of country, I called the attention of President Taylor to the conditions of the people as they had been explained to me, anticipating that he would say that it would be necessary for the Church to lend some financial aid when it came to transferring those people and getting them started to making a living for themselves." He admitted to surprise when President Taylor replied, "Brother Stewart, the lord will open up the way." In his written account of the encounter, Stewart remembered his reaction to the statement: "Well, I knew that 'the Lord could do it,' but I must confess that I thought it was the hardest mission that I had ever been called upon to perform." As he was offered no financial assistance, Stewart borrowed sixty dollars to finance his mission. In his conversation with Stewart, President Taylor mentioned the possibility of settling the Saints in southern Colorado, rather than New Mexico or Arizona; in fact, Taylor had already solicited advice from Lawrence Marcus Peterson of Cebolla, New Mexico, regarding the southern converts. Elder Peterson, who had once lived in Los Cerritos, Colorado, along the Conejos River, recommended the San Luis Valley for settlement. President Taylor immediately solicited Peterson's help in establishing the new colony.[31]

James Stewart, charged with locating the specific settlement site, insisted that John Morgan travel to Pueblo to prepare the southern converts for the final leg of their journey. So in early March 1878 and prior to his planned return to the South, Elder Morgan visited with the Pueblo Saints and found them impatient for a permanent home. By working at various occupations in and around the city, they had survived the winter and earned enough to provide support for the group. However, Morgan learned that they had been unable to put aside any of their earnings, as "they had been too trustworthy of others and had been defrauded of some of the little means they had." Even more concerning, Pueblo residents had attempted to dissuade the southerners from their religious path. Despite the isolation of the barracks, which Morgan hoped would shield the converts from disruptive influences, strangers occasionally appeared in camp, including one Mormon apostate described by Morgan as "a man who had turned from the truth and endeavored to cause dissension." Gratefully, Elder Morgan reported that he had "yet to find the first person who was in least affected from this."[32]

Still, the weary would-be colonists bickered constantly, and Elder Morgan reluctantly predicted that the rebellious Georgians who initially rejected life in the barracks "will probably fail to continue the journey," a mission misstep he was forced to address in a letter to the *Deseret News*. In it, he acknowledged the difficulties faced by the southerners, though he likely minimized their suffering, and assumed some responsibility himself: "They were entirely unacquainted with the country, its manners or customs, which was an obstacle of no small magnitude to overcome. They had no Elder to advise them and were left to their own resources to obtain food and raiment, but they tell me they have had plenty to eat and wear; no one has suffered. Another difficulty was they were thrown into very intimate relation with each other in their winter quarters and the natural weaknesses and frailties of human nature would, of course, prominently develop themselves; differences would naturally arise, and inexperience would make blunders."[33] Bickering and discomfort aside, real heartache accompanied life in the barracks. Alabama convert Bird Jackson Kirtland died there, as did the tiny daughter of Samuel Sellers, and for the southern converts nothing reinforced the strangeness of their new circumstances more than consigning their loved ones to the Colorado soil. They remembered burial as an agonizing process, even for infants whose small bodies required relatively limited space. A fire would be built on the spot selected for the grave. The bereaved relative waited by the fire until the frozen earth had been sufficiently warmed to allow some soil to be scraped away. In the slight depression thus created a new fire was built, then more soil removed, the process repeated again and again until there was a cavity large enough to cradle the tiny casket. But in the midst of such melancholy, births also offered renewed hope to those wintering in Colorado. The arrival of Hugh Sellers's baby daughter cheered the converts, as did the realization that young Pack Haynie and Henrietta Bagwell of Georgia seemed to have fallen in love.[34]

To those eager for news of a final settlement site, Elder Morgan could offer very little. A desire to guarantee employment for the southern converts still chief among his concerns, he turned again to the officials of the Denver and Rio Grande Railroad for advice. From Pueblo, he penned a letter to Alexander Cameron Hunt, the territorial governor of Colorado from 1867 to 1869, now a promoter of the extension of the Denver and Rio Grande line into the San Luis Valley near the southern boundary of Colorado. Hunt responded cordially enough and offered to meet with Morgan and United Order president Daniel Sellers in Garland City, Colorado, the end of the Denver and Rio Grande line. The trip to Garland City they accomplished via a narrow-gauge railroad that was, for a time, the highest rail line in the world. In a report to the *Salt Lake Herald*, Morgan recalled his delight when the train stopped on the eastern side of the La Veta Pass through the Sangre de Cristo Mountains, where he encountered "a settlement of Georgians, who have recently left the sunny south and cast their lots in this far-off land." The Georgians he met, non-Mormons all, expressed contentment with their decision to move west and buoyed Morgan's confidence that his expedition of southerners would experience similar success.[35]

From La Veta, the train continued to climb in a dizzying ascent. "Still up and up we go," Morgan wrote, "until in the dim distance we can see the narrow thread of road that makes the route we have come over, thousands of feet below. The cars swing and sway to and fro, at places where it seems as though the least displacement of equilibrium would topple us over the side of the mountains into the top of the tall pines, so far below that they assume the look of mere shrubbery." One imagines that Daniel Sellers of Sand Mountain, Alabama, may have clutched at his seat a time or two before the little train chugged into a depot that Morgan noted was nearly ten thousand feet above sea level, then "the highest railroad post in the known world." A more gradual descent carried them into Garland City, the temporary end of the track where they planned to meet with former governor Hunt.[36]

Hunt shared plans to extend the railroad during the summer, first forty-five miles west to Alamosa, then south toward Wingate or Santa Fe, New Mexico. If the southern converts relocated, Hunt assured Morgan and Sellers, the railroad extension would furnish employment to all willing to labor. He also recommended for settlement the Colorado lands that lay directly in the line of the railroad extension—at the southern end of the San Luis Valley in Conejos County, near the mouth of the Conejos and Antonito rivers. Though enthusiastic about the promise of employment, Morgan believed the elevations and conditions of life in the railroad towns between Pueblo and the San Luis Valley prohibited a series of relocations. Instead, he recommended to President Taylor that the company remain in Pueblo until the acquisition of land for settlement had been accomplished, but he also stressed haste, as he estimated that the converts had only six weeks, perhaps until the end of April, to plant a spring crop. Negotiations with the Denver and Rio Grande Railroad produced reduced fares of $1.22 per adult to the end of the track at Garland City, an affordable fare as most of the southern laborers collected wages of $1.25 per day, lower than promised, but sufficient for travel costs. Morgan did request that the LDS Church send teams of cattle to the settlement, as they would be immediately needed to put in a crop of spring wheat. "If not," he wrote, "we will need means from some source to buy cattle with, to plow our ground, and gather together enough material to build houses."[37]

Assured of employment and with a possible final destination in sight, Morgan and Sellers departed for Pueblo and shared their news with Elder Stewart, intercepted in Denver as he also made his way to the southern colonists. On his arrival at the barracks, Stewart remembered, he "found the Saints in just the condition I had been told they were," all maintaining their faith, but "anxious to get permanently located somewhere." He wasted little time in preparing a party to survey the recommended San Luis Valley and selected three of the Pueblo Saints—Milton Evans from the Alabama contingent and George "Jesse" Wilson and Tobe Bagwell of Georgia—to join him "in hunting a place to colonize." The party of four, carrying rations for twenty days as well as axes, spades, and guns, left Pueblo for Garland City by the same narrow-gauge rail line that had transported Morgan and Sellers.[38]

Upon his arrival in Pueblo, John Morgan circulated among the southern Saints, mediating differences and encouraging the "lukewarm" to continue the journey. To the delight of the assembled converts, Morgan officiated at the marriage of Pack Haynie and his bride, thirteen-year-old Henrietta, eight years his junior. Two days later Morgan boarded the train that would carry him back to Georgia. As he moved east, Stewart's expedition reached Garland City, then set out on foot, beginning a three-day trek "part of the time in snow, rain, and mud" toward the Rio Grande. A Mexican freighter ferried them across, and they found their western Zion the next day, in southern Colorado's San Luis Valley, near the village of Los Cerritos and a few miles north of the New Mexico border.[39]

Elder Stewart acquired property for the Mormon colony by purchasing two farms from Mexican ranchers on the south side of the Conejos River. The first parcel, with a "good adobe house ... and 120 acres of land," he obtained for thirty-five dollars, which he paid with a note cosigned by the governor of Colorado. The second, described only as "a good farm," he acquired for fifty dollars, on Stewart's personal note alone. From local residents, the four men purchased a plow and a team of oxen to pull it, and by the end of May, Stewart reported to John Taylor by letter that they had managed to sow seven acres of wheat and to plant an acre of potatoes as well as a variety of other vegetables. Of "Conejos," Stewart wrote, "the land and water are good, and timber plentiful, but the climate is cool ... good crops are generally raised, but are sometimes cut off by frost." He estimated the altitude to be seven thousand feet; in reality, he was about seven hundred feet short. Later, in response to Taylor's request for a more detailed description, Stewart elaborated, "There are three or four nice streams flowing through the country, along which are nice bottoms of meadows and farming land." Along the banks of the rivers grew cottonwood trees, large willows, and wild currants. In fact, Stewart wrote, "the natural growth of the country is similar to that of Utah." The southern converts would prosper there, he believed, assuring Taylor that Colorado's state officials welcomed the Mormons and that the Denver and Rio Grande Railroad would "run directly through the Valley, from one end to the other in the coming year," which promised employment and prosperity.[40]

Despite Stewart's assurances, President Taylor expressed his misgivings to Elder Morgan, laboring again in Georgia and already planning a second expedition to the West. "We have but one fear" about the Colorado settlement, Taylor wrote, "and that is that it is somewhat too cold for Southern folks." Morgan heard similar concerns from the Georgians but dismissed them, writing, "I am of the opinion that Conejos will not be so extremely cold as some of the brethren conjecture. It will at least furnish a base, to enable us to stand upon until such time as the Saints can look up a more favorable locality."[41]

Elder Stewart, who thought it best to send settlers a few at a time, selected the families in Pueblo who would leave the barracks first—the Daniel Sellers family, the widow Kirtland, Pack Haynie and new bride Henrietta, and her mother, Carolyn Bagwell. He left behind laborers with good jobs in Pueblo, as they would continue to earn money to benefit the colony. Southern converts later remembered that Pack Haynie constructed the first house in the settlement. The Haynies set up housekeeping in a hut measuring twelve feet by twelve feet and "built of quite large trees," with walls "about 3 logs high," and a roof of wooden poles, straw, and dirt. Another southerner constructed housing from Haynie's cast-off tree limbs.[42]

According to Mormon accounts, the southerners desired the assistance of those more experienced in establishing settlements. Certainly Morgan and Taylor believed they would benefit from the counsel of other church members. Answering the call, a group of church members from New Mexico immediately relocated to the new Colorado colony. Bishop Hans Jensen accepted the call, too, and departed Manti, Utah, with a party of eighteen. They reached Los Cerritos in October 1878, only days after the final group of southern brethren arrived from Pueblo.

In that same month, a local branch was organized with Bishop Hans Jensen as presiding elder.[43]

During the summer of 1878, Daniel Sellers—still representing the southern emigrants—sounded optimistic. Declaring "things generally in good shape" in Conejos County, he compared past to present. He evaluated the progress of the southern Saints and reported that "the health of the Brethren and Sisters is generally good at this place." The weather he described as "nice" with warm days, "but not hot and sultry," and the July nights were cool. However, frost persisted until mid-June, and Sellers predicted a somewhat disappointing harvest. The wheat promised a light crop, but the potatoes, peas, and beets grew well; still, he wrote, "most of the other garden stuff looks rather sorry." He declared himself "well pleased with this country" even though the colonists missed some of the fruits and vegetables they had raised in the South. "Upon the whole," he concluded optimistically, "I think it is a much better country than I left."[44]

As Sellers warned, the fall harvest failed to produce enough to sustain the colonists. When they had been reduced to meals of ground wheat and Mexican beans, Bishop Jensen requested emergency assistance from the church. Help arrived, appropriately enough, on Christmas Eve. President Taylor provided forty-five dollars, and with that money, Jensen purchased flour, which was divided among all. From their Mexican neighbors, who were apparently sympathetic to their suffering, they solicited a loan of twenty-one dairy cows to produce milk, butter, and cheese.[45]

Though the emergency provisions satisfied immediate needs, there was trouble brewing in the western utopia. The United Order of Pueblo, the communal organization introduced so painfully in winter quarters, persisted in the Colorado colony, but for only a short time. Citing unspecified "misunderstandings and difficulties" that made cooperation impossible, Bishop Jensen thought it best to disband the United Order.[46]

CHAPTER FOUR

"Women Is the Only Subject to Be Talked On"

Threats of Violence in North Georgia

After successfully shepherding the first company of southern converts west, John Morgan expected to return to his Salt Lake City home. Instead, the church rewarded Morgan's efforts by naming him president of the entire Southern States Mission. So in the spring of 1878, as members of the first expedition fought to establish a foothold in the new Colorado colony, Morgan returned to Georgia to assume his new responsibilities. Having relinquished the care of the southern brethren to others, Morgan turned his attention to problems that had erupted over the winter within the northwest Georgia mission field.

A flurry of winter correspondence from Georgia Saints to Elder Morgan carried news that a missionary from the Reorganized Church of Jesus Christ of Latter-day Saints was at work in northwest Georgia. Having battled Methodists, Baptists, and Presbyterians for the hearts of Georgians, Morgan realized that he now faced an unexpected foe—Joseph Smith III of the Reorganized Church. Headquartered in Plano, Illinois, the RLDS represented the bitter political struggle occasioned by Joseph Smith Jr.'s death. The majority of Mormons chose to follow Brigham Young, but a smaller group ultimately appointed Joseph Smith III, the prophet's son, to head the rival church. The "Reorganites" or "Josephites," as Georgians variously referred to them, rejected the principle of plural marriage as divine revelation, and apparently Haywood Valley branch president John Barbour, one of Morgan's first converts, also questioned the principle. Determined to go to the authority, he penned a letter to Smith III, and from Smith's reply it is obvious that the issue of polygamy prompted Barbour's inquiry. In his letter, Smith denied that polygamy originated with his father but did admit that he was "not positive nor sure that he was innocent." Smith preferred to blame Brigham Young for introducing the practice. In his first sermon as leader of the Reorganized Church, Smith had articulated his distaste for Young and his followers: "There is but one principle [polygamy] that I hold in utter abhorrence; that is a principle taught by Brigham Young and those believing in him." In his reply to John Barbour, Smith explained further that if plural marriage *did* originate with his father, "it could not have been a revelation from God," but "either of man or of the Devil." The 1870s saw an intense and bitter rivalry between the Utah Saints and the Illinois Saints, and apparently the leader of the Reorganized Church resolved to battle Mormons who accepted the principle, even on grounds as remote as Appalachian Georgia. In Morgan's absence, Reorganized Church representative John H. Hansen moved among the Georgia Saints to offer a counterargument to the Southern States missionaries. Morgan fought back as best he could, noting in his journal that "[I] have been writing letters in reply to some from the Georgia Saints, who are being much disturbed by a Josephite preacher." Morgan assessed the threat as real and he was correct.[1]

The dissension created by preacher Hansen—and confused Georgians—plagued John Morgan in the first weeks after his return in March. In April he sought out John Barbour for an intense overnight discussion, which concluded most unsatisfactorily. Barbour, he wrote, "showed a bad spirit, a spirit of contention," code words for someone disagreeable, argumentative, or inhospitable. The exchange proved so confrontational that at one point Barbour suggested they send for the "Josephite" John H. Hansen to debate Morgan in person, but Morgan angrily refused any such exchange with the "apostate." Two weeks later, he returned to Barbour's home for another overnight stay with a similar outcome, declaring himself "pained to see John's condition."[2]

Scholars of the Southern States Mission have argued that Mormon elders typically avoided the subject of plural marriage. As mission president, John Morgan downplayed the principle's importance, reassuring a newspaper reporter in 1881 that Mormon elders "preach faith, repentance, baptism for remission of sins, and the laying on of hands for the reception of the Holy Ghost. They very rarely refer to polygamy, and then only in response to inquiries." Local newspapers appeared to buttress his claim, confirming that Mormon missionaries, as far as they knew, "have not preached licentious doctrines at all, but have kept the polygamic feature of their religion in the background."[3]

Such a claim is unlikely, as LDS marriage practices held a prurient fascination for most nineteenth-century Americans. Mormon elders could not escape questions about polygamy, even in Appalachian Georgia. Morgan prepared himself to confront such inquiries, arming himself with Bible verses that seemed to offer support for the practice. Morgan's papers, which document his mission to the South, contain a collection of Bible verses carefully organized by topic. One imagines that he assembled the list for easy retrieval at times when his arguments required scriptural proof. Of the four topic headings, three concern the "Gathering" of the Saints. The fourth is "Plural Marriage," which suggests that these issues—emigration to the western Zion and polygamy—represented topics that must be addressed. In his defense of Mormon marriage practices, he relied chiefly on the Old Testament. From Genesis 4:19, for example, "And Lamech took unto him two wives," and the account in Genesis 16:1-3 of Sarai, who urged her husband Abram to take Hagar as another wife. Exodus 21:10 instructed, "If he take him another wife; her food, her raiment, and her duty of marriage, shall he not diminish," while Deuteronomy 21:15-17 offered advice "if a man have two wives." In citing the multiple wives of Bible patriarchs, Morgan's conclusion seemed inescapable—what the Scriptures mention but do not condemn cannot be a sin. Such an argument may have been familiar to southerners, as a similar Bible-based argument for slavery often came from southern pulpits.[4]

It is more accurate to conclude that LDS elders, though forced to address private questions about polygamy, generally avoided public pronouncements regarding plural marriage. While representatives from the Reorganized Church made north Georgia home throughout the spring and summer and continually challenged Elder Morgan to publicly debate points of doctrine, he summarily declined all invitations. From sad experience, Morgan knew that such encounters usually devolved into messy spectacles. Only weeks into his first mission, Morgan found himself in a pitched battle with the editor of the Bloomington, Illinois, *Leader*. The *Leader*, in its coverage of one of Morgan's public lectures, summarized the missionary's views: "His very argument seemed to be that because Solomon and David had a plurality of wives, therefore every man in these latter days should increase his responsibilities in the same direction." Morgan responded in a December 1875 letter to a more-sympathetic Bloomington newspaper, the *Pantagraph*. He railed against the *Leader* and mounted a vigorous defense of polygamy. Of his critic, Morgan wrote, "He asserts polygamy to be a sin. I ask him to point to one single passage in his Christian Bible, from Genesis to Revelations, denouncing it a sin!" The *Leader* responded by taunting Morgan with Joseph Smith III's Reorganized Church: "Mr. Morgan tells us that polygamy is a Divine Institution, while the followers of Joe Smith [the Reorganized Church] tell us that polygamy is an institution introduced by imposters to gratify the lust of the flesh; which shall we believe? Why doesn't Mr. Morgan pitch his tent at Plano, Illinois, and preach polygamy to the Monogamous Saints, whose eyes have not yet been opened to the beauties of a system that proposes to cure prostitution by establishing a system of concubinage in its place?"[5]

Morgan did not arrive back in Georgia in time to prevent a similar public spectacle. Elder David Williams of Salt Lake City, handpicked by Morgan for the Southern States Mission, reached Georgia in early 1878 and found himself drawn into just such a combative situation. He had arrived weeks in advance of the mission president so could not benefit from Morgan's advice, and when Reorganized Church missionary Hansen invited him to engage in public debate at Cave Spring Church in Walker County, he accepted. In February, before the assembled Georgia Saints and curious onlookers, Williams lost his temper and did not acquit himself well. As a pained John Morgan later admitted, Williams "appeared to have run contrary to the spirit" in the heated exchange, "and the result was not at all pleasant, but we hope to overcome the evil influence engendered in the discussion." Morgan waxed optimistic in his journal, writing that Georgians "are apparently paying but little or no attention" to the Reorganized Church, but reluctantly acknowledged that John Barbour appeared "still shaky in the faith. He does not know which is right, and I think is about as likely to go one way as another." The work of the "Josephite preacher" in provoking Barbour's questions certainly reveals that Morgan's Georgia converts were not as strong in the new faith as he might have hoped.[6]

Despite Barbour's internal struggles, Morgan believed the Georgia mission field to have been stabilized by May 1878. After a visit with the Georgia branches in Chattooga, Floyd, and Walker counties, Elder Morgan reported "a good feeling existing on all sides." To church authorities in Salt Lake City he conceded that "the storm that swept over the branches caused many to tremble and fear, but they are righting too, and once more getting into shape, and the final result will, I think, be that their trials have only strengthened them."[7]

Violence and threats of violence had dogged John Morgan's heels during his first mission to Georgia, and he expected little change in the second. Warnings of trouble had come during the summer of 1877, when Morgan visited with converts in Walker County. "Some pistols fired near the house after night," he wrote in his journal at that time. In the autumn that followed, Jesse Bartlett Faucett, also of a Walker County branch, reported a midnight visit from "devils" claiming to represent the Ku Klux Klan (KKK). They asked for Elder Morgan, but upon learning that the missionary was not in residence, they left. They reappeared days later at an outdoor meeting hosted by convert William Dixon Bailey. Morgan remembered that the meeting had barely begun when one of the Bailey daughters "rushed in from a neighbor's house and informed her father that the KKK were preparing to break up the meeting and forcefully drive the elders from the community." After a moment's deliberation, Morgan asked if Bailey possessed firearms. Bailey then walked into his home, reemerging moments later with three loaded weapons "which Elder Morgan stacked immediately beside the table he was using as a pulpit." The Klansmen retreated.[8]

Nineteenth-century Appalachian Georgia was a dangerous place. It is impossible to divorce the mountain counties from the violence inherent in antebellum racial slavery as that institution existed, at least marginally, in north Georgia. The Civil War also unleashed destructive and devastating guerrilla warfare in northwest Georgia counties, as Confederate sympathizers and Unionists clashed on the home front. Whether described as raiders, Independent Scouts, or guerrilla bands, brutal marauders prowled northwest Georgia, inciting fear in Unionists and Confederates alike. In the months immediately following the war, guerrillas continued to plague the region, claiming that they worked on behalf of local residents and the maintenance of law and order. Reconstruction saw renewed violence as the Ku Klux Klan worked to "redeem" Georgia from Republican rule and return control of the state to white conservative Democrats.[9]

Chattooga County boasted the largest group of Klansmen north of the Chattahoochee River, attracting members from Floyd, Walker, and Chattooga counties who worked to suppress the Republican vote in northwest Georgia. Although the KKK had officially disbanded by the time Mormon missionaries appeared in the state in the mid-1870s, men identifying themselves as members of the Klan continually harassed Mormon elders, describing themselves as protectors of public morality. Whether they had represented the terrorist group in the past is unknown. The illegal liquor trade also provoked shooting wars in the Georgia mountains, as it did in 1877 when armed conflict between moonshiners and U.S. revenue officers broke out on the border of Fannin and Gilmer counties. As historian Edward

FIGURE 2. Warning to the Mormon elders. Southern States Mission president John Morgan found this warning tacked to a tree. John H. Morgan Photograph Collection (P0605), box 1, folder 11, Special Collections, J. Willard Marriott Library, the University of Utah.

Ayers pointed out, "the New South was a notoriously violent place." Lynching reached a peak in the last decades of the nineteenth century, with the southern mountain region experiencing a disproportionately high rate of extralegal violence, usually atrocities inflicted upon African American men.[10]

Morgan reserved his bitterest recriminations for those he believed responsible for inciting violence against Mormons: Georgia's clergy and press. He communicated Georgia threats to the Saints in Utah, an effort to emphasize both the perils of his mission and the sweetness of success, which led the *Deseret News* to report, "Alarmed on account of so great progress being made, notices were posted warning Elder Morgan to leave the country, and ministers from the pulpit advocated mobbing, hanging, and other violent measures." For an 1878 issue of the church journal *Juvenile Instructor*, Morgan wrote a first-person account of an event that took place in the shadow of Floyd County's Lavender Mountain. The Floyd County Saints, he wrote, typically gathered at dusk, seating themselves "upon the rough planks and benches that have been hastily brought together for the purpose." Morgan remembered that the small church was crowded with converts and curious family and neighbors who had come to hear him preach. His words were met with such close attention, he said, that "a pin can almost be heard to drop upon the floor." However, the peaceful service was suddenly and shockingly interrupted. To journal readers, he described the scene:

> "Bang, bang, bang, bang!" go a lot of guns. The boards that cover the crevices between the logs rattle, and we hear the heavy thud as the lead strikes the solid logs. The shots rattle alongside of and against the weather boards while the hurried tramp of feet on the outside tell us that our disturbers are fulfilling scripture, in that they are fleeing "where no man pursueth." For a moment only does the audience show signs of uneasiness. One or two start to their feet, while a frightened word or two falls from the lips of the most excitable. Uncle Billy Manning, sitting directly in front, without ever turning his head, or deigning to notice the alarm, speaks slowly and calmly: "Keep quiet!" The tones of his voice show that he is cool and collected as though at the table asking for polk greens, his favorite dish. A word from the Elder of assurance is offered, and

the thread of the discourse is taken up, and continued to the close without any allusion to the incident.[11]

John Morgan expected the opposition to resume upon his return to Georgia in 1878, so he was not surprised to learn that Klansmen intended to welcome the elder by disrupting LDS meetings in Walker County's McLemore's Cove Branch. Though he never acknowledged fear, Morgan found it prudent to travel between Chattooga and Walker counties in the hours between midnight and morning. Forewarned of a particular threat, Walker County branch president William C. Kilgore summoned Morgan to the cove. Resolving to meet violence with violence, the two "sent for some of the brethren and armed ourselves for a fight." The anticipated showdown never occurred. "More or less talk of K.K.K.," Elder Morgan wrote in late May, "but we have not been troubled yet."[12]

The arrival of new missionaries from Utah buoyed his spirits—especially the arrival of Joseph Standing, called by the church in March 1878 to take up his second mission to the South. Morgan assigned two elders to Virginia, including nineteen-year-old Matthias Cowley, a former student at Morgan College and welcomed affectionately as "Brother Mattie" by his old headmaster. Morgan asked missionary David Williams—he of the disastrous debate—and Andrew S. Johnson to remain in Georgia, where they had made tentative inroads south into Polk and Haralson counties, though Morgan generally preferred Georgia missionaries to go into the counties to the north. Four missionaries would labor in Georgia, including Morgan and the young man he selected as his missionary companion. Of Standing's responsibilities, Morgan wrote simply, "Joe will stay with me for a while." The elders had labored together briefly in Indiana and Illinois before Standing relocated to Tennessee to complete his mission and Morgan welcomed the opportunity to renew their friendship.[13]

Perhaps the strengthening of his mission force led Morgan to downplay local resistance. "The opposition has been strong and bitter," he wrote in a mission report, "but so far has not had any perceptible influence to retard the work. I am satisfied that thinking people throughout this part of the country are more in the spirit of investigation than they heretofore have been, and if we but have the patience to teach steadily along, good results will follow." Oddly enough, he believed the South uniquely receptive to religious outsiders. This was due, he believed, to southerners' Reconstruction-era exposure to "carpet-bag governments and imported officials" from the North. Further, he argued, southerners understood and sympathized with Utah's efforts to achieve statehood and its ongoing battle with the federal government as both the South and Utah had "felt the iron heel of the oppressor." As proof Morgan cited a growing receptiveness to Mormon preaching and religious tracts, which he interpreted as a lessening of hostility.[14]

Few, if any, contemporary historians would support Morgan's image of a South that welcomed "spiritual carpetbaggers." At Reconstruction's end, Georgians had driven blacks and northerners from positions of power as quickly as possible, returning the state to native southern Democrats. However, Morgan correctly predicted that at least some southern politicians would remember that the Republican Party had once identified slavery and polygamy as the "twin relics of barbarism" and view the government's repression of the LDS Church as reminiscent of the South's own struggle against the United States. Regardless, the majority of Georgians likely believed, as the majority of Americans did, that polygamy violated the sanctity of marriage. If they had any doubts, they need look no further than local pulpits for answers, as north Georgia's ministers preached earnestly an anti-Mormon and anti-polygamy message. At this point, no face-to-face violent confrontations between elders and locals had occurred, largely because the first branches of the LDS Church in Georgia—those in Chattooga, Floyd, and Walker counties—primarily represented nuclear families, some of them constituent families within a larger network of kin. In these counties, the presence of male heads of household seems to have successfully deterred serious efforts to confront directly either Georgia's new Saints or the LDS missionaries who often relied on their protection. When patriarchs assumed a prominent role in branch leadership, their participation appears to have diffused, at least partially, objections from local critics.

Four Mormon missionaries now labored in the Georgia mountains, including John Morgan, who intended to direct the efforts of the Southern States Mission from Floyd County. Thus reinforced, Morgan announced plans for an aggressive fall and winter campaign. He believed the cool weather seasons were best suited for proselytizing in the South and anticipated spreading from the established branches in Chattooga, Floyd, and Walker counties into new fields of labor. He intended to rely upon the leadership of new Saints to maintain established branches, so selected John B. Daniel of Floyd County, assisted by Joan Manning, to organize a Sunday School. Sister Manning also expended much energy in the production of a new publication, a missionary tract written by John Morgan and titled *The Plan of Salvation*. Morgan ordered three thousand copies printed locally and enlisted Joan's assistance to stitch the pages together. The coming campaign would be launched from a conference to be held in Haywood Valley in August. John Morgan set the tone, and an optimistic spirit dominated the summer gathering.[15]

The Georgia brethren assumed their duties willingly enough—as branch presidents, counselors, and teachers—and when Morgan organized a Relief Society in 1878 for the benefit of Georgia's female converts, the sisters were given new opportunities to serve. Created by Joseph Smith in 1842 as a fundamental part of the LDS Church, the Relief Society provided adult women an opportunity for religious education, service, and leadership and emphasized the sisterhood of female Saints. The organization of a Relief Society followed that of the general Relief Society headquartered in Salt Lake City and mirrored that of a branch, so leadership consisted of a president and her two counselors, a secretary, and a treasurer. New members were elected into the fellowship. Though profoundly patriarchal, the LDS Church expected women of the Relief Society to play a significant role in their branches, offering advice regarding the material and spiritual needs of the community. Sisters devoted themselves to a service ministry, administering to the poor and infirm, but also bore responsibility for "saving souls" so were instructed in church principles in much the same manner as the men.[16]

Georgia's mountain women found opportunities for religious service but generally exercised domestic skills. They traditionally provided hospitality, food, and shelter to visiting preachers and missionaries, and just as they had cooked and laundered for Methodist circuit riders, they willingly assumed similar duties for Mormon elders. In an 1877 journal entry, Elder Lisonbee praised one of the sisters "who had been doing his washing" and expressed gratitude for a pair of socks she knitted to accompany his new boots. Morgan also benefitted from the care of female Saints, thanking Mary Kilgore for similar tasks.[17]

LDS missionaries repaid that devotion by ministering to the women's physical and emotional needs. Elders Morgan and Lisonbee reported their first healing after receiving a summons from Tabitha Marshal in 1877. They anointed and blessed the woman then claimed "she was healed in a few minutes of spinal disease in the back, not being able to get up when she was down." A similar but more urgent appeal drew the pair to Martha Bailey's Walker County home to minister to her newborn son. "Rode back through a terrible rain storm and found the child very sick," Morgan wrote in his missionary journal. He attempted a healing that night and for three additional days "continued to watch around the baby . . . night and day." By the fifth day Elder Morgan began to abandon hope, and on the sixth he confided to his diary that the baby "continued to sink away until at 1:25 PM he passed away. My heart bled with pity for the poor mother and sisters." Later, he and Elder James Lisonbee assisted with the funeral of "little Millard" Bailey.[18]

Beyond cooking and cleaning, the Latter-day Saints' Relief Society offered women more direct opportunities for religious service. Morgan believed the labor of women important to the success of the southern mission, as they "could be a great help to the Elders in spreading the gospel . . . by writing to their friends, distributing tracts and disseminating the principles of truth among their associates and friends." Elders frequently relied on the women within branch organizations to identify potential converts and thus provide potential openings into new fields of labor. But Morgan also considered the Relief Society to be critically important as it linked Georgia's female Saints "with the sisters in Zion," a supportive sisterhood that—intentionally or not—transcended and supplanted traditional networks of kin and neighborhood. In 1878, when Morgan extended an invitation to any female "who wishes to do good," female converts eagerly stepped forward to join the first Relief Society in Georgia. At the conclusion of the three-day conference, highlighted by a picnic within a grove of trees, Morgan crowed that it was "the best conference I ever attended away from Zion." Conference minutes noted that by August 1878 the South had produced over 500 branch members; of that number, 261 had already relocated to the West. Morgan, who had directed the first company to Colorado, anticipated a second expedition from Georgia in November.[19]

Morgan dedicated the remaining warm months to expanding the mission field, creating openings that could be exploited during the prime cooler months. An invitation to preach in Catoosa County shaped the direction of that campaign. Ironically, the invitation came from Nathaniel Connally, a non-Mormon whose brother had converted to Mormonism. Connally believed the Utah missionaries deserved a fair hearing and once sided with Morgan in Walker County against the KKK. According to Morgan, Connally proved a tremendous asset, as he was well known and well liked but a member of no church, which implied a certain neutrality. Nathaniel advanced the Mormon cause with energy and enthusiasm, encouraging Morgan to carry the LDS message to family members in Catoosa and Whitfield counties. Somewhat bemused by Connally's efforts on his behalf, Morgan praised the Georgian by name in a mission report published in the *Deseret News*, writing that Connally "has for some time been taking an active interest in behalf of the Gospel, and devoted much of his time in talking to the people and securing places for us to preach, a business for which he is well qualified as his acquaintance is quite extensive and he spares no pains. He distributes our tracts and pamphlets and papers everywhere he goes and altogether has been a great help in disseminating the truth."[20]

A yellow fever epidemic curtailed missionary efforts during the summer of 1878, including potential visits to Catoosa and Whitfield counties. The disease depopulated nearby Chattanooga, sending residents of that city to Dalton and other unaffected communities. Morgan wrote to Salt Lake City readers of traveling the north Georgia countryside and finding refugees in "outhouses, tents, temporary barracks, and often wandering aimlessly through the woods." Though he believed the onset of cold weather would halt the spread of the disease, fears of contagion and the unfavorable economic climate ultimately forced him to abandon his plans for the November expedition to Colorado, which he intended for departure from Chattanooga. Morgan placated the approximately one hundred prospective colonists, many in receipt of letters from Colorado settlers urging their southern brethren to come West, by pointing out that the Colorado colony was "scarcely strong enough" to support its current residents, but would be stronger by spring.[21]

Disappointed, Morgan delayed the second expedition until March 1879, assuring potential emigrants that they would still have time to establish homes and put in crops before the cold Colorado weather set in. He hoped the delay might add to the company's number, as it provided additional time for the poorest Georgia Saints to raise money for train fare. As he had done in the past, Morgan attempted to solicit aid for migrating southerners. In a letter to church president John Taylor, Morgan described those seeking aid as "eminently worthy of help," pointing out that men with large families desired to go, but could pay only a portion of the travel costs. They would accept a loan from the church, he wrote, if allowed to repay it over time. The church did not extend such help; in fact, Morgan would be forced to leave destitute families behind when the second company left the South.[22]

With no fall expedition forthcoming, Morgan accepted Nat Connally's invitation. John Morgan and Joseph Standing left Walker County in mid-September, Connally traveling with them as he intended to personally introduce the missionaries to family members living along the border separating Catoosa from Whitfield County. Connally delivered the missionaries first to the Catoosa County home of his niece, Elizabeth Elledge, who welcomed the missionaries cordially, as did her husband and children. Elizabeth, in turn, directed the elders to the residence of her married daughter and son-in-law, Mary and Henry Huffaker, a short distance away in the railroad town of Varnell's Station, where Henry and his father-in-law ran a store. Just as the Elledges had done, the Huffakers opened their home for public meetings, and soon the Mormons were also holding services for Whitfield and Catoosa citizens at nearby Smith's Chapel.

The first baptisms to occur in Varnell's Station came only six weeks after the elders' initial visit, when Mary and Henry were baptized, along with Mary's mother, Elizabeth Elledge. Dillingham Elledge gave consent for his wife's baptism but did not join her, perhaps due to the influence of his brother-in-law and Baptist minister Brittain Williams. Local residents had always considered Dillingham and Elizabeth Elledge to be "good Baptists," so word of her defection quickly spread. Brittain Williams was especially outraged. According to family members, when the preacher heard of Elizabeth's baptism, he exclaimed forcefully, "I'll soon straighten her out!" Williams's comment may suggest that evangelical church discipline persisted, especially as an effort to correct women and prevent disruption of the family and community. Interestingly, Elizabeth Elledge refused to accept the correction offered by Brittain Williams, in either role of patriarch or preacher. His effort to "straighten her out" proved singularly unsuccessful, as both the Elledges and Huffakers were soon inviting neighbors to attend meetings with the Mormon elders at their homes and nearby Smith's Chapel. Among those giving the missionaries careful consideration was David Williams, the son of the Baptist preacher. "I think we are moving something," Morgan enthused after a meeting at the Huffakers', noting that there had been a "full house" and "good attention" given his message.[25]

Morgan also found "a good spirit" at the home of John Nations, who had married into the Huffaker family and was, in fact, a cousin to Elizabeth Elledge. However, the visit to John Nations illustrates the selectivity of the conversion process and the potential for family disruption. The oldest child of Elizabeth Elledge's paternal uncle, Manley Nations, John was the only member of Manley's family to receive a call from the elders. There is no record that Mormon elders visited Manley Nations or any other member of his household, which included a wife, a daughter, and grown sons. Similarly, the missionaries made no call at the home of Elizabeth Elledge's stepmother. By indirectly choosing her coreligionists, Elizabeth appears to have rejected her deceased father's extended family even as she embraced the new religion brought to her by members of her mother's family.[24]

Seventeen-year-old William Lonzo Kaneaster recalled that the arrival of the missionaries rescued him from his mid-September boredom. The northwest Georgia weather was fine—warm and sunny, with no hint yet of an autumn chill—but the pastimes William most enjoyed, like floating on his back in a small pond nearby, had been put aside for familial obligations. The young man was charged by his parents with the care of his paternal grandfather, who had broken his shoulder in a fall from a wagon, and his interest was piqued by the announcement that Mormon elders would be holding services at nearby Smith's Chapel. "That was news to me," he wrote later, and with a curiosity appropriate to news of a visiting circus, he immediately "went home to fix to go to hear the strange people." When his mother, Sarah Kaneaster, asked where he was going, he replied simply, "to hear the Mormons." She declared herself not interested. But William's great-grandmother was keenly interested. He found eighty-eight-year-old Sarah "Granny" Fullbright, who lived next door to the Elledges and so near Smith's Chapel that some of the church gravesites extended onto her property, "shining herself up to go," William remembered, as curious as he to see "what kind of people they are."[25]

Kaneaster escorted his great-grandmother to the meeting, where they found friends and neighbors already assembled. Joseph Standing opened by singing a Mormon hymn, "O, Say What Is Truth," then John Morgan rose to speak. "He spoke two and a half hours as fast as he could talk," Kaneaster wrote, "and he wasn't slow." When services ended, William returned his grandmother to her home, where Elviny Hamblin, Sarah's daughter and William's grandmother, waited. "What did you hear?" she wanted to know. According to William, Granny Fullbright pointed her finger for emphasis and declared, "I heard the first sermon I ever heard in my life," meaning, of course, the best sermon she ever heard in her life. At his own home, William's mother also waited for an account. Like his great-grandmother, he reported it as the best sermon that he had ever heard.[26]

Granny Fullbright's finger wagging would not have surprised her Catoosa County neighbors, as she enjoyed a reputation for outspokenness. When a Catoosa County debating society organized evening meetings at the chapel, Fullbright found her sleep disturbed by the angry male voices that carried through her windows. Late one night, she rose from her bed and resolved to put an end to the debates. Wearing "only snow white gown and cap," she walked across her yard and through the church's graveyard, then burst through the door of the chapel. Fullbright opened her mouth to berate the young men she saw assembled there, but it was not necessary as "the audience looked around and saw what they took for a ghost coming out of the cemetery, and promptly fled through the windows. There were no more debates at this place."[27]

In John Campbell's classic 1921 study of Appalachian culture, *The Southern Highlander and His Homeland*, mountain "grannies" are afforded much respect. "There is something magnificent in many of the older women," Campbell wrote, praising their "deep understanding of life" born of hardship and perseverance. "Patience, endurance, and resignation are written in the close-set mouth and in the wrinkles about the eyes," he observed, "but the eyes themselves are kindly, full of interest, not unrelieved by a twinkling appreciation of pleasant things." This "Granny"—as he referred to the mountain matron—"has gained a freedom and a place of irresponsible authority in the home hardly rivaled by any man in the family. Her grown sons pay to her an attention which they do not always accord their wives; and her husband, while he remains still undisputed master of the home, defers to her opinion to a degree unknown in her younger days. Her daughters and her grandchildren she frankly rules."[28]

One suspects that Granny Fullbright, the first in her family to embrace the new religion, exerted a considerable influence over her daughter and granddaughter. William's mother, who had initially expressed no interest in the Mormons, soon joined her mother and grandmother in attending Mormon meetings, an activity apparently tolerated by her husband, Josiah Kaneaster, though he displayed little interest. For weeks, the women—William referred to them as his "three mothers"—regularly attended and hosted meetings conducted by Elders Morgan and Standing. So impressed was Standing with elderly Sarah Fullbright that he mentioned her by name in a mission report, noting in amazement that "she read the Book of Mormon through in one week." As 1878 came to a close, the women expressed a desire for baptism. It was a simple matter for both Sarah Fullbright and Elviny Hamblin, who had no husbands to consider. The matter was more complicated for Sarah Kaneaster, who required permission from her husband.[29]

Mormon missionaries routinely refused women's requests for baptism if the ritual lacked the approval of male heads of household. When two men claimed authority over females, the decision proved more complicated, and occasionally explosive. Morgan's missionary journal reveals that just such an uncomfortable situation occurred in Walker County, Georgia, when a woman's request for baptism pitted father against husband. Mary Faucett Haggard and her husband, Albion, often accompanied family members to neighborhood meetings conducted by Elder Morgan. Mary and her family displayed only eagerness to join the Saints, but Albion initially proved unreceptive to Mormon advances. Morgan recalled his first, difficult encounter with Albion in the summer of 1877, when, he wrote in his journal, "a young man by the name of Haggard got mad." But Mary's desire for baptism increased when first her mother, then her father, sister, and brother received the ordinance. She confronted Morgan directly to request baptism, but he refused, advising the young woman that she must ask Albion's permission, a common practice among missionaries sensitive to public opinion. Mary Haggard eventually gained Albion's permission, as Morgan noted in a journal entry: "Last night Albert [sic] Haggard, who has been very bitter against us, came up to me and asked me to baptize his wife, which I did." Ultimately, Albion joined his extended family in Mormonism, his reservations about the new religion overcome by the dedication of his wife and in-laws.[30]

Elder James Lisonbee reported a similar domestic situation while laboring on Sand Mountain in Alabama when Mrs. Sariahann Uptain requested baptism. She was told by Elder Lisonbee to obtain the permission of her husband, which she did. Unfortunately, as Mr. and Mrs. Uptain made their way to the creek, they encountered Sariahann's father and a group of his friends. "They came to forbid me baptizing Mrs. Uptain," Elder Lisonbee wrote. Harsh words soon turned to physical confrontation, and the missionary could only watch and await the outcome as Sariahann's husband and father "had a small fight over the matter." The younger Uptain prevailed, and Lisonbee continued with the baptism, but Sariahann's religious choices clearly divided and disrupted the family unit.[31]

Neither Granny Fullbright nor Elviny Hamblin required any man's permission for baptism, and apparently Josiah Kaneaster had no strong feelings about the matter, for no controversy accompanied Sarah Kaneaster's request for baptism. On New Year's Day 1879, Elder Standing led the three women into the cold waters of a nearby creek for baptism. So delighted was he that he could not resist sharing the news with Elder Matthias Cowley in Virginia. He would have baptized the women in late December, he wrote, but the weather had been too cold—"Isn't this fearful cold weather? 'Sunny South,' ugh!"—so he postponed until January 1, 1879, when it was, one assumes, warmer. To "Brother Matty," Standing gently boasted, "I baptized the old lady and her daughter and her daughter, making three generations." The Varnell's Station Branch now claimed six members, five of them women. Henry Huffaker, the lone male participant, served as branch president.[32]

More Mormon elders joined the northwest Georgia mission field with the arrival of Ralph Smith, Edlef Edlefson, and Andrew Johnson. Morgan assigned them to the maintenance of existing branches and an exploratory foray into Polk County; he and Standing tested the waters in Murray County, but continued to maintain a headquarters in Varnell's Station. Standing, waxing optimistic, declared that he was "getting to like the work first rate. One can enjoy it when he sees the people desirous of leaving and who are not so full of prejudice, that you can't get within 400 rods of them." But his comment speaks to the persistence of anti-Mormonism in the region. Missionaries routinely received warning letters, including one from Methodist minister Henry Green, which they ignored. Standing tended to dismiss the opposition of rival ministers, believing that their personal shortcomings prevented serious objections, even to plural marriage. He pointed out the hypocrisy of an ex-minister of the Baptist Church who had recently scheduled a public meeting in order to dispute the Mormon teachings. Standing attended and watched as the lapsed preacher arrived in a wagon along with "his legal wife and a woman that he has kept as a wife for years," making the subsequent tirade against polygamy seem ridiculous.[53]

At this point, the young elder betrayed no fear. Judging from his correspondence, Standing's chief complaint was loneliness. He pouted when John Morgan left Georgia to see to mission duties elsewhere. When bereft of his missionary companion, Standing complained to his friend, Matthias Cowley. "I assure you that I *sigh for one glance of his eye*," he wrote of Morgan. "This single blessedness is not so nice as I would wish, but one cannot have everything he wants." On another occasion, when Morgan left him in order to visit the Alabama Saints, Standing complained to Cowley again: "So you see how I am situated—alone." He battled the solitude and homesickness by maintaining a busy schedule of preaching and visitations and "thus I am kept out of mischief, and my thoughts are engaged on other matters than home." When he learned that youngsters in Varnell's Station especially loved Mormon hymns, he loaned out hymnbooks and set aside two nights of each week for singing, "with pleasing results."[54]

Morgan continued to shuffle elders into the mission field, calling Thomas Higham from his Tennessee post to travel with Standing into Murray County. Elder Charles W. Hardy came from Mississippi to maintain the Varnell's Station Branch. Joseph Hyrum Parry, just completing a mission to Wales but en route to Georgia, also planned to join Morgan's mission. A former student at Morgan College in Salt Lake City, Elder Parry avidly read Morgan's mission reports in old copies of the *Deseret News*. As his Welsh mission neared completion, he requested a transfer to Georgia, to work with his "old friend and college teacher," John Morgan. "In this field I felt that I should get some real old-time missionary experience," he later explained, "and I was not disappointed." After the two-week journey from Wales, Parry landed in New York City in mid-February, where he purchased a train ticket for Rome, Georgia. Inquiries in Rome led him to a convert family in Floyd County, residing seven miles out of town "in the woodsey country," but Morgan was not there. The mission president had traveled to Fannin County, in response to a call to preach. He located the John D. Harrison family, "who live in the highest rocky place I ever saw people live," at the top of John Dick Mountain, near the headwaters of Noontootla Creek. In return for the visit, Harrison promised to escort the elder farther north to western North Carolina. For weeks Morgan moved across the border between Georgia and North Carolina, dividing his time among new converts in Fannin County and the branch he established in Brasstown, North Carolina.[55]

The planned spring expedition drew Morgan back to Varnell's Station in mid-March. It would be his last expedition, he hoped. He anticipated an end to his southern mission; in fact, church president Taylor had released him to return home to Utah, which he intended to do once he had seen the southern company safely to Colorado. Calling the Georgia missionaries together to Varnell's Station, Morgan saw to a new distribution of labors, his chief concern the maintenance of branches already established and continued efforts in those mountain vicinities newly opened to Mormon visits. Elder Parry also made his way from Rome to the meeting at the Elledge home, where he felt immediately welcome. Morgan greeted his former student effusively, and Parry also recognized Standing, whose father he knew from the Monday evening prayer circle Parry had attended as a youngster. After much affectionate back-slapping, Morgan assigned Elders Parry, Higham, and Edlefson to go to North Carolina, where they would continue the work he had begun in Brasstown. Standing, who had been working for two months in Murray County with very little to show for it save "a number of friends," he directed to Fannin County. Elder Hardy would travel "with Brother Joe into the mountains east."[36]

When he evaluated the earnest faces of his elders, Morgan was dismayed by their youth, the youngest of them only eighteen years old. In a letter to church president John Taylor he fretted about leaving the Georgia mission in the hands of elders who "are inexperienced in the work and are quite young." However, his anxiety could not cloud the festive occasion. With six young Mormon elders gathered together in the Elledge home, neighbors crowded in, prevailing upon the missionaries to lead them in some Mormon hymns. The young men complied, and Joseph Standing and Joseph Parry took the lead, acquitting themselves so admirably that they resolved to meet a few days in advance of the next conference in order to practice for the public singing. They arranged to rendezvous in Varnell's Station on July 20 and travel together to the planned Haywood Valley Conference in August, "singing at the various branches as we traveled through."[37]

On March 21 Elder Morgan bid the elders goodbye, satisfied that he had successfully completed his second mission to the South. Perhaps he would have lingered with Standing, who had served with him so faithfully and cheerfully, had he known what the future would bring. Instead, he turned his face toward the West and departed for Colorado with sixty southern converts, among them Henry and Mary Huffaker. In anticipation of the move, Huffaker sold his Catoosa County farm, accepting a partial payment of five hundred dollars but relying upon his wife's uncle, Thomas Nations, to collect the remaining five-hundred-dollar balance. The Elledges' son George replaced Henry and assumed management of the store in Varnell's Station, a temporary expedient as the Elledges intended to follow their daughter and son-in-law to the western colony. Though they remained in residence on their Catoosa County farm, they had already transferred the property to Nathaniel Connally, who agreed to dispose of the real estate. The Fullbright-Hamblin-Kaneaster women also began to prepare to emigrate.[38]

Standing noted, with a fine sense of irony, that this second exodus of Georgia Saints coincided with excitement surrounding the "Second Coming" of William T. Sherman, who returned to Georgia for a well-publicized tour in 1879, then praised north Georgia as a region suitable for settlement by those from the North or West. Though one Georgian suggested to the *Atlanta Constitution* that Sherman's arrival in Atlanta should be marked by the ringing of the city's fire bells, curious Georgians crowded the train depot in hopes of spying their famous foe. At the conclusion of Sherman's tour, he was invited to share his observations of the state, and he obliged in writing, singling out north Georgia as a "naturally beautiful and most favored region of our country." He praised the climate, general healthfulness, and abundance of natural resources, and declared Georgia's upcountry open to newcomers: "North Georgia is now in a condition to invite emigration from the northern states of our union and from Europe, and all parties concerned should advertise widely the great inducements your region holds out to the industrious and frugal of all lands," he wrote, adding that "two or three millions of people could be diverted from the great west to this region with profit and advantage to all concerned." Surprised by the generosity of Sherman's letter, Editor Howell of the *Atlanta Constitution* reproduced it in its entirety. It became so popular that the *Constitution* advertised extra copies for sale "in wrappers ready for mailing" at five cents per copy. Dalton's *North Georgia Citizen*, whose editor acknowledged himself as "no admirer of the man who desolated so many of the homes of this beautiful section of the State," nevertheless issued thanks for

Sherman's "kind words about our country," and expressed confidence that the letter "may do much towards attracting immigration in this direction." Standing, who had just waved goodbye to west-bound Georgians, wryly commented that the Utah Board of Trade should "apply for the services of W. T. Sherman in inducing immigration to Utah."[39]

On March 25, Elder Standing added four new members to the Varnell's Station Branch. "We now have a Branch of eight," he reported to Matthias Cowley, "all Sisters." The development, though not unwelcome, created a dilemma for Standing and Hardy. "We are undecided as to what steps to take," Standing wrote. "Bro. Huffaker, who was the only male member of this branch, and its president, is on his way to Zion, so that there are eight lone women, and all young in the Church." With no male at the head of the branch, meetings would not be possible and communion could not be provided. Instead, Elder Standing mused that they might "let the sisters hold their own meetings," perhaps through the organization of a Relief Society or similar woman's organization. At least three of the sisters were married, but their husbands—Dillingham Elledge, Josiah Kaneaster, and Riley Loggins—had not been baptized, so they may not have shared their wives' commitment to the new religion. "I would like to see some men step forward and take hold of the Gospel so that meetings could be held in the branch," Standing complained to Cowley, moaning "the men, oh, the men!"[40]

Standing's disappointment in the men of Varnell's Station continued into April, so, perhaps resigned to the men's recalcitrance, he organized the women into a Relief Society. Elizabeth Elledge agreed to accept the presidency, with Granny Fullbright and Sarah Kaneaster serving as her counselors; Elizabeth Loggins assumed the office of secretary. That spring, eight sisters from Catoosa and Whitfield counties came together regularly in an exclusively female religious organization, bound together by gender and belief, but excluding those, even friends and family, who did not accept Mormonism. To those unfamiliar with LDS religious organizations, the Relief Society may have seemed a female prayer group, which many community members would have viewed as improper. Or, when Elizabeth Elledge—who rejected Brittain Williams's correction—assumed leadership of the women, it may have suggested a female-headed church, with no male authority supervising the sisters and no spouses to exercise husbandly authority. Instead, the sisters worshipped under the solicitous care of the young male representatives of a polygamous faith.[41]

Standing simply hoped that the organization would be enough to "encourage and sustain" the women "until the time shall come that they may gather to the body of the Church" in the West. Satisfied that he and Elder Hardy successfully resolved the problem, Standing noted his intention to leave Varnell's Station to go "up among the mountains" of Fannin County, "where the pure breezes blow and the clear streamlets flow." An Atlanta newspaper would later report that he fled Varnell's Station to avoid accusations of seduction, but there is no evidence of that. Instead, Elders Standing and Hardy hoped to fulfill John Morgan's desire to build on an opening he had made in that area. In Fannin County, the elders found a receptive audience, but Standing soon faced the loss of yet another missionary companion.[42]

"Elder Hardy left me to return home, having been released," Standing complained in an 1879 letter to Matthias Cowley. "This was by no means pleasant to my feelings, for not only had I become greatly attached to Brother Hardy, but here were scores of people seemingly interested in the gospel, and it now devolved upon me to teach and instruct them." He then noted gloomily the possibility that John Morgan would remain in the West and compared Cowley's long-term relationship with his missionary companion to his own unfavorable circumstances. "It seems to me that you and brother Barnett are married. I get a companion for a short time, then am left alone, and then another one is given me, and he goes, and so adfinitum," Standing complained, then added a plaintive postscript to the bottom of the missive: "Write."[43]

Later, Standing learned that Elder Hardy barely achieved his departure. Hardy left Fannin County for the Varnell's Station depot but missed the train by minutes. With time to spare, he decided to call the Varnell's Station Saints together for one last meeting. Sarah Kaneaster agreed to host the event, but at the conclusion of the meeting, one of the Georgia Saints "looked out and saw a bunch of men coming." According to young William Kaneaster, whose "three mothers" were in attendance, it was the first mob to move against the Mormons in Varnell's Station. If the assembled men intended to apprehend the missionary, they were thwarted in their effort by the sisters gathered inside. Just as the men approached the front of the Kaneaster house, the women led Hardy to a rear window that opened into a field of corn. Hardy, who said he "didn't want to cause any trouble," escaped, invisible among the tall stalks.[44]

The immediate arrival of Rudger Clawson, Hardy's replacement and the new missionary companion to Standing, further prompted the ire of anti-Mormon forces. Clawson had not anticipated a mission call that would carry him to Georgia. In his memoir he remembered sitting quietly in the great Mormon Tabernacle on Temple Square in April 1879, when his name was announced as a new missionary to the Southern States. "You can very well believe that this was like a bolt from a clear sky," he remembered. "It nearly took me off my feet—it would have taken me off my feet had I been standing, but fortunately I was sitting."[45]

Standing and Clawson were not friends prior to their Georgia mission, but would become so; in fact, their names are forever linked in tragedy. Both were unmarried, the children of LDS Church members who resided in Salt Lake City's Twelfth Ward. The similarities end there. Clawson grew up in a polygamous household that included one father and two wives, as well as a noisy brood of fourteen children and two female domestics from Europe who helped care for them. A good student, Clawson enjoyed the Wasatch Literary Society and at eighteen earned an enviable position as secretary to the president of the Utah Western Railway Company. His job required travel, which took him from Utah for two years and exposed him to major urban centers of the East. New York City introduced him to dancing,

FIGURE 3. Elders Joseph Standing and Rudger Clawson. Records indicate that this photo was likely taken in Georgia. John H. Morgan Photograph Collection (P0605), box 1, folder 10, Special Collections, J. Willard Marriott Library, the University of Utah.

which he enjoyed so much that he hired a dancing master upon his return to Salt Lake City. He learned the popular round dances of the period—the waltz, the mazurka, and the gallop—which earned him the disapproval of church authorities. Though Clawson claimed he would "prefer to engage in the round dance rather than to sit down to an elaborate and sumptuous banquet," he gave up the hobby "and thus abandoned one of the real pleasures of social life."[46]

Rudger Clawson, blessed with all the social graces befitting prominent young men, hastily prepared for a mission to the

Georgia mountains. With barely enough time to purchase sturdy new boots, Clawson boarded a train to the South. Clawson disembarked in Varnell's Station in early May, expecting to find Standing there, only to learn that Standing remained in Fannin County, perhaps seventy miles away via dusty wagon roads. "It was a hot summer day," Clawson remembered, "the air was sultry and the heat well-nigh unbearable." But he believed that he should present his most polished appearance to the Georgia public, so he struggled with only partial success to get his new boots back onto his feet, as perspiration had caused the leather to shrink. He managed to wedge his toes into the boots, but his heels would not go down. "I was a cripple," he described himself, "hobbling along through the hot sand and the heat, with a knapsack over one shoulder containing literature and a knapsack on the other shoulder containing personal supplies." He trudged along, virtually on tiptoe, before finally removing the offending boots, tying them together, and throwing them over one shoulder. He continued his journey barefooted, a summer style very familiar to backwoods Georgians but strikingly at odds with Clawson's neatly tailored suit.[47]

He emerged from the rough path in Gilmer County, where he quickly acquired a crowd. He responded to queries honestly, introducing himself as a Latter-day Saint, which earned curious stares. Commentaries regarding the church and its most controversial practices had featured prominently in Georgia newspapers for years. Georgians had snickered at Ann Eliza Webb Young's divorce suit against Brigham Young in 1873, when she accused the Mormon prophet of neglect, cruel treatment, and desertion. "Ann Eliza is fairly sweeping away the old man's property," the *Atlanta Constitution* reported. "If he had but been content to clamber up the hill with seventeen or eighteen, all this might have been avoided." The divorce suit was later thrown out, at which point Brigham Young's apostate plural wife embarked upon a national publicity tour, delivering strident anti-polygamy lectures while promoting her book *Wife No. 19; or, The Story of a Life in Bondage, Being a Complete Expose of Mormonism, and Revealing the Sorrows, Sacrifices and Sufferings of Women in Polygamy*. She also testified before the U.S. Congress and may have influenced the passage of the 1874 Poland Act, which reorganized the judicial system of Utah Territory and made it easier for the federal government to prosecute polygamists. Similarly, the *Constitution* celebrated the 1877 execution by firing squad of John D. Lee, "The Mormon Butcher," convicted of masterminding an 1857 attack in which 125 Arkansas settlers were killed at Mountain Meadows in Utah. Georgia readers eagerly followed when the LDS Church resolved to go forward with a test case of the Poland Act. In 1878, Utah polygamist George Reynolds appealed his conviction to the U.S. Supreme Court, arguing that plural marriage should enjoy protection under the First Amendment to the Constitution. The court disagreed. The conviction was upheld and Reynolds was summarily dispatched to the penitentiary. Occasionally, anti-Mormon sentiment was masked as humor. In 1878, for instance, one writer quipped, "A Mormon has just married, at one swoop, a mother and a daughter. Has he a mother-in-law?"[48]

In some cases, news articles focused on the licentiousness of local missionaries. Following the departure of the Georgia Saints to the West in the spring of 1879, the *Atlanta Constitution* reported on the progress of that expedition, reprinting an interview that appeared in the *Memphis Avalanche* under the heading, "Mormon Converts from Georgia." The *Avalanche*'s reporter intercepted the company only days out of Georgia, describing the party as "squalid in dress, ignorant looking," and "taken from the poorer and lower walks of life." The Memphis newspaperman sought out one attractive young woman to ask why she had undertaken the journey. She had only barely responded that she was on her way to the West "after a husband" when John Morgan, according to the reporter, intervened to "put an end to the conversation." The reporter directed the same question to Morgan: "Why is it that these people wished to leave?" Morgan allegedly replied that "the men go because it is the religion of the world, and it will finally prevail." Of the women, he said, they go "because they cannot get husbands here." For the benefit of the newspaperman, Morgan explained that Georgia possessed thirty-three thousand unmarried women. "As soon as we get to Utah," he said, "all will be married to as many as we want to." Morgan then pointed out that the newspaperman was young and handsome. "This young lady," Morgan indicated the young Georgia Saint, "is also young and pretty," adding slyly that "if you will go along with us you may have her." According to the reporter, his superior morality prevented him from accepting Morgan's offer. Whether or not the writer accurately reproduced Morgan's remarks or character is uncertain. The *Atlanta Constitution* simply reprinted the article with no comment.[49]

Morgan often complained that newspapers stirred anti-Mormon sentiment in Georgia, explaining that articles carried in the *Atlanta Constitution* were routinely reproduced by smaller county newspapers, becoming fodder for local ministers' sermons against the religion. In some cases, the opposite was true. On May 1, 1879, the *North Georgia Citizen* included a small and suspect, but incendiary, item: "Within the past year eight Mormon girls have married colored men in Salt Lake." The same appeared, word for word, in the May 15 issue of the *Atlanta Constitution* and then was reproduced exactly in the May 21 issue of Murray County's *Gazette*.[50]

Unfamiliar with the newspaper coverage that generally denigrated Mormonism and portrayed Georgia's women as the victims of lascivious elders, Rudger Clawson accepted a Gilmer County physician's invitation to take shelter from the heat, but hesitated when the doctor offered to arrange a meeting at the local courthouse. "The judge and the lawyers and their ladies and all the important people of the court are here," he told the young elder. "If I can get the court room tonight for a meeting, will you be the speaker?" Clawson gave a weak affirmative, having had no experience in public speaking, but the doctor returned quickly, a celebratory smile in place. And despite the objections of a burly sheriff, the physician delivered a packed audience. Directed to "take the rostrum," Clawson realized that "I had no choice but to take it." He read some hymns to the crowd and then launched into his impromptu sermon. He had spoken for thirty minutes when a man shouted from the audience, "We want to hear something about polygamy." Clawson obliged, saying, "I have been raised in a polygamist family, I am a polygamist child, my mother was a second wife" and "a noble woman she was too." A sudden loud rustle from the room startled him. He watched as "the ladies of the court officials, those grand society ladies who were occupying the front seats, all with one accord rose to their feet and made for the door." Clawson attempted to halt their rush by promising to say nothing further on the subject, but they "fairly swept out of the room, and nearly swept me off the rostrum."[51]

Elders Standing and Clawson finally connected in mid-May. Clawson described Standing as "kind and affable," even though Joe occasionally mocked Clawson's ignorance of his mountain mission field. "I had to laugh at him the other day," Standing confided in a letter to Matthias Cowley, describing a recent dinner at the home of Georgia converts. "At night we had corn bread, bacon, and some gravy—for drink we had thick clabber milk, cream, and half sour," while the next morning "we indulged in a change—heavy wheat bread, bacon and gravy with sour skim milk minus the clabber." Curious, Clawson wondered aloud if they had been served "the same to drink as we had last night, having taken the thickening out." Unfamiliar food often provoked homesickness, especially for Standing, who once advised missionaries to the South to "fill their valises with wheat bread" before leaving Salt Lake City. What began as a joke at Clawson's expense ultimately revealed Standing's yearning for home. "Won't it be jolly when we can have wheat bread two or three times a day and can get to gnaw a shank bone?" he asked Cowley. "Oh! the luxuries one can picture out!"[52]

Their work in Fannin County produced six converts, among them a couple who acknowledged the elders' devotion by naming their newborn son Joseph Rudger Stover. However, news from Varnell's Station overshadowed the joy occasioned by such an event. Though Clawson escaped confrontation upon his arrival in Whitfield County, a mob emerged to successfully drive away new elders Charles W. Hulse and Thomas Lloyd, who arrived in Varnell's Station seeking mission assignments. Hulse and Lloyd fled the state to North Carolina in early June, which prompted

Standing, who had assumed the position of president of the Georgia Conference, to seek the intervention of authorities.[53]

On June 12, 1879, from his headquarters in Fannin County, Elder Standing penned a letter to Governor Alfred Colquitt of Georgia. He informed the governor of the situation in Varnell's Station and asked his assistance, writing that Mormon elders "have been obliged at times to flee for their lives, as armed men to the number of 40 and 50 have come out against them." Additionally, Varnell's Station Saints reported that mobs had, on occasion, "entered their houses in search of said elders." He acknowledged the unpopularity of Mormonism but reminded the governor that "the laws of Georgia are strictly opposed to all lawlessness, and extend to her citizens the right of worshipping God according to the dictates of conscience." In return, Elder Standing received what he described as "a very respectful letter" from J. W. Warren, secretary of the Executive Department, which officially decried extralegal violence that attempted to inhibit the free practice of any religious faith, so long as the practice of that faith conformed to the laws of the state. "The Governor regrets to hear the report you give from Whitfield County," the letter continued. "He will instruct the State Prosecuting Attorney for that district to inquire into the matter, and if the report be true, to prosecute the offenders." The governor's reply apparently reassured Standing, who reported its contents to other elders.[54]

What Standing did not tell the governor was that when the new Mormons of Whitfield and Catoosa counties found angry mobs at their doors, familiar faces dominated the groups. Community members later testified that neighbors and kin of the Varnell's Station Saints frequently patrolled the community in their search for elders, if necessary bursting into homes where they may have once been welcomed as family. Both the Kaneasters and the Elledges reported nighttime visits from men who demanded the whereabouts of Mormon preachers. So fearful was Riley Loggins—whose wife was a member of the Relief Society—that he forbade his children to accompany William Kaneaster to school in Varnell's Station, as was their practice. Children of the

Kaneaster and Loggins families attended a school run by the Huffaker family in Whitfield County, along with children from the Nations and Elledge families, an association that echoed religious beliefs. William Kaneaster, who typically sang the hymns he had been taught by Mormon elders on the way to school and back, said Loggins "stopped his son and daughter from going to school for fear the mob would take action on me for singing Utah Mormon songs along the road."[55]

Standing and Clawson, reassured by the governor's letter and hopeful that the potential for violence had been snuffed out, remained securely remote from the immediate threat as they labored in Fannin and Pickens counties. In the first week of July, Standing sounded an optimistic tone when reporting to Morgan, who remained in the West to welcome another company of fifteen Georgians who planned to leave from Chattanooga in mid-July. Standing wrote that he and Clawson would remain in Pickens County until mid-July, when they would travel to a church conference in Chattooga County. They intended a brief stop in Varnell's Station, where Elder Parry planned to join them before continuing to the conference, the long walk providing a perfect opportunity to practice their hymn singing. Parry anticipated that at the conclusion of the meeting he would be released to return home.[56]

A letter from Morgan interrupted Elder Parry's conference plans. The last paragraph of the letter especially disturbed Parry, who had already written his family to anticipate his return: "As the time draws near for you to leave the Mission," Morgan wrote, "the more I regret your departure; still, I suppose you have been away from your family so long that it would be cruel to say anything; but I feel that you could do so much good by a little longer stay." After prayerful deliberation, Parry decided to remain in North Carolina and "finish my work, whatever it was, and forget my temporary disappointment."[57]

Unaware that Parry's plans had changed, Standing and Clawson proceeded toward Varnell's Station. The summer heat slowed their progress. The *Rome Tri-Weekly Courier* reported on the steady increase in temperature, which topped off at a hundred degrees on July 15. The mountain district offered no relief, and the *North Georgia Citizen* concluded that "evidently, the torrid zone has got out of place and slipped up this way." Drought accompanied the heat. The *Citizen* suggested it was "the hottest summer for two hundred years," with "only a few slight showers in spots." Depression plagued farmers, who found the dust and heat "intolerable."[58]

On July 18, 1879, a small company of Georgians successfully reached Colorado. The Elledge family dominated the summer expedition, which traveled unaccompanied by a Mormon elder. On that same day, Standing sat down to pen the last letter he would ever write. To a friend in Utah, he reported the terrible summer heat: "Talk about hot, it is simply awful. Yet we have considerable walking to do." He worried about the condition of Georgia's farms and speculated that "there are hundreds and thousands who will suffer for food" in the coming months. Still, he reported that "last night we had a genuine treat," when he and Clawson "visited a house where there is a piano as well as those who play it." Standing enjoyed tunes such as "Auld Lang Syne," the first instrumental music he had heard for months. For a time, he wrote, he "was conscious only to the sweet tones of the instrument and the long ago scenes, that came fresh to my memory, as the familiar airs one after another were played." Overwhelmed by nostalgia, and likely exhausted by his Georgia mission, Standing described to his friend the unhappy challenges he faced: "How would you like it," he asked, "after having preached to have two ministers get up and lie about you and shake their fists nearly in your face, and that before an audience of 150 people?"[59]

In the wake of the last expedition, threats against the missionaries escalated in both number and intensity, and according to Clawson, Elder Standing had grown increasingly troubled. "Brother Standing had a dream which made a powerful impression upon his mind," Clawson recalled, "and caused him to have forebodings of approaching trouble." In his dream, Standing traveled to Varnell's Station, "when suddenly clouds of intense blackness gathered overhead and all around me." He dreamed that he visited a family of Georgia Saints, which did little to alleviate his distress. The Georgians, who seemed frightened and fearful, "made it clear" that Standing's visit was unwelcome. Standing told Clawson that the dream concluded when "I suddenly awoke, without my being shown the end of the trouble." So it may have come as no surprise to the missionaries when they arrived in Varnell's Station on Saturday, July 19, 1879, to find the Saints frightened and fearful and doors firmly shut against them.[60]

CHAPTER FIVE

"The Day of Grace Is Gone"
The Murder of Joseph Standing

The sun had set by the time Joseph Standing and Rudger Clawson reached Whitfield County and knocked at the door of Riley and Elizabeth Loggins, where they hoped to find shelter for the night. Instead, Mr. Loggins brusquely "turned them away and would not keep them." When the bewildered missionaries asked where they should go instead, Loggins directed them to Henry Holston's home, about a mile and a half away. Holston enjoyed a local reputation for fairness and had opened his home to Mormon elders on more than one occasion, though he expressed no interest in baptism. Standing knew he could trust Holston's hospitality, but the missionaries dreaded the nighttime walk. They left the Loggins house, reassured by the prospect of a night's lodging but disturbed by their inhospitable greeting. After proceeding only about a half mile, they decided to try their luck again, this time at the Josiah Kaneaster home.[1]

William Kaneaster answered the knock at the door and later claimed to have invited the elders to stay all night, an offer he said was refused by Standing. Clawson's account differs. Clawson noted that the household "seemed to be in a state of great excitement." The Kaneasters reported that "threats had been made" against the elders, and "the feeling toward them in the neighborhood was bitter and murderous." Clawson remembered that their request to stay overnight was refused, just as it had been by Riley Loggins, "because if anything happened, they would have to share the trouble." In fact, evidence suggests that Sarah Kaneaster may have been especially fearful, as she and her husband, Josiah, had recently separated. Her embrace of Mormonism and determination to go west with her sister, mother, and grandmother strained her marriage to the breaking point. Though she would not allow them to stay, the elders did leave their valises at the Kaneaster home, planning to return for them the next day.[2]

William Kaneaster accompanied the elders to Henry Holston's house, directing them to take a less dangerous, albeit longer and less direct, route, but when they arrived Holston only reluctantly opened his door to the missionaries. He explained that "there was danger in the air. Threats of mobbing, whippings and even killing the Elders had been freely made, and he expected to get into trouble on account of entertaining them." Kaneaster, too, feared retaliation, especially when he learned that his detour stymied the mob's effort to intercept the elders. Though the night passed without incident, Standing woke Kaneaster at first light to urge the young man to seek the intervention of local authorities. The elders intended to remain at Holston's, who agreed to open his home for Sunday services. Kaneaster went willingly enough, but his mission failed. He located the sheriff, who said he could do nothing as no harm had been done to the LDS missionaries or local converts. Kaneaster returned to Holston's house, burdened by an unhappy report, to find his female kin—Sarah Fullbright, Elviny Hamblin, Sarah Kaneaster, and aunt Mary Hamblin—assembled there, perhaps the only Varnell's Station Saints willing to attend Sunday services with the elders. The women lingered until nearly dusk, but prudently departed for home before darkness could settle. Clawson recalled that Standing appeared "pale, anxious, and determined" throughout the visit, preoccupied with thoughts of impending danger and unnerved by the prospect of an encounter with the mob. He double-checked the doors and windows to make sure all were carefully secured. Still, Sunday night passed without disruption, just as Saturday had.[3]

The missionaries left Holston's early Monday morning, intending to retrieve their suitcases from the Kaneaster house, unaware that Varnell's Station was already astir. Sarah Kaneaster later told William that the elders returned only minutes after he left for school. Local resident Jonathan Owenby noticed the two missionaries at the Kaneasters' and described their hasty departure from the house, though he claimed to be unaware of any threats against the elders. Others noticed a flurry of morning activity in Varnell's Station. Henry Holston, who saw the elders off before departing for a local sawmill, found several armed men gathered there who inquired as to the whereabouts of the Mormons. Kate Cleaveland, Holston's daughter, also suspected trouble when she saw armed men pass near the Holston home. Local resident Alfred Clark remembered that he was "at work on a ditch" nearby when four or five men approached him to ask "how many Mormons I had seen." He recognized them immediately. "Saw same men on same business before," he said, "when they went to Elledges and searched the house." Henry Holston later confirmed that "it was the same armed crowd" that invaded and searched the Elledge house.[4]

By midmorning only Standing and Clawson were unaware of the impending confrontation. Valises in hand, they left the Kaneaster home and began the walk back toward Mr. Holston's house. Clawson described the road they traveled as curving and "densely wooded on both sides," so the missionaries were unprepared when they rounded a bend and found their way blocked by three horsemen who presented weapons and ordered the elders to halt. Within minutes, nine other men joined their three compatriots. "Some were mounted, the remainder were afoot," Clawson remembered, though "all were armed," and when they recognized the two young elders as the Mormons they sought, they unleashed whoops of joy.[5]

Even at a distance, Jonathan Owenby recognized the celebration. He saw "two men going in gallop" down the road; one of them, waving his hat, yelled out twice, "We've caught them! We've caught them!" Detained in the middle of the road, Standing demanded to know why and by what authority they had been stopped. The question prompted one Georgian to dismount and brandish his weapon threateningly before retorting that "the government of the United States is against you, and there is no law in Georgia for Mormons." Standing and Clawson were directed at gunpoint back down the road, in the way they had come.[6]

Standing walked briskly and argued incessantly with his captors, attempting to persuade them that the missionaries intended immediately to vacate north Georgia. From his precarious position at the rear of the jostling assembly, Clawson sadly listened to Standing's appeals. He understood that Standing's promises to abandon the mission field were pointless as "it was not what the missionaries might do for which these base fellows had resolved to punish them, but for what had already been done." In fact, their captors shared a personal grievance with the representatives of the Church of Jesus Christ of Latter-day Saints. Though Clawson had only a passing acquaintance with the residents of Varnell's Station and so did not recognize the armed men, Standing likely understood that the mob represented the families and neighbors of Whitfield and Catoosa County converts.[7]

Four of Elizabeth Elledge's cousins rode with the mob. The oldest, thirty-three-year-old Jasper "Newt" Nations, Clawson described as "tall, dark and swarthy" and sporting a "pointed black beard." Dave Nations, his younger brother, rode alongside, motivated by a perceived injury that extended beyond the loss of the Elledge family. Married to Josiah Kaneaster's sister, Dave likely viewed the destruction of the Kaneaster marriage as the result of Mormon conversion. Bill and Joe Nations also participated in the apprehension of Standing and Clawson.[8]

Hugh Blair, a neighbor of the Brittain Williams family, also numbered among the group assembled to punish the Mormon elders. Blair anticipated the loss of two sisters due to the proselytizing of LDS missionaries. One sister, Nancy, was married to David Williams, who now planned to abandon his Baptist father in order to join his aunt and uncle, Elizabeth and Dillingham Elledge, in the western Zion. Another of Hugh Blair's sisters, Martha Blair, planned to accompany them to Colorado. Blair's neighbor, Andy Bradley, described by Clawson as "a coarse and brutal specimen of humanity," rode with the mob. David Smith, neighbor to Andy Bradley and the now-emigrated Huffakers, also joined the armed group, as did A. S. "Jud" Smith, who possessed a reputation for violence. Accused of killing a black man in Whitfield County, Smith successfully eluded capture until his sweetheart urged him to attend a Methodist camp meeting in Varnell's Station. Local resident James Tinsley recognized Smith and approached him in the guise of shaking hands, then captured him in order to collect the thousand-dollar reward. Jud Smith went to jail, but jurors believed his self-defense claim and acquitted him of the charge. Gang members Jefferson Hunter and Mac McClure were linked by marriage, not blood, but both had lost neighbors to Mormonism. Jim Faucett of Catoosa County, kin to numerous Walker County converts, declared himself the leader of the armed group. Ben Clark was a Baptist deacon and related by marriage to John S. Martin, who had left the Baptists for the Mormons.[9]

Resentful at the family and community divisions that resulted from conversion to the LDS Church, mob members resolved to punish Elders Standing and Clawson. They ushered the two missionaries down the road, pausing occasionally to curse and pummel them. Baptist deacon Ben Clark struck Clawson a powerful blow in the head before being restrained by others in the group. A brief encounter with local resident Jonathan Owenby diverted the mob's attention and provided an opportunity to mock the missionaries' faith. Noticing that Owenby, a large man, rode astride a woefully thin horse with legs that seemed liable to collapse beneath Owenby's weight at any moment, an armed man called out for Owenby to halt. "Is there anything the matter with your horse?" the man asked. If so, he laughed, the Mormon elders "will heal it by the laying on of hands." Smiling grimly, Owenby declined the offer on behalf of his horse and passed by, but not before scanning the faces of the assembled group.[10]

While no north Georgia men intervened on the elders' behalf, women did. Just as the female Saints of Varnell's Station had spirited Elder Charles Hardy out a rear window and to safety, they tried to prevent the capture of Elders Standing and Clawson.

Apprised of the danger, Elviny Hamblin and her daughter Mary set out from home in a vain effort to intercept and warn the missionaries. Mary Hamblin was the first to locate the two, but by the time she reached Standing and Clawson, they were already in the hands of the mob. Clearly, the gang understood that she intended to help the missionaries, for when she emerged from the woods and attempted to pass them on the road, Jud Smith issued a threat: "We've got your brethren," he warned, "and we'll tend to you hereafter." Clawson recalled the young woman's quiet response: "The Lord is with them and my prayers are forever for them." She was allowed to leave but feared punishment for having interfered.[11]

It is not certain that the mob intended murder. At one point, Jim Faucett told the elders that "if we ever again find you in this part of the country we will hang you by the neck like dogs," suggesting that their lives would be spared. However, Clawson recalled that "they told us they were going to whip us and that we'd be limber when it was over." Standing, described by Clawson as fearing the whip more than death, was terrified. When the group reached a shady hollow by a spring, the July heat forced the men to a halt. Standing drank twice from the spring, perhaps an indication of his extreme anxiety. "Some of the men sat down," Clawson recalled, "and one of them laid his pistol down." Standing realized his opportunity and seized the weapon. Directing the pistol toward the men still on horseback, Standing ordered them to surrender. It was at that moment, Clawson said, that "one man raised up from under the tree" with a weapon of his own. A shot was fired and Standing fell. Clawson would later testify that he believed the shooter to be a man who had lost a daughter to the Mormons, but he could not be sure. At first it seemed that Clawson would be shot as well, and the elder braced himself. Unaccountably, the group lowered their weapons.[12]

Clawson later attempted to explain why the mob spared his life. Questioned by a *Denver Tribune* reporter, Clawson explained that in the confusion following the gunshot, the mob rushed toward Clawson. He remembered that one man shouted,

"Shoot the other one, too." Clawson claimed to have folded his arms and addressed the group, saying, "Gentlemen, I am ready to die." He believed his demeanor calmed the men and saved his life. An article in England's *Liverpool Mercury* offered an alternative explanation, suggesting that the elder successfully begged for his life, but evidence supports Clawson's account. His testimony, given only hours after the incident, supported the account givenced by the *Tribune* reporter.[13]

Having escaped injury, Clawson knelt in the dust beside Standing and examined his friend, finding him still alive but suffering a mortal wound to the head. Standing's injury horrified Clawson. He noted that the bullet tore off the bridge of Standing's nose before entering his forehead and destroying the right eye. Ghastly sounds issued from Standing's throat. As Clawson tenderly placed his hat under Standing's head to keep it out of the dust, a member of the Nations family approached the body and said, "Well, he shot himself, didn't he?" Perhaps it was because Clawson carefully replied, "I don't know," that the mob agreed to let him leave the scene to summon help for the dying man. "It is a burning shame to leave a man to die in the woods in this manner," Clawson told them. "Either some of you must go for assistance that his body may be removed ... or let me go."[14]

The Georgians stepped aside and Clawson departed immediately, casting apprehensive glances over his shoulder, though he understood that nothing could be done to prevent Standing's demise. He only hoped that the law could be brought to bear against Standing's murderer and wondered at his own good fortune at escaping. Clawson ran toward Henry Holston's house and intercepted Kate Cleaveland, who had heard the gunshot. She loaned the elder a horse and directed him toward Catoosa Springs, where the coroner resided. By now the community had been alerted. Henry Holston hurried toward the scene and found Standing not yet dead, but he became alarmed when he noticed that armed men still lingered nearby, watching his movements. "Fearing injury," he left. Holston then sent his daughter Kate and farm worker "old Grandad" Seatherwood to minister to the dying missionary, apparently convinced that gender and age would shield them from violence. They found Standing "yet alive" but unconscious and paused long enough to cover Standing's body with a protective bower of tree branches; however, "there were so many men running from one tree to another and from one thicket to another" that the pair left, afraid for their own lives.[15]

Eventually, gang members vacated the scene. Matilda Huffaker, the sister of Mormon converts, encountered Jud Smith as he emerged from the woods. Unaware that Standing had been shot nearby, she extended a cordial greeting. "It's a good day," she observed, but an agitated Smith shook his head in disagreement. "Ah, law, the day of grace is gone," he muttered before making his escape. As Clawson rode toward Catoosa Springs to fetch the coroner, he encountered seven of the mobbers. Like Clawson, they were in a hurry, making their way north toward the Tennessee border in order to evade capture. At their approach, the elder slowed, wondering if he would survive this second encounter. He pointed toward Catoosa Springs, and the men apparently interpreted the gesture as a sign that the missionary intended to flee the country. "Some of them smiled" with satisfaction, he remembered, "and all rode on." Clawson stopped at a Catoosa Springs hotel long enough to compose a terse telegram to Georgia Governor Colquitt in Atlanta: "Joseph Standing was shot and killed to-day, near Varnell's, by a mob of ten or twelve men." He sent the same message to John Morgan in Salt Lake City, with the addendum: "Will leave for home with the body at once. Notify his family."[16]

It was sundown when he returned, having fetched coroner Amos S. Sutherland to the scene. In short order, Sutherland impaneled a jury for the inquest of Standing's body. Some jurors, like Endymeon Martin and J. H. Huffaker, were related to Varnell's Station converts. Several members of the Kaneaster family attended the outdoor inquest, including Josiah Kaneaster, whose female kin played such a significant role in the controversy. The coroner conducted the inquest, asking questions and writing down the testimony of witnesses. Perhaps no witness suffered more than Alfred Clark. Related to the Nations family by marriage, Clark served the Confederacy with Dillingham Elledge and Henry Huffaker, so family and political loyalties should have influenced him in favor of the Mormons. Having witnessed the mob's activities earlier that day, he felt obligated to testify against the mob but grieved upon learning that his nephew Ben was among the accused.[17]

Clawson noticed that Standing's hat had been removed from under his head and placed over his face. The removal of the hat verified that Standing was lifeless; further, new injuries had been inflicted. Clawson's examination of the body revealed more gunshot wounds to the head and neck. He observed, too, that "the fiends had stabbed the body repeatedly and fired a charge of shot into his left cheek." William Kaneaster, who shooed flies from the body of the slain missionary, believed some of Standing's injuries due to the blast of a double-barreled shotgun "at close range," one load entering Standing's head where the original wound was inflicted, then "one above." Kaneaster observed that "the two holes in his forehead were about large enough to turn a man's thumb around in without touching the fractured parts." He also reported that Standing's right hand was peppered with shot, a fact he found inexplicable.[18]

Clawson believed that he understood the mutilation of Standing's body. He surmised that the members of the mob had "agreed to stand upon an undoubted common ground," so each had fired into the body. A closer inspection confirmed that they had fired into Standing's head and neck from close proximity, as the wounds were also "powder-burnt." Coroner Sutherland and the jury simply counted the obvious wounds and issued their verdict: "We the jury, having made examination of the dead body find that the deceased came to his death by gun and pistol shots or both inflicted upon the head & neck of deceased said wounds consisting of twenty shots or more from guns or pistols." Henry Holston, Mary Hamblin, Jonathan Owenby, and Alfred Clark produced the names of the accused, and a warrant was issued for the arrest of twelve men.[19]

Henry Holston proved himself a friend to the Mormons again by opening his home to Standing for one last time. From an abandoned cabin nearby, volunteers obtained a plank large enough to support Standing's corpse. Four boards crossed underneath to allow eight men to transport the dead missionary. They hoisted their sad burden and began to walk. Clawson later remembered that the journey to Holston's was accomplished in the dark and that the evening had gone quiet and still. "There was no symptom of a breeze," he wrote, "not even enough to stir a leaf," and no words passed between the men as they bore the body along.[20]

Clawson refused to consign Standing's body to Georgia soil, and, despite the objections of the coroner, he resolved to transport the body back to Utah. The corpse rested upon its makeshift bier in Henry Holston's front yard, and with only a tallow candle to illuminate the lifeless missionary's head, Clawson began to wash the clotted and dried blood from Standing's face and hair. He paused frequently to rinse his grisly cloths in warm water, but finally dressed the body in fresh garments and placed a sheet over the corpse. The men of the coroner's jury attended the scene, as did neighbors who had begun to gather as the news spread across the small community. A shop in Dalton produced a metal casket, and on July 22 Clawson and Standing began the long journey home. Clawson feared that those sympathetic to the mob might interrupt the short trip to the train station, so he waited until dark to make the move. He hired an armed guard to accompany him as the wagon rattled through Varnell's Station to Dalton, where Standing's body would be conveyed by rail to Utah.[21]

From Utah, John Morgan directed a letter to the "Elders and Saints in the Southern States Mission," instructing them that "no act of recrimination, on the part of any one, either by word or deed" should "mar the hitherto bright record that the Saints have made in the mission." But he also advised southern converts—"those who are in a situation to do so"—to emigrate and "gather where they can be protected." The letter did not reach Georgia in time to be read aloud to the elders and Saints who assembled at the Haywood Valley Conference on July 25 as planned. Five Mormon missionaries attended, including three elders who had left Utah only a week before and arrived in Georgia in time to learn of Standing's murder. One of the men, Teancum William Heward, wrote in his diary that Standing's death brought "a terrible gloom" to the assembled Saints. Despite that, the conference continued, and Elder Heward reported that they "had a good time, considering the circumstances under which we were placed."[22]

In Utah, the LDS Church prepared to receive the body of the slain missionary. With frequent dispatches from Clawson, the *Deseret News* tracked Standing's progress from Georgia to Salt Lake City. The newspaper noted that when the missionary's remains reached Ogden, Utah, on July 31, "an immense concourse of people" gathered to witness the transfer of the body to a Utah Central railroad car. Morgan and a committee of Southern States missionaries joined the train in order to accompany the body on the final part of the journey. Standing's casket was placed upon "a bier draped with black and white" and decorated with garlands and banners reading, "Joseph Standing, another Martyr for the Cause of Truth" and "Freedom, Where is thy Domain?" A brass band accompanied the casket to the train, playing *Webster's Funeral March* as the body was placed on the train car that would bear it to Salt Lake City. Outwardly stoic, Morgan expressed his personal feelings of loss in private correspondence. To Matthias Cowley in Virginia he described himself as "bowed down with grief" following the death of Standing.[23]

Another brass band greeted the train's arrival in Salt Lake City on August 1. Standing's funeral service was conducted at the Salt Lake City Tabernacle two days later, in the presence of ten thousand mourners. Pallbearers included Morgan, Clawson, and C. W. Hardy, who had himself only barely escaped a Varnell's Station mob. According to published descriptions, "the stand was tastefully draped in black," with a vase of beautiful flowers at each corner, and flowers covered Standing's casket. Several speakers delivered remarks during the lengthy ceremony, including church president John Taylor. His speech seemed especially relevant, as he had been wounded in the attack on Joseph and Hyrum Smith and only narrowly escaped martyrdom himself. Though he led the Saints in mourning Standing's loss, he also used the occasion to rally church members against the perceived legislative persecutions of the U.S. government. At the conclusion of his speech, mourners filed out to join a carriage procession "over half a mile in length." Standing's parents and siblings accompanied the hearse as it left the east gate of Temple Square, following the band, which "discoursed sweet and solemn music" along the road to Salt Lake City's cemetery, where Standing was laid to rest.[24]

As Salt Lake City grieved its newest martyr, the murder garnered local, state, and national attention. The *Chicago Times* reported, erroneously, that "ten indignant servants of the Lord" dispatched "the heathen . . . with shot-guns." The *New York Herald* predicted that the murderers would never be punished and expressed a belief that evading the law entirely was likely as "more than half the houses in Georgia would offer them refuge." Not that the *Herald* was unsympathetic to the plight of north Georgians. Indeed, even as New York writers denounced the mob as "savage, bloodthirsty, and cowardly," they offered an explanation for the murder: "There were many men and women who had become converts to the polygamic faith and had expressed a determination to leave for Utah. This incensed their friends and relatives, who several times threatened the Elders with summary treatment, if they did not leave the country." Connecticut's *New Haven Register* deplored the murder—"Violence is not the remedy for Mormonism"—but pointed out that "families are the composite units which are the foundation stones of society," arguing that "the state must protect the family from corruption and disintegration" that accompanied Mormon conversion efforts.[25]

In the immediate aftermath of the murder, the *Atlanta Constitution* rushed to defend Georgia's reputation. Arguing that "the killing was entirely unwarranted," the newspaper reassured its readers that the mob did not enjoy popular support. "The quiet people of the county are determined that a fair and full trial shall be had, and the parties committing this murder be brought to justice." By comparison, local newspapers rallied to the defense of the accused. The *North Georgia Citizen* placed the blame for the murder on the Mormons, explaining that the elders had been "in that portion of the county for several weeks proclaiming their plurality of wives doctrine, with a view to working up a colony of women to send to Utah. The boldness with which they proclaimed this doctrine incensed the men of that neighborhood against them." Similarly, the *Catoosa Courier* justified the attack on Standing as a defense of household and womanhood, arguing that the "good citizens" of north Georgia "could not stand any longer the bad influence that his preaching had upon the female portion of the neighborhood."[26]

The *Atlanta Constitution* countered that "the plea of the *Courier* is not sufficient," as the reputation of the whole state was at stake, but conceded that the Mormon missionaries "were audacious and aggressive, and invaded household after household for the purpose of preaching their polygamous creed." The paper quoted a "sturdy farmer," who evaluated the Mormon threat and said, "I would shoot a man just as quick for talking polygamy to my wife or daughter as I would if he tried to seduce her." The reporter confirmed that "this feeling has been shared by many, and it is really a wonder that there has not been trouble before," but, officially, the newspaper maintained that the murder of Standing was "almost without excuse." Even if Standing had grabbed a pistol and threatened the mob, the reporter reasoned, "he could have been disarmed without being shot through the head."[27]

Popular humorist and newspaper columnist Bill Arp responded irritably to the *Atlanta Constitution*'s criticism of the local response in Rome's *Tri-Weekly Courier*, writing, "Not long ago some of our editors were apologizing about that Mormon affair. Well, if I wasent as meek as Moses the like of that would make me mad. The fact is, I'm mad anyhow—who are they apologizing to? Can't we build a wall around our State some way? Is there no way to keep impertinent people from overlookin and interferin with our private affairs. . . . We can't . . . kill a vagabond Mormon, nor find a dead nigger in the woods, but what five hundred sanctified editors get on a Radical stump and blow a horn."²⁸ Georgia's Governor Colquitt, who had turned a blind eye to anti-Mormon mobs in Varnell's Station, now authorized a five-hundred-dollar reward for the arrest and conviction of the murderers. The *Atlanta Constitution* applauded the action as evidence that "efforts are being made to capture the murderers, and if caught they will be prosecuted vigorously." But the newspaper also tempered its condemnation of the mob by suggesting that "there were personal reasons that led many of the attacking mob to try and drive Standing out. . . . He had endangered the peace and integrity of many homes, and he was attacked in defense of these homes."²⁹

By the time the sheriff of Whitfield County assembled a Dalton posse, most of the mob had slipped over the border into Tennessee and evaded capture. Thomas Nations, Elizabeth Elledge's brother, suspected that his cousins fled to the home of Tennessee kin, so he would not have been surprised to learn that seven of the accused huddled there in Charley North's Bradley County barn. When a month had passed and his cousins continued to evade justice, Nations offered to lead the search, and accompanied by a deputy sheriff and Henry Holston, Nations rode out against his cousins. His decision to hunt down his murderous kin allied Thomas with his sister Elizabeth and the Mormon elders, a decision that proved very unpopular in the Varnell's Station community.³⁰

The trio rode for the better part of a night, crossing into Tennessee just before daybreak. A quick survey confirmed that seven mobbers rested inside the barn. They invaded the scene with weapons drawn, surprising the sleeping men. Four fugitives managed to escape through a cornfield, but Thomas Nations, Henry Holston, and the deputy managed to apprehend one man each: Jasper N. "Newt" Nations, Andrew Bradley, and Hugh Blair. They bound their prisoners together by looping a length of chain around the neck of each man, each loop secured by a padlock. Thus secured, the captives marched back to Georgia on foot, after being warned that any effort to free them would provoke certain death. When an angry crowd did gather, threatening to intervene on behalf of the accused, the deputy sheriff shouted that any rescue attempt would be seen as "the signal for us to shoot them down." Tom Nations's role in the apprehension of his own kin provided further evidence of the fractured family unit and earned special disgust from Varnell's Station residents. When the small party of men, three securely padlocked together, stopped for dinner, Tom Nations volunteered to guard the captives, arousing the ire of a Whitfield County woman. She accosted Nations as he reclined in the shade of a tree. "Tom Nations," she shouted, "aren't you ashamed of yourself to be guarding your own blood cousin to jail?" If the attack disturbed him, it was not evident in his reply. He said simply, "No, all I am ashamed of is that I haven't got the others." Tensions ran high in Varnell's Station, especially when Nations, Bradley, and Blair appeared in chains. William Kaneaster watched as men on horseback rode from house to house, attempting to stir a mob and mount a rescue. The prisoners, realizing that such an effort placed them in serious danger, now worked to discourage extralegal violence, crying out to everyone they passed, "Don't come with a mob, they will kill us first."[31]

The posse accomplished the trip to Dalton without incident and delivered the three fugitives to Whitfield County's jail on August 13. Manley Nations, Jasper's father, visited his son, then made his way to Dalton's King Street—known as "Lawyers Row" for the number of attorneys who kept offices there—where he hired five defense attorneys to represent his son, Andrew Bradley, and Hugh Blair. On August 16, the accused appeared before Judge Cicero D. McCutchen in response to a writ of habeas corpus filed on their behalf. Bail was requested, and Judge McCutcheon obliged, but placed bail for each at five thousand dollars, a significant sum that was well beyond the reach of the three captives. The jailer escorted them back to jail, but sympathetic citizens soon obtained their release. According to John Morgan, it was "the leading members of two or three denominations" who "immediately came forward" to offer bail.[32]

The actions of church members in securing the prisoners' releases heightened Mormon suspicions that local ministers deserved a share of the blame for Standing's murder. The *Deseret*

News quoted Clawson in his belief that "the horrid act was instigated by the preaching of three 'Christian' ministers, two Methodist and one Baptist," who were jealous of Mormon successes in north Georgia. Their sermons, he believed, incited the passions of their Georgia listeners. Latter-day Saints seized on the remark, publicly calling upon "Elders and Saints throughout the world" to identify ministers who actively opposed the LDS Church. Newspaper announcements urged Mormons to "write their names in full. Give the names of the Churches, the character of the opposition, the dates and places where it occurred, and the approximate number of witnesses." Morgan needed no urging in preparing a list, as he had already begun the task. "I find in getting a list and the religious status of the men" accused of Standing's murder, he wrote, "that out of the twelve [accused], seven were members of so-called religious bodies: four Baptist and three Methodist." He added, sarcastically, "They will doubtless in the future be looked upon as bright and shining ornaments in their respective churches."[33]

Anti-Mormon sentiment in Georgia intensified when it was announced that Nations, Bradley, and Blair would stand trial for the killing of a Mormon elder. The editor of the *Marietta Journal* warned of public dissatisfaction if the state sided with Mormons against Georgia citizens: "It may be the right thing to invoke the strong arm of the law to protect Mormons, in disseminating their licentious doctrines in Georgia, but we cannot see it in that light. Mormonism is the embodiment of licentious lawlessness; and if the authorities intend to guarantee it full sweep in Georgia, the people will have a controversy with the authorities."[34]

The strength of public disapproval may have prompted an abrupt change in the *Atlanta Constitution*'s coverage of the case. On August 24, responding to the interest shown by "the press throughout the whole country," the newspaper produced an article that described Elder Standing's true mission as the deflowering of virgins across several northwest Georgia counties. The column labeled Standing as the "Lustful Lout," an unfortunate alliterative device that would be similarly employed against "black beast" rapists accused of attacks on white women. Elder Standing appeared first in Walker County, the paper reported, residing in the home of a widow with two grown daughters. Though the location was incorrect, this was likely a reference to Elizabeth Hamblin and her two daughters. In his time there, "he succeeded in accomplishing the ruin of both of the young ladies," then moved on to the home of Dillingham Elledge in Catoosa County. The newspaper reported the conversions of the Elledge women, but added new and tantalizing information. Elizabeth Elledge's daughter Jane, the article claimed, reportedly gave birth to a child by Standing, "which mysteriously disappeared immediately after its birth," causing "considerable excitement in the neighborhood." Apparently Elizabeth Elledge's cousins—who justified the attack on Standing as a defense of family and womanhood—were now content to participate in the public destruction of Jane Elledge's character. The newspaper also implicated Standing in further indiscretions:

> We are pained to say that his intimacy with [Whitfield and Catoosa County] women was not by any means confined to this one family. Some three or four, if not more, young ladies living in the vicinity of Varnell's Station, whose names we prefer not now to mention, met with their ruin by this man; one of the young ladies is the daughter of one of the murderers. Nor does this tale stop here, as he has caused trouble in several families by being too intimate with their wives, and trying to get them to adhere to the Mormon faith and persuading them to emigrate to the Mormon country. So great were the troubles in one family on account of Standing's intimacy, that it caused the husband and wife to separate.[35]

Though he did not mention them by name, the writer clearly referred to the strained marriage of Josiah and Sarah Kaneaster. Many dismissed the article as a "lawyer-looking," albeit effective, device crafted to arouse public sympathy for the mob, especially as an earlier article in the *Atlanta Constitution* had claimed that no man could be found who believed the Mormon elders guilty of "immoral practices, even in the families of their 'saints.'" North Georgia converts leaped to Standing's defense, unleashing a flurry of letters in response to the accusations. In an interview with the *Chattanooga Times*, Morgan revealed that "statements signed by good citizens . . . have been forwarded, including a letter from Capt. Elledge, whose family came in for a portion of the unjust assertions heaped upon Elder Standing." Still, the defense was a powerful one, and most north Georgians believed the accused would escape justice.[36]

Morgan returned to Rome in October 1879 to hear testimony offered to the Whitfield grand jury in the Standing case. "It remains to be seen what steps they will take to punish the murderers," he wrote, but he looked forward to Clawson's testimony in the matter. He remained skeptical that the Latter-day Saints would receive a fair hearing and doubted that any Georgia jury would produce a conviction for murder, "owing to the general public sentiment on the matter." He hoped for a conviction on the charge of riot, a lesser crime.[37]

Clawson joined Morgan in Rome on October 6, in anticipation of his appearance before the grand jury. The missionaries sought out Henry Holston, also scheduled to appear as a witness. Holston's efforts on behalf of the Mormons and his participation in the capture of the fugitives made the Georgian a target. He confided to the elders that "the whole community where I lived turned against me, so that it appeared as if I had no friends," and he feared that "the friends of the men who murdered Standing thirst for my blood." Threats to his life prompted the purchase of additional weapons, Holston reported, and only a sturdy watchdog and the promise of violent retaliation protected him.[38]

The grand jury subpoenaed Jonathan Owenby and Mary Hamblin, but they chose to remain out of Whitfield County until they were needed. If Jonathan Owenby experienced threats similar to those faced by Henry Holston there is no record of it, but Elizabeth and Mary Hamblin, like Holston, suffered ostracism and intimidation from fellow north Georgians. Men threatened the two women, William Kaneaster remembered, warning them that their house would be burned as reprisal for their attempted rescue of the elders, a threat that prompted Henry Holston and Tom Nations to confront individuals sympathetic to the mob. The two men "rode out to public places," William wrote, spreading the word that "when these old ladies were burnt the fire was just started." They issued threats of their own: "We will burn 'til you will be sick of fire." The situation became so precarious, hovering on the brink of new violence, that it captured the attention of wealthy landowners. Land speculator William L. Hedrick, who had recently purchased the Elledge property, and local physician William B. Wells circulated in the community to deliver warnings of their own. They "told people to hush that fire talk, nobody wanted his property burned," reassuring angry neighbors that the Whitfield and Catoosa County converts would soon be leaving the community for the West.[39]

Despite promised recriminations, Henry Holston, Jonathan Owenby, and Mary Hamblin testified before the grand jury, as did Rudger Clawson. From Clawson, Solicitor-General A. T. Hackett obtained the sad story of Standing's shooting; from the others, he elicited the names of those who participated in the mob. On October 8, Whitfield County's grand jury returned indictments against the twelve members of the mob, charging them all with murder and the lesser charge of riot. "The finding of a true bill in the case caused considerable surprise," Clawson remembered, "as it was popularly expected that the charges would be ignored." The trials of Jasper N. Nations, Andrew Bradley, and Hugh Blair would commence on October 13. Georgia law allowed a separate trial for each of the defendants, an option they chose. The other accused were also free to offer testimony on behalf of their fellow defendants, which would also be the case.[40]

Though Solicitor-General Hackett impressed both Morgan and Clawson with his determination to see justice done, Morgan thought it expedient to hire additional legal services to assist him in the prosecution. To that end, they engaged the services of Dalton attorney W. K. Moore. Described by locals as a fine lawyer and good Christian, Colonel Moore served as a deacon in the First Presbyterian Church of Dalton. Moore agreed to assist Hackett, but they were outnumbered by the *five* defense attorneys—W. H. Payne of Catoosa County, Johnson and McCamy of Dalton, and Shumate and Williamson, also of Whitfield County. Judge Cicero D. McCutchen presided.[41]

Locals flocked to the Whitfield County courthouse on October 13, joined by a reporter from the *Atlanta Constitution*, who described the scene as "densely thronged with curious spectators." Disappointed to hear that the trial had been postponed to October 16, most vowed to return, as the proceedings promised high drama. It was not the prospect of a north Georgia murder trial that excited Georgians, as such things were not uncommon. Accused murderer Alex Rataree moved through the Whitfield County justice system in tandem with members of the mob, but with a decidedly dissimilar outcome. The county accused Rataree, a railroad brakeman, of causing the death of a man by striking him in the head with a stick during an altercation that erupted as both enjoyed "a house of ill fame" on the outskirts of Dalton. No crowds jostled for seats at Rataree's trial, which ended with a conviction for the lesser charge of involuntary manslaughter and a sentence of three years of hard labor while confined in the state penitentiary.[42]

The trial of Jasper "Newt" Nations, on the charge of murder in the first degree, began early on Thursday, October 16, when Nations entered a plea of not guilty. In its coverage, the *Atlanta Constitution* declared that no case had ever "excited the interest which has invested this trial," and, as a result, the courtroom boasted a capacity crowd for each session. Family and friends of Nations crowded around that portion of the courtroom set aside for his counsel, while Morgan and Clawson, and others sympathetic to the elders, seated themselves behind the prosecutors. One attorney was overheard boasting that "we are now engaged, gentlemen, in making a part of the history of this country." Such a statement likely created anxiety for the unhappy souls waiting in the jury pool. One hundred forty-two potential jurors were questioned and one hundred thirty rejected, reflecting, Clawson thought, "a general reluctance to serve on the case."[43]

At ten o'clock on Friday morning, the jury was complete. An anticipatory flurry erupted in the courtroom when Solicitor-General Hackett finally called Clawson, the first witness for the prosecution, to the stand, but when he began his testimony, "the courtroom was hushed in perfect silence." For those unable to attend in person, the *Atlanta Constitution* provided a detailed description of the witness:

> He is an intelligent looking blonde, with clear cut rather handsome features, and bright blue eyes. He wore what college girls would call a "lovely" mustache. When he smiled, as he did once or twice on cross examination, he displayed white and perfectly formed teeth. His hands are small and symmetrically shaped, and he appeared to wear a No. 6 boot. He was dressed in genteel taste and would pass for one of our popular society young men. His language was accurate and concise, his enunciation clear and distinct, and his manner graceful and self-possessed. He certainly evinces education and culture training. . . . No wonder the quiet quaint old-fashioned folks . . . thought him dangerous.[44]

The description of Clawson is curious and clearly designed to emphasize his position as outsider. The emphasis on his small hands and feet suggests femininity; however, his delicacy may also suggest refinement and sophistication, evidence of the "education and culture training" that provoked suspicion. In his first mission, Morgan faced similar comparisons when an Indiana speaker publicly attacked the elder "by warning the audience against allowing educated and learned divines coming into their midst and deceiving them with the sophistries." Morgan managed to laugh off the description, assuring the audience that, like most in attendance, he had been raised on a farm. Indeed, he reminded them, most of his day had been occupied in grinding corn for a gentleman in the audience. Clawson could make no similar claim. Further, Clawson's blond hair, blue eyes, appealing smile, and "lovely" mustache—all likely to attract feminine attention—could be seen as physical tools of the seducer. In emphasizing the difference between Clawson and the unsophisticated and uneducated mountain folks who believed him "dangerous," the *Constitution* thus managed to malign both.

Solicitor-General Hackett guided Clawson through his account, then offered him to the defense for cross-examination. The missionary bristled at the questions asked by young defense attorney Williamson. Fair, with light hair and mustache, the lawyer may have resembled Clawson, but the missionary noted that Williamson lovingly stroked his mustache as he questioned witnesses, an affectation the elder despised. Clawson later pointed out that the defense team barely mentioned the killing of Standing; instead, they focused on controversies associated with the LDS Church, introducing, he felt, "a great deal of irrelevant matter" into evidence. "The object of this," he believed, "was to prejudice the jury against the prosecution and in favor of their client."[45]

On only one occasion did Judge McCutchen intervene on behalf of the prosecution—when Clawson was asked, during cross-examination, "Are your parents living in the practice of polygamy and are you a polygamous child?" Thoroughly angry by now, Clawson refused to answer, and Judge McCutchen overruled the question. But the defense scored points by directing another question at the witness. Referring to Clawson's description of the shooting, one of Nations's attorneys asked if the missionary remembered a particular verbal exchange. Clawson did and replied that one of the mob said, "The government of the United States is against you and there is no law in Georgia for the Mormons." Had he stopped there, his answer would likely have worked in the prosecution's favor. But Clawson elaborated. "Judging from the manner in which this trial is being conducted," he sneered, "I see no reason to question the correctness of his assertion." The room erupted in indignation, and Judge McCutchen attempted to gavel the courtroom to silence without success. One of the most respected men in north Georgia, Cicero McCutchen counted many lawyers and judges within his family and was frequently praised for his judicial experience and fairness, but he also valued his association with the First Methodist Church of Dalton, which may have inspired Clawson's outburst. In order to bring the proceedings to order, the judge ordered a brief recess.[46]

When the prosecution rested, Andrew Bradley was called to the stand for the defense; in fact, the only witnesses offered in Nations's defense were Andrew Bradley and Hugh Blair. Asked to explain why he had been carrying a weapon as part of the armed mob that apprehended the Mormon elders on July 21, Bradley offered an excuse, testifying that he had concluded to "go hunting turkeys on that day." Asked how he found himself part of a murderous mob, he had no answer. The same question was put to Hugh Blair, who explained that he was out that morning because his gun "was out of order." He intended, he said, to visit his brother-in-law, a blacksmith, to ask him to repair the gun. It was on his way there that he met with the others.[47]

No further witnesses were called. The defense concluded, W. K. Moore rose to speak on behalf of the prosecution. In an address to the jury that consumed the better part of three hours, Moore appealed to the better natures of the jurors. "Calmly and earnestly he insisted that the State of Georgia could not afford to do this great wrong, that she could not afford to allow the blood of innocence to cry unavenged from the ground," Morgan remembered. "In a most logical manner he reviewed the evidence," pleading for the right of a man "to worship God according to the dictates of his conscience, as guaranteed by the Constitution of our common country."[48]

Solicitor-General Hackett added a brief concluding remark, and Judge McCutchen delivered his charge to the jury. Morgan objected to the wording of the charge, which appeared, he believed, "to furnish a plausible excuse for them to acquit the defendant." McCutchen instructed the jury to consider whether or not the mob intended to murder Standing. If one member of the mob went "beyond the original purpose and intention" to commit a homicide, that individual alone would be guilty. Further, the jury must be convinced beyond a reasonable doubt "that the individual defendant had intended to kill Standing himself."[49]

"It seemed impossible to avoid conviction," Morgan wrote to the editors of the *Salt Lake Herald*, "but the judge, in his charge to the jury, left so wide a loophole, that had they been willing to convict, they could scarcely have done so." W. K. Moore, working with the prosecution on behalf of the Mormons, waited until the court adjourned to approach Judge McCutchen. Moore pointed out that the judge "had utterly failed" in making the appropriate

FIGURE 4. Joseph Standing's grave in Salt Lake City, Utah. Photo by the author.

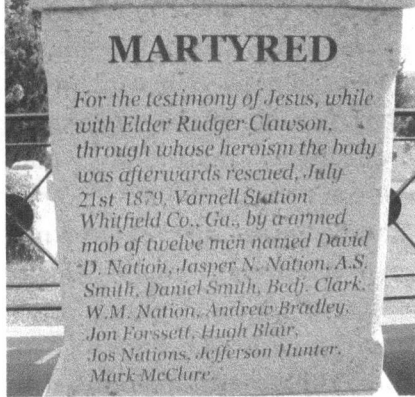 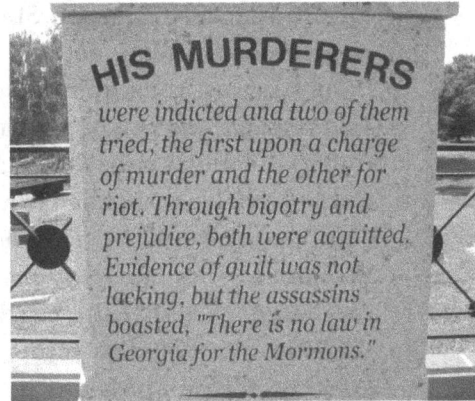

FIGURE 5. Face of the Standing Monument naming members of the Georgia mob. Photo by the author.

FIGURE 6. Face of the Standing Monument declaring, "There is no law in Georgia for the Mormons." Photo by the author.

charge by ignoring "the nature of the crime committed—when twelve men band together and destroy the life of a human being, and when it cannot be proven who struck the fatal blow." To Moore's astonishment, the judge seemed to admit his mistake, replying that the proper charge "slipped his memory." On Saturday, after nearly three days of testimony, the case went to the jury. Despite the judge's prejudicial charge, Morgan later learned that four jury members advocated ignoring the charge and finding Nations guilty, but in the end "finally succumbed" to pressure brought by other jurors. At eleven o'clock on Saturday evening, the jury returned with a verdict of not guilty.[50]

The failure convinced Solicitor-General Hackett to drop murder charges against Andrew Bradley and Hugh Blair. He did, however, charge the three defendants with riot, the lesser charge that Morgan had predicted. Blair's trial began on Tuesday morning, and he was quickly found not guilty. On Thursday, a jury declared Andrew Bradley innocent of charges of riot, then the grand jury absolved the entire mob of blame. "In consideration of the verdicts of the various juries in the trials of persons for the murder of Joseph Standing, the Mormon elder, and for riot in the same connection," the presentment read, "the indictments against the other persons accused of participating in the said murder and riot be not pressed." The community thus sanctioned the mob's behavior as appropriate. On that same day, the grand jury also responded to a charge of libel, brought by Thomas Nations on behalf of his niece Jane Elledge, against attorney William L. Shumate. Nations declared Shumate responsible for the *Atlanta Constitution* article that alleged an immoral relationship between the young woman and Joseph Standing. In keeping with its previous decisions, the grand jury refused to bring an indictment against attorney Shumate.[51]

Less than a year after the trials, members of Salt Lake City's Young Men's Improvement Association erected an Italian marble monument over Standing's grave. It was later replaced. A poem decorates one face of the current monument, its words the work of Orson F. Whitney:

> Beneath this stone, by friendship's hand, is lain
> The martyred form of one, untimely slain,
> A servant of the Lord, whose works revealed
> The love of Truth for which his doom was sealed.
>
> where foes beset—when but a single friend
> stood true, nor shunned his comrade's cruel end
> Deep in the shades of ill-starred Georgia's wood,
> Fair freedom's soil was crimsoned with his blood.
>
> Our brother rests beneath his native sod,
> His murderers are in the hands of God.
> Weep, weep for them, not him whose silent dust
> Here waits the resurrection of the just.

Another face of the monument declares Standing "MARTYRED For the testimony of Jesus, while with Elder Rudger Clawson, through whose heroism the body was afterwards rescued, July 21st, 1879, Varnell Station Whitfield Co., Ga., by a armed mob of twelve men." The names of the accused follow, chiseled permanently into stone. "HIS MURDERERS," continues on another face of the monument, "were indicted and two of them tried, the first upon a charge of murder and the other for riot. Through bigotry and prejudice, both were acquitted. Evidence of guilt was not lacking, but the assassins boasted, 'There is no law in Georgia for the Mormons.'"

CHAPTER SIX

"Think Not When You Gather to Zion, Your Troubles and Trials Are Through"
Georgia and the Mormon Question

Only four days after Joseph Standing's murder, the *Baltimore Gazette* predicted that "Mormon missionaries will give Georgia a wide berth, now that one of their number has been murdered in that state." Elder Rudger Clawson expressed a similar belief that the church would abandon Georgia to move to safer missionary fields. As he transported Standing's body back to Utah for burial, Clawson was asked by a newspaper reporter, "Do you think the work of proselyting will be resumed in Georgia by emissaries from the head church?" Clawson answered without hesitation, "I hardly believe we shall send any more workers into that field. The territory of the United States is large enough to obviate the necessity of sacrificing personal safety in the work of conversion."[1]

Both the *Baltimore Gazette* and Clawson were wrong. Though Clawson fled Georgia shortly after the disappointing murder trial, in order to avoid rumored perjury charges and a possible prison sentence, John Morgan had no intention of abandoning the state. In 1880, ten additional elders were called to the Southern States Mission and assigned to Georgia, which meant that as many as sixteen elders labored in the state at one time. The *Atlanta Constitution* reacted with consternation, reporting incredulously that "the field is not to be abandoned . . . it will be filled even more vigorously than ever before by new Mormon priests." Morgan confirmed this supposition in an interview given to the *St. Louis Post and Dispatch* and reprinted in the *Constitution* on October 31, 1879. Asked if Standing's murder had driven Mormon missionaries from the state, Morgan responded, "Not at all." In fact, he believed Standing's murder "beneficial" to the Mormon cause: "It caused agitation, created comment, and the result is that we have made double the number of converts throughout the southern states on account of that murder." In the interview he pointed out that the violence in north Georgia had produced another salutary effect, as it convinced many converts to leave Georgia for the new Mormon settlement in Colorado. "We scarcely need to preach in the Southern States the principle of emigration," Morgan added, "so anxious are the people to escape from their surroundings."[2]

Certainly those from Whitfield and Catoosa counties seemed eager to leave. In November 1879, a company of over one hundred southern converts arrived in Colorado, among them the three generations of Georgia women at the heart of the Varnell's Station controversy. Sarah Fullbright completed the journey with her daughter Elviny Hamblin and three granddaughters—Mary and Martha Hamblin and Sarah Kaneaster. At some point, Sarah's husband Josiah must have intended to emigrate too, for he and Sarah signed a quit-claim deed in August 1879, giving up his land and house to his father in exchange for a cash advance. But locals remembered that "Joe was plowing in the fields" when his wife and children boarded a train to the West. Sarah left behind one child, ten-year-old Robert Cochran Kaneaster, perhaps the Kaneaster son whose unspecified malady had been prayed over by John Morgan in the spring of 1879, but she carried an unborn daughter with her.[3]

In Colorado, considerable progress had been made. A town named Manassa would soon emerge, carefully surveyed into thirty-two blocks, each block further subdivided into four separate residential lots. In the center block residents planned to build a temple, and the southern converts envisioned tree-lined streets emanating from the center, reminiscent of Salt Lake City. Such optimistic visions aside, the poverty of the southern immigrants remained an impediment to quick development.

More distressing, many of the Georgians had been stricken by illness—the measles, as well as another condition described by John Morgan as similar to the mumps. In a report on Manassa conditions to Elder Matthias Cowley, Morgan minimized the ailments, writing that "the Saints here are feeling well and doing well, though they have been sorely tried for some length of time with sickness, scarcely any of a fatal character, but generally measles, bad colds, etc. etc."[4]

Despite such reassurances, the measles proved especially deadly for recent arrivals from Georgia. Ninety-year-old Sarah Fullbright successfully escaped the violence in northwest Georgia but succumbed to measles in Colorado on April 14, 1880. When Sarah Kaneaster's baby daughter arrived on that same day, it must have seemed especially appropriate to bestow the name "Sarah" on the infant. But loss likely overshadowed any joy at the birth, for on April 14—such a melancholy day—Sarah Kaneaster's four-year-old daughter Fanny also died. The new mother contracted the disease too and passed away six days later, at the age of thirty-eight. Sarah's newborn daughter languished nearly five months before finally following her mother to the grave. Georgians reported that Joe Kaneaster tracked his family to Colorado, pleading unsuccessfully for them to return to Georgia, but William Lonzo Kaneaster refuted that. He insisted that after leaving north Georgia he never saw his father again. Nevertheless, Joe Kaneaster apparently learned of his wife's death, for he described himself as "widower" on the 1880 Georgia census, and in 1881 he remarried. Despite her losses, Sarah Hamblin did not return to Georgia. She remained in Colorado with her surviving daughter and grandchildren, settling into a small house just blocks away from former Georgia neighbors, the Huffakers. Pack Haynie and his young wife Henrietta, veterans of the first westward expedition, lived nearby and next door to Henrietta's mother and brother, and the union of Pack and Henrietta ultimately produced many children, as did his marriage to Mary Elma "Ellie" Wilson, his second, illegal, wife. Pack Haynie settled both wives in Manassa, but at a judicious distance, one occupying block 2 and the other block 38 of the town. Joseph

Haynie and his wife resided near Haynie's father-in-law Francis Marion Weldon, who had since returned to Georgia to retrieve additional family members. Another brother, Robert Haynie, met and married Georgian Lydia Belinda Stover in Manassa. In this way, Georgians began to re-create, though not precisely replicate, the northwest Georgia community they had abandoned.[5]

Had they known that members of the murderous Georgia mob also suffered, the Georgia Saints may have tolerated their western hardships better. North Georgia's converts left the state, but Standing's accused murderers—those who could—also deserted the mountains. The 1880 census located several of the gang in Arkansas. James Faucett moved his family to Dorsey County in the southeastern part of the state, and Manley Nations relocated to Johnson County, Arkansas. He and son Joseph shared a domicile in Howel Township, while son Jasper N. Nations settled nearby in Pittsburg, as did David D. Nations and wife Isabella Kaneaster Nations. Interestingly, Manley Nations's son John and his wife, Mary Huffaker Nations, who had both expressed interest in Mormonism and received missionaries hospitably, also left Georgia for Pittsburg, Arkansas, as did Riley and Elizabeth Loggins and their children. Though their relationship to the Manley Nations family remains unclear, it seems likely that kinship played a role in their migration. Elizabeth Loggins, an LDS convert and one of the females of the controversial Varnell's Station Branch as well as an officer in the Relief Society there, dutifully followed her husband, leaving Georgia and the Mormons behind. The other members of the mob remained in Georgia, at least in the immediate aftermath of the murder and trials, though their lives were reportedly far from happy. Hugh Blair's role in Standing's murder did not dissuade Nancy Blair Williams and Martha Blair from leaving Georgia. The Blair family splintered—just as the Nations, Kaneaster, and Huffaker families had—when their female kin moved to Manassa with David Williams and settled next door to David's uncle, Dillingham Elledge.[6]

Mormon missionaries continued to pour into the South throughout the 1880s, most destined for the southern mountains, a preference noted by those even outside the region. The *Atlanta Constitution* reprinted a news item from St. Louis that reported "the passage through their city of seventeen Mormon elders en route to the mountain districts of the southern states." The specificity of the destination the newspaper considered a "libel upon the mountain people, for the Mormon elders select only the ignorant when they go out to make converts and to secure emigrants to Colorado." Indeed, a reporter for the *Atlanta Constitution* confirmed that the Standing tragedy, "far from frightening [Mormons] away from north Georgia, has only made them redouble their efforts to make converts there." After a tour of the north Georgia region, the reporter observed that "there are now several of these priests or prophets roaming about the mountains, earnestly pleading for their church, holding out brilliant prospects to the poor people of that section." He conceded that "they take converts of either sex, but their first desire is to GET ALL THE WOMEN they can." Of a recent expedition to the West, he counted only four or five men, but "several widows went along. About a dozen old maids joined the excursion, and a few blooming lassies, in the May-day of young womanhood, went also." He claimed to have witnessed a conversation between one of the "blooming lassies" and a friend, "who told her that in Utah she would be the wife of some man who had at least another spouse." According to the reporter, "She had evidently calculated on this, and promptly replied that she supposed 'half a loaf was better than no bread at all.'"[7]

The continued proselytizing of Latter-day Saints and perceived loss of north Georgia's women galvanized the *Atlanta Constitution* to launch a bitter campaign against the LDS Church. The newspaper dedicated a great deal of paper and ink to calls to rid the state of Mormon missionaries in order to protect mountain families. In mid-1881, the newspaper reminded Georgians that "the disgraceful fact remains that the emissaries of Mormonism find north Georgia a profitable field for the propagation of their vile doctrines," claiming further that "hundreds of families have been broken up and many innocent women and young girls have been hurried off to Utah to be 'sealed' to some lecherous 'saint' in the great temple dedicated to lust and concubinage." The *Constitution* appealed for legal action: "The other states may do as they please . . . but Georgia wants no Mormonism in its borders. The state cannot afford to tolerate such an insidious form of crime and corruption. Neither can the United States afford to temporize with Mormonism in Utah. It must be rooted out and destroyed by law wherever found." Several days later, the same newspaper called for renewed violence, imploring that LDS missionaries be forcibly "driven out of the state," declaring that "the Mormons must go."[8]

It is likely no coincidence that Morgan decided to move the mission's headquarters from Rome, Georgia, to Nashville, Tennessee, in 1881. Though he claimed the location to be more convenient for traveling elders, Georgia was proving increasingly inhospitable to Mormons. The *Atlanta Constitution* issued repeated warnings about the "Mormon organization in north Georgia." Describing female converts as "ignorant," "unfortunate," and "grossly deceived" by the fact that Mormon missionaries avoided the topic of polygamy, the newspaper reminded readers that although the emigrating women "may be accompanied by their brothers, their husband or their fathers," they were destined for lives of ruin at the hands of the lecherous Saints. In August 1881 Georgia's legislators applied themselves to proposed anti-Mormon legislation, a development that the *Constitution* hailed as progress. In order to spur the Senate's efforts, the newspaper continued to report on the growth of the north Georgia mission, the perceived immorality of the Latter-day Saints, and the consequent damage to Georgia's reputation in the eyes of the rest of the nation. On August 12, the periodical repeated a salacious—though partially true—tidbit about the Colorado Saints from the *Chicago Herald*: "It is not uncommon to find the Georgia Mormons living with a plurality of wives" in the West.[9]

On August 13, 1881, an anti-Mormon bill that made the preaching of polygamy a crime was introduced in the Georgia legislature. The first reading of the bill prompted some laughter, especially when Senator William B. Butt, a prominent bachelor, rose to offer an objection. As he "had never been able to capture even one of the fairer sex," he said, he "did not wish to trespass upon the rights of any man." Such initial levity aside, a vigorous debate quickly ensued. Some questioned the constitutionality of the bill and pointed out that state laws against bigamy and polygamy already existed. Senator DuPont Guerry cautioned that "the spirit of the constitution does not mean that we shall pick out what is good religion and what is bad religion." Further, he argued, a bill prohibiting the preaching of polygamy would restrict speech, and the freedom of speech—even in support of an unpopular belief—enjoyed constitutional protection. "I shall vote for the constitution," he said, "it matters not what the speech is about." Senator James G. Parks countered by asserting that the proposed legislation was akin to laws against attempted crime: "We propose to punish the men who seek to induce others to violate this law of God and man." Further, he argued that the missionaries ("in league with hell and the devil") and the church's practice of plural marriage "saps the life of all domestic happiness which is the great bulwark of constitutional liberty." That opinion ultimately prevailed: on August 18, the anti-Mormon bill passed the senate by a vote of thirty-four to five. On that same day, the Georgia legislature enacted the law, which read,

> Be it enacted by the General Assembly of the State of Georgia, that from and after the passage of this act, it shall not be lawful for any person in this state, in any address to a public or private assemblage of persons, to counsel, advise, or encourage in any way the violation of the laws of this state forbidding polygamy or bigamy. Be it further enacted that any person or persons who shall be guilty of the violation of this act shall on conviction be punished by confinement at labor in the penitentiary for any time not less than two nor longer than four years.[10]

Popular humorist Bill Arp, whose columns regularly appeared in the *Atlanta Constitution*, registered his support for the bill, writing, "I am glad the legislature passed the Mormon bill. Intolerance in religious matters is a bad thing, but there is no religion in polygamy or bigamy, and no good ever came of it since the world was made. . . . I don't like these Mormons. They are slipping around here trying to demoralize our ignorant people, and I shall rejoice to see 'em slip into the chain-gang." A more aggressive solution was proposed by a "Red-Hot Colonel" in Emanuel County, who dismissed the legislation. He favored other remedies: "We say shoot 'em, lynch 'em, hang 'em, and burn 'em. We don't want 'em in our midst." As justification for the violence, he professed his desire to protect his wife from the Mormon elders, writing, "We haven't got but one wife, and we solemnly declare we intend to keep her, if we have to do it at the point of the bayonet."[11]

Mission president John Morgan minimized the impact of the legislation at first, interpreting the controversy as a tribute to Mormon successes in the state. In Missouri when he learned of the law, Morgan chortled to a St. Louis reporter that "we are getting along so well that the lawmakers are now getting after us." Church president John Taylor viewed the matter more dimly. In a letter to Matthias Cowley on September 6, Taylor described the Georgia law as "against Polygamy, Bigamy, and Emigration," adding his fear that the legislation would be seen by Georgians as a "license to mobocracy." Curiously, Morgan simply denied the law's passage, despite newspaper reports to the contrary. In October, he wrote to the governor of Georgia to request details on the legislation; lacking that information, he reported to Taylor that the bill "failed to become a law, and in fact only passed its first reading, and the vote of 35 to 4 was on that reading, after which it was never called up again." Once Morgan's remarks were made public, the denial incensed the editors of the *Atlanta Constitution*, and in an article addressed to him, a reporter taunted the Southern States Mission president: "If Elder Morgan will take advantage of his belief to preach polygamy in Georgia, he will soon discover whether the bill has become a law."[12]

Morgan did admit that by early 1882 the *Constitution*, "although friendly in the past, now carried on a serious campaign of vilification." In fact, the newspaper aimed to vilify all Mormons—missionaries and Georgia converts alike. Items that targeted the LDS Church began to appear between longer columns of news. "Fifty persons left Rome for Utah on Wednesday morning," one such item read, but "they were mostly snuff-dipping women who had become Mormons" (particularly ironic as the LDS Church forbade the use of tobacco). Similar items appeared interspersed among the newspaper's classified ads. If a sickly Georgian scanned the classifieds in search of a cure for consumption, he might find an advertisement for "Dr. Wm. Holt's Balsam for Lungs," followed by this catchy rhyme: "Wherever vice and ignorance abound, the Mormon missionaries may be found." If one needed a supply of "Burnett's Cocoaine" or "Rough on Rats" rodenticide, it was impossible to miss, "The next point to try on the Mormons may be the point of a bayonet!" which was sandwiched neatly between ads for the two products. Concluding perhaps that those seeking "Dr. Fuller's Youthful Vigor Pills" to cure impotence would naturally be interested in Mormon marital practices, the *Constitution* followed the ad with a short editorial: "The Mormon church divides its territory into 'stakes' and the Mormon women are kept tied to those stakes." Attracting the attention of southern readers became simpler yet when the periodical accepted advertising for "The Mormon Elder's Damiana Wafers, The Most Powerful Invigorant Ever Produced," which prominently featured a bare-breasted woman.[13]

For those not interested in eradicating vermin or seeking cures, the *Constitution* commissioned a serial adventure, "Sealed unto Him," described as "Thrilling Adventure among the Mormons!" Written by Joaquin Miller, the story ran for several weeks in 1884, under a banner that suggested its relevance: "With Mormon Elders Desperately at Work in every Southern State practicing their infamous doctrines, *This Powerful Story is Timely*." When Morgan moved the headquarters of the Southern States Mission again in 1882, this time to Chattanooga, Tennessee, he deliberately removed himself from the state, but posted himself only miles from the profitable north Georgia missionary field.[14]

Frustrated by the failure of local and state efforts to end Mormon proselytizing, Georgians became increasingly strident in their calls for federal intervention. The *Constitution* warned that northern states were misguided in believing Mormonism to be "a Georgia problem" and urged a national effort against the church: "Everywhere they are active, energetic, plausible and untiring. Everywhere they are supplied with funds; and everywhere they so conduct themselves as to make a profound impression upon ignorant people. Not a day passes that fresh squads of emigrants do not join the tide of converts that is flowing . . . from every state in the union. What do the people of the country propose to do about it?"[15]

Georgia's intolerance of Latter-day Saints, expressed at the local level by a murderous mob and at the state level by antipolygamy legislation, was hardly atypical. Both Tennessee and Mississippi eventually passed anti-Mormon legislation, which prompted the *Constitution* to point to the continuing exodus of Georgians from the state and perceived deficiencies in Georgia's law. "The Tennessee legislation . . . has dealt more wisely with the Mormon nuisance than the general assembly of Georgia" as "it gives the officers of the law an opportunity to arrest those who are engaged in sending caravans of ignorant people to the West." In late 1881, the U.S. Senate also considered legislation to punish Utah polygamists. In December of that year, Vermont's senator George F. Edmunds proposed legislation that defined polygamy, or "unlawful cohabitation," as a crime, with penalties including a fine and imprisonment. In addition, Edmunds proposed a measure that restricted polygamists (or those who believed in polygamy) from voting, holding office, or serving on juries and assigned the supervision of Utah's elections to a five-member commission appointed by the president. Few expected any serious opposition to the bill, as it was an amendment to an existing 1862 anti-bigamy law. But several southern legislators raised objections to the proposed legislation, including Georgia's senator Joseph E. Brown.[16]

Senator Brown, the former Confederate governor of Georgia elected to the Senate in 1880, had been raised in north Georgia. A lawyer and prominent businessman, Brown served as president of the Western and Atlantic Railroad Company as well as the Dade Coal Company, which included iron mines in north Georgia and Chattanooga. Senator Brown issued the first challenge to the bill, not as a defense of polygamy, but because he believed the Edmunds Act to be unconstitutional, in that it seemed to establish a religious test for voting and holding office. In a speech delivered in the U.S. Senate on February 16, 1882, Senator Brown pointed out that the bill effectively disfranchised not just those Mormons who practiced polygamy, but also all Mormons who *believed in* polygamy's lawfulness:

> There are those in the Mormon territory who believe that there is a divine revelation later than the New Testament which authorizes a member of the Mormon Church to have more wives than one. They believe in the revelation, as they term it, made by God himself to their prophet, Joseph Smith. I do not believe in it, but they religiously believe it. Many of them are as earnest and honest in their faith as I am in the Baptist faith, or as other Senators are in their Methodist or Presbyterian faith. I think they are greatly in error; but I have no more right if they do not practice it, to disfranchise them on account of that belief than I have to disfranchise any Senator in this Chamber or any man out of it who believes that the New Testament does not forbid polygamy.[17]

The bill threatened to disfranchise "almost the entire people of a Territory," Brown argued, as most people in Utah believed in polygamy, whether they followed the principle or not. He pointed out that the bill seemed to replicate those once leveled against the defeated Confederacy. At the end of the war, he said, "I had then a little taste of the rule that we now propose to apply to Utah. I stood by the polls, disfranchised and not permitted to vote, while my former slaves, emancipated, walked up and deposited their ballots." He had no power to challenge his disfranchisement at the time, he acknowledged, as Georgia had seceded from the Union and "the conquering power had the right to dictate the terms." However, the Mormons had not seceded from the Union and, as it stood, Brown believed, the bill established a religious test that disfranchised Mormons from voting and holding office "on account of their religious opinions." He succeeded in having the bill amended to reflect disfranchisement only in the event of a legal conviction of bigamy, an important distinction.[18]

Brown also objected to the proposed election commission—he noted its similarity to a Reconstruction-era "returning board"—and its ability to control the outcome of elections. Concerned that the measure could effectively transform a Democratic territory into a Republican state, he denounced the returning board system, which, he said, "stinks in the nostrils of honest men." His objections were addressed when the Senate accepted Brown's amendment requiring that no more than three of the five members of the election commission would represent the same party. Though southerners challenged the bill again when it reached the House of Representatives, President Chester A. Arthur signed the Edmunds Act into law on March 23, 1882. The Utah Commission, which consisted of two Democrats and three Republicans, went to work in the fall and disfranchised more than twelve thousand Saints within the year.[19]

Though he declared himself opposed to the "evil practices" of Utah's Mormons, Georgia's senator Brown continued his opposition to the Edmunds Act. On January 11, 1884, he made another speech in the U.S. Senate. In it, he challenged the constitutionality of the test-oath administered by the Utah Commission. The oath required the prospective voter (male *and* female as women in the territory were allowed to vote) to swear that he was not currently—and never had been—a bigamist or polygamist. If he refused to take the oath, Brown pointed out, his guilt was presumed and he was denied the right to vote or hold office. The Georgia senator pointed out several reasons why this was an unconstitutional violation of rights—to due process, a jury trial, and so on. As a result, Brown argued, Congress "put the feet of the power of this Government upon their necks and crush[ed] them because there have been found among them 12,000 men and women who will not take an illegal oath which has been tendered to them, and who are therefore presumed to be guilty of bigamy or polygamy.... We punish 138,000 people who have not practiced polygamy in order to make sure that we have punished 12,000 who are believed to be guilty of bigamy or polygamy."[20]

Four months later, Senator Brown addressed the Senate again. On the issue of the government's attention to the "preservation of the purity of the family by the suppression of polygamy," Brown said, why not also protect the family from "illegal" divorce (divorces granted on spurious legal grounds) and subsequent "adulterous" marriages? Drawing explicit comparisons between Utah and New England, the Georgia senator argued that the rising rate of divorce in the northeast also posed a significant moral threat. "If reform is necessary," he said, "and I think it is, let it apply to all sections where the same evil exists." In his view, both Utah polygamists as well as those who divorced a first wife without legal cause in order to take a second were guilty in the eyes of God: "They stand side by side alike condemned by the divine lawgiver of the universe. They are both bigamists, and they both live in a state of adultery; and the moral guilt of the husband in Utah who lives with two wives, one of whom he has no right to have, is not greater than the moral guilt of the husband who in Georgia or in Massachusetts has two wives and cohabits in a state of adultery with the one he has no right to have." He spoke passionately against government persecution of the church and issued a surprising defense of the Latter-day Saints, describing Utah's Mormons as "a quiet, peaceable, orderly people, who have comfortable homes, work hard, and make an honest living, and who worship according to the dictates of their own conscience, and, as a mass, believe they are right."[21]

Georgia periodicals followed Senator Brown's speeches with great interest. They welcomed his condemnation of polygamy and thoughtfully considered Brown's argument that the Edmunds Bill was unconstitutional. But they viewed skeptically Brown's plan to counter the Latter-day Saints by sending missionaries to "Christianize the Mormons." Reporting that Brown opposed government force and favored the intervention of mainstream denominations "to point out to the wicked Mormons the error of their polygamous ways," the *Douglasville Star* countered that "the Mormons are already sending missionaries among the Christians to convert them to Mormonism and with very gratifying success. If Senator Brown's suggestion is acted upon, the proselyting will begin with vigor, and no doubt both sides will meet with success enough to ensure the existence of polygamy for years to come." Bill Arp, writing in the *Atlanta Constitution*, openly chided the ex-governor: "They say that Governor Brown made a good speech against the Mormon bill," Arp wrote, "but if he pulled it down he had better build up another one that will regulate them fellows." Why not turn loose the power of the U.S. military, he wondered. "If our government is strong enough to subdue the southern states and set four million niggers free, I reckon it can regulate affairs in Utah and free those white women. I reckon so."[22]

To the consternation of many southern antipolygamists, Brown's challenges to the Edmunds Act on constitutional and biblical grounds gained the enthusiastic endorsement of Latter-day Saints. John Morgan ordered printed copies of Brown's speeches; these he distributed to Mormon elders, who used them to great effect in proselytizing. In the weeks following the debate in the Senate, Morgan reported happily that "the bitter nature of the opposition is gradually giving way and a much more liberal spirit being manifested; this caused, to a great extent I think by the judicious distribution of the speeches made in Congress on the Edmunds Bill, and distributed in pamphlet form. We find these speeches ... sought after with avidity."[23]

Atlanta's *Constitution* noted bitterly that the new legislation—both state and federal—failed to halt the spread of Mormonism in Georgia. "The Mormons in Utah are laughing at the Edmunds law," a columnist reported, and "they are also laughing at the law of Georgia." Georgia's legislation, which had been aimed at Mormon missionaries who preached polygamy, was, according to the newspaper, "a dead letter." This, because "no Mormon missionary ever so far forgets himself as to preach polygamy to those whom he proposes to convert." The writer predicted that the missionaries "will continue to laugh at the Georgia law until four or five of the genial elders are treated to a free ride on a rail by the indignant people of north Georgia, and then they will fail to enjoy the humor of the situation." In fact, a Georgia mob turned on Elder John T. Alexander in 1883, shooting and wounding him seriously enough to send him back to Salt Lake City to recover. The most serious of all the southern anti-Mormon violence occurred in Lewis County, Tennessee, in 1884. In what became known as the Cane Creek Massacre, a mob shot to death two Mormon elders and two Tennessee converts. Again, Atlanta's *Constitution* weighed in, offering a similar defense to that afforded Elder Standing's killers: "Perhaps the law itself is responsible for much of the lawlessness with which the country is afflicted. People find themselves hedged about by grievous evils for which no remedy exists. They murmur, grow restless, and finally remove the evil in their own way. Frequently public opinion sustains them and their violations of the law are tacitly ignored."[24]

Despite the renewed violence in Georgia, Mormon missionaries persevered and southern converts continued to pour from Georgia to the West. Each year saw two or more expeditions from the southern states, and by late 1883, the population of the Colorado colony reached nearly eight hundred. In that same year, Manassa returned some of its southern converts to Georgia as missionaries. Georgian Samuel Echols was among the young men who accepted the call to a southern mission. A Polk County native, Echols had been twenty-five years old, with wife and baby, at the time of his conversion in 1881. Echols's conversion to Mormonism strained the marriage, and for a while Sam and his wife Mary separated. After a time they reunited and Mary was baptized along with the entire Echols clan—Sam's mother, father, and siblings—who then made plans to emigrate to Colorado. In March 1882, as the Echols family prepared to leave Georgia, Mary begged for one last extended visit with her parents who lived three miles away. Sam agreed and planned to fetch his wife when it was time to go. Two days later, after the Echols family had already begun their move, Sam went to collect his wife and baby from his in-laws. According to Echols's memoir, he and his wife "had arranged to go also but when I went by after her she would not go with me. Her people had persuaded her not to go with me." In his account, he did not go into detail about what was surely an ugly scene, but concluded by writing, "So I left her and the baby and went on my way."[25]

Sam and his parents arrived in Manassa in the spring of 1882, but in early 1883 church authorities called Echols to return to the South. Echols made his way first to north Georgia, where he apparently sought out his wife and child, who resided in Floyd County with Mary's parents. He intended a reunion with his family, but Mary refused to see her long-absent husband. In February 1884, Echols took legal action against her. According to the *Atlanta Constitution*, Echols "sued out a writ of habeas corpus for the child, which he wishes to take with him to Colorado." The newspaper predicted a lively legal battle. Sam and Mary Echols appeared before a judge in Rome on February 15, 1884. Echols testified first that he "had never given his wife cause of complaint." He recalled that after joining the LDS Church, he and his father decided to go to Colorado "to better their fortunes." His return to north Georgia, he testified, was prompted by a desire to spread the Mormon doctrine and to rejoin his wife and child. Though he was an emissary of the Mormons, he added, he did not practice polygamy. A reporter covering the trial wrote that "Echols gave his testimony in a quiet and modest manner with apparent frankness." Witnesses—two Georgia Mormons and one non-Mormon neighbor—came forward to testify on his behalf, declaring Echols to be "a man of good character, moral and upright."[26]

Mary Vincent Echols appeared on the witness stand next, and in a "cool and self-possessed" manner, shared her account of the marriage. For a while her married life had been happy, she said, but "then came some slight jars." Her husband had forced her to work in the fields when her health was poor, she testified, and neither she nor the baby received a physician's care as often as needed. After her husband joined the LDS Church, she joined too, she admitted, but only because of "the constant persuasion of her husband, and for the sake of peace." It was her discovery that Mormons practiced polygamy that persuaded her against emigrating to Colorado. She and her child—"a bright, fair-haired boy" according to the newspaper—relied on her parents in Sam's absence, she testified, as "for two years she did not see her husband, nor did he contribute one cent to the support of herself and child." Mr. Vincent, her father, swore to the truth of her statements, and told the court that he was willing to continue his support of his daughter and grandson. After hearing the testimony and arguments on behalf of each side, the judge ruled that the child should stay with his mother in Georgia.[27]

The case received no further coverage, but a month later Elder Echols came to the attention of reporters again, when a correspondent from the *Brunswick Herald* happened to encounter the missionary, described as "a real Mormon," on a train from Paulding County to Nashville, Tennessee. According to the reporter's account, Echols's missionary labors seemed to be "confined to converting handsome young women and escorting them to Utah," a conclusion based solely on the young woman seated next to Echols. The reporter dedicated seven lines of type to a physical description of the woman, which suggests that the newsman also possessed an eye for the ladies. He described the elder's companion as "a decidedly handsome, modest looking young woman, perhaps twenty years old, fine complexion, dark eyes and hair, and a splendid figure, perhaps a little inclined to robustness," concluding that "her face denoted all that a physiognomist would declare strong and perfect." Two days later, the *Nashville World* repeated the account, augmented with fresh details. When Echols returned to Georgia, the story went, he returned to his wife and child, but then "took up with another woman as his wife and decamped for Utah with her, leaving his lawful wife in tears and heart broken." While it is doubtful that Mary Echols grieved her husband's return to the West, it is true that he did not go alone. According to family accounts, Elder Sam Echols met and fell in love with Arminta Missouri Lee of Paulding County during his Georgia mission and convinced her to return with him to Colorado, where they were married.[28]

Sam Echols finally managed to acquire one wife; at the same time, John Morgan was considering adding a second. He confided to his journal that he faced mounting pressure from church authorities who had subjected him to "quite a talking" concerning his failure to follow the principle of celestial or plural marriage. On January 12, 1884, after a long talk with wife Mellie, John Morgan acquiesced, taking a second wife, Annie Mildred Smith, only weeks later. By the end of the year, he found himself evading federal marshals who actively sought out polygamists for prosecution. During Christmas week, he penned a quick report in his journal: "Have been in hiding these days to keep out of the way of Marshalls." In 1885, he decided that it would be prudent to take his second family "underground" (Annie produced a child with Morgan in December 1884), so he began construction on a house in Manassa. On land purchased from Silas Smith Jr., the husband of Jane Elledge, Morgan built a home for Annie and their new daughter. Annie's neighbors would be the southerners Morgan apparently trusted to look after his second family when he was away.[29]

Manassa's continued growth, in spite of its divisions, may be seen as the consequence of both Mormon success and persecution. New converts continued to arrive in the township, their numbers augmented by a steady flow of Utah refugees fleeing from federal marshals as, in the years following the passage of the Edmunds Act, the San Luis Valley accommodated illegal plural wives forced into hiding by the aggressive legal pursuit

FIGURE 7. Mary (Molly) Hamblin in Colorado. Mary Hamblin and her mother attempted to warn Joseph Standing and Rudger Clawson prior to Standing's murder. This photo was taken in Colorado in the early 1900s. John H. Morgan Photograph Collection (P0605), box 1, folder 3, Special Collections, J. Willard Marriott Library, the University of Utah.

FIGURE 8. Group portrait from the LDS Sunday School in Colorado. John H. Morgan Photograph Collection (p0605), box 1, folder 12, Special Collections, J. Willard Marriott Library, the University of Utah.

of their husbands. If apprehended with their children, the illegal wives "were deemed sufficient evidence to convict their husbands." So many of the plural wives—or "widows" as Saints often referred to them—made their temporary home in Manassa, more than five hundred miles from Salt Lake City.[30]

Rudger Clawson, missionary companion to the slain elder Joseph Standing, did not choose to hide his plural wife in Manassa, among the southern converts who very nearly cost him his life. Instead, Clawson earned notoriety as the first Mormon imprisoned under the Edmunds Act. He had been apprehended at a Utah boardinghouse with plural wife Lydia Spencer, and his prosecution was the first to include a jury that excluded those who practiced or believed in polygamy, a provision of the Edmunds Act. At his trial, Lydia Spencer refused to testify against the man she considered her husband, a stance that earned her a stay in the penitentiary. Despite her refusal, in late 1884, a jury convicted Clawson of polygamy and unlawful cohabitation. On November 3, the day Clawson was to receive his sentence, the judge asked "if he had anything to say why sentence should not be passed upon him." Clawson chose to respond defiantly: "I very much regret that the laws of my country should come in conflict with the laws of God; but whenever they do, I shall invariably choose to obey the latter." His first conviction carried a sentence of imprisonment for three years and six months as well as a fine of five hundred dollars; the second, lesser charge fetched Clawson an additional six months in prison and an additional fine of three hundred dollars. In commenting upon the landmark trial and harsh sentence, the *Atlanta Constitution* noted approvingly that "the impudent Mormon must pass his time behind prison bars." He served most of his sentence in the Utah Penitentiary.[31]

Mormon defiance prompted consideration of yet another federal anti-polygamy bill, and again Senator George F. Edmunds led the opposition. Cosponsored by Congressman John Randolph Tucker of Virginia, the new legislation represented a shift in that it resolved to punish both plural husbands and wives as well as the church that was complicit in shielding them. The Edmunds-Tucker Act of 1887 prohibited the practice of polygamy, but also disincorporated the LDS Church and confiscated church property. When news of the legislation reached Morgan, he reacted bitterly, writing, "This is another link in the chain of bondage sought to be thrown around the saints." At the same time that he divided his time between the southern mission, Utah, and Colorado, he worried about a possible indictment against him.[32]

Again, the LDS Church appealed to the U.S. Supreme Court, but in May 1890 the court upheld the dissolution of the church corporation and the seizure of church property. In that same year, church president Wilford Woodruff issued his famous Manifesto, which officially ended the practice of plural marriage. By that time, Morgan had been relieved of his responsibilities in the South, though the Southern States Mission continued under the leadership of William Spry. Morgan had accepted new responsibilities—he had been chosen and ordained one of the First Seven Presidents of the Seventy, a significant leadership position in the LDS Church, and also served in the Utah

Territorial Legislature. In that capacity, he worked on behalf of Utah statehood. Political concerns carried him to the White House in January 1892, where he met with U.S. President Benjamin Harrison. Of the president he wrote, "His head was evidently set on the Utah question against us. He expressed fear that the Mormons were not going to give up Polygamy."[33]

The same political imperative motivated another trip to Washington, D.C., that year. And it also afforded former federal soldier Morgan the opportunity to view the Grand Army of the Republic as they paraded down Pennsylvania Avenue. From nine thirty in the morning to six in the evening, veterans—eighty thousand of them, Morgan believed—marched past. "It was a grand display and one doubtless that will never be witnessed again. The day was a very fine one with bands of music and soldierly tread." In September 1903, when a monument commemorating the heroism of Wilder's Brigade was unveiled at the fortieth anniversary commemoration of the Battle of Chickamauga, General John T. Wilder called on the old soldiers of his command to gather in Georgia. Though others who rode with the 123rd Illinois rallied to Wilder's side, Morgan was not there. He had died on August 14, 1894, at the age of fifty-two. The cause of death was officially listed as "typhoid-malaria," a malady blamed on his years of service in the South, first as a federal soldier, then as a Mormon elder.[34]

By the time of Morgan's death, America's Protestant churches had already begun the rush into the southern highlands, establishing Christian missions to benefit needy and backward mountaineers. But when they made their way into the most distant mountain hollows, they encountered Mormons.

Much has been written about the work of Presbyterian missionaries Edward O. Guerrant and Samuel Tyndale Wilson in Appalachia; however, a careful reading of their mission accounts reveals that by the time they began the quest for souls in the southern mountains, Mormon elders were already there. Presbyterian Guerrant, who labored in the mountains of Kentucky, Tennessee, and North Carolina in the 1880s and 1890s, reported that he encountered Mormons "in the most distant and inaccessible parts of the mountains. They have more missionaries in Kentucky (and probably in every Southern State) than all other denominations together." In 1906 Presbyterian Wilson confirmed that he had "personally and repeatedly seen the emissaries of the Mormon abomination plying their mission of perversion and seduction" among the southern mountains.[35] The nineteenth-century battle between Protestant America and the Mormons was far from over.

Conclusion

Joseph Standing's body rests in Salt Lake City Cemetery, interred with the dignity appropriate to a religious martyr. His monument bears bitter recriminations against the men accused of his murder and the state that denied him justice—"There is no law in Georgia for the Mormons." Another memorial to Elder Standing exists in north Georgia, on a small patch of donated land believed to be the site of Standing's murder. The July heat had forced the unhappy procession to a halt in a patch of shade. Standing knelt to drink from the small spring that still runs there today. In his account of the murder, Rudger Clawson described it as "a lovely spot—a spring of clear water, overshadowed by a huge, outspreading tree." It is still a lovely spot, though somber reminders dampen the visitor's appreciation. A bronze plaque affixed to a large stone slab tells the story; in the grass nearby, a small rock engraved with the initials "JS" marks the spot where Standing fell.[1]

From this vantage point it is easy to imagine the community as it would have been in 1879. White settlement in northwest Georgia followed a familiar frontier pattern. Relatives and friends joined original settlers in the area, and over time, intermarriage among constituent families drew the settlement clusters into an extensive kinship system. Intermarriage and marriage alliances further strengthened the system, as did community relationships between friends, neighbors, trading

FIGURE 9. Stone that marks the spot in Whitfield County, Georgia, where Standing fell. The stone is located in the Joseph Standing Memorial Park, established in 1952 and maintained by the LDS church. The road leading to the park was also named Standing Road. Photo by the author.

partners, and coreligionists. When Italian novelist Italo Calvino wrote *Invisible Cities*, he imagined a similar web of relationships. In a city named Ersilia, he wrote, "the inhabitants stretch strings from the corners of the houses, white or black or gray or black-and-white, according to whether they mark a relationship of blood, of trade, authority, agency." The pattern of strings thus "establish the relationships that sustain the city's life." If, like Calvino, we allow our imagination free rein, the evocative description could be applied to the mountains of northwest Georgia. The comparison is not particularly apt, especially as the discussion of Ersilia is part of an imagined conversation between Marco Polo and Kublai Khan in the thirteenth century. But it is possible to imagine similar strings stretching from household to household, and county to county, each with a distinctive hue symbolic of relationships—familial, neighborly, economic, or religious—all of them mingling in a multicolored canopy in the north Georgia sky.[2]

That complex web of relationships that linked northwest Georgians in antebellum times, often influencing or determining wartime political loyalties, largely survived into the postwar period. When Elder John Morgan and other representatives of the Church of Jesus Christ of Latter-day Saints moved into the region to attract converts, they deliberately negotiated the ties of family and friendship in order to advance their gospel and promises of a better life in the Mormon West. Such promises proved seductive as, by the 1870s, both men and women found it increasingly difficult to scratch a living from the ridges of northwest Georgia. With few options for upward mobility, the poorer classes of whites—men *and* women—experienced the familiar push-pull of migratory forces. Economic hardship and diminishing social status pushed them to look beyond the southern mountains, while religious imperatives and the lure of new lands pulled them to the West.

On those occasions when families unilaterally accepted Mormonism, few serious disruptions occurred. The Chattooga, Floyd, and Walker County branches primarily represented nuclear families, some of them constituent families within a larger network of kin. In these cases, the presence of male heads of household within the branches seems to have successfully deterred serious efforts to persecute either Georgia's new Saints or the LDS missionaries who often relied on their protection. When patriarchs assumed a prominent role in branch leadership, it appears to have diffused, at least partially, objections from local critics. The situation proved very different in Varnell's Station, which drew converts from both Catoosa and Whitfield counties. When the lone male member of the Varnell's Station Branch departed for Colorado, he left behind a religious organization populated solely by women. In the absence of male leadership, Mormon patriarchy, as profound as any found in southern households, demanded the creation of a female Relief Society instead of a branch organization, but few northwest Georgians would have understood the difference. Most would have seen only an exclusively female religious organization—consisting primarily of widows and young unmarried women, as well as one sister whose adherence to the Mormons prompted a crisis in her marriage—under the solicitous care of the young male representatives of a polygamous lifestyle in the West. So as the Mormon elders moved among the strings that linked family, kin, and neighbors, the tiny cords were disturbed. Some frayed; others simply snapped.

The tragic death of Elder Joseph Standing lays bare the bonds that existed among northwest Georgians. In the process, family and community are illuminated, and Standing's murder is revealed as the consequence of the tensions resulting from separating converts from loved ones and dependents from heads of household. Such tensions existed to some extent in all of the northwest Georgia branches, but the women of Varnell's Station, in asserting their rights to their religious beliefs and declaring their intentions to abandon Georgia for the West, especially offended their families and neighbors. It was in Whitfield and Catoosa counties that women openly defied men—ministers, fathers, brothers, and husbands—by claiming the new religion for their own. It was in those same counties that men felt justified in resorting to violent action against both the representatives of the disruptive faith and the women who continued to intervene on behalf of the missionaries, deliberately shielding them from harm whenever possible. The mob's elimination of Joseph Standing must therefore be seen as more than an attack on Mormon missionaries. It was also an effort, mostly unsuccessful, to control women's religious beliefs as well as their sexuality.

In the aftermath of the murder, members of the mob framed their argument in familiar language, justifying their actions as a defense of home and womanhood. In portraying Standing as a licentious male and themselves as defenders of family, the accused men gained sympathy. The message would not have been lost on those inclined to tolerate Mormons, or the north Georgia women who placed religious belief above spousal devotion. The argument proved a particularly effective one, as Georgians justified the behavior and absolved them of blame. Georgia's press cooperated with anti-Mormon vigilantes in their characterization of Standing as "a lustful lout" and Mormonism as the construction of salacious and satyric males. Institutional solutions to the state's "Mormon problem" followed in the years subsequent to Standing's murder, as Georgia legislators created legislation intended to discourage the teaching of polygamy, thus protecting, they argued, Georgia families and the institution of marriage. In speeches delivered before the U.S. Senate, Joseph E. Brown propelled the state to the center of a national debate.

This history of an encounter between two "peculiar" peoples—Appalachian Georgians and Mormons—provides the historian with an unusual vantage point from which to examine social networks, but there is an additional benefit to such a concentrated study of social life. As noted earlier, a prominent Georgia historian once referred to the state's poor white farmers as the "little" men, the "forgotten" men, of the nineteenth century.[3] By studying the Latter-day Saints' mission to Georgia's "little" men and women, we restore the poor to history and reveal them on a national stage as Americans debated the "Mormon Question" and the limits of religious freedom.

Appendix 1

North Georgia Converts Organized by Branch

The individuals listed in this appendix were identified on conversion and branch membership records maintained by Elder John Hamilton Morgan. The branches appear in order of establishment.

HAYWOOD VALLEY BRANCH
Chattooga County

Caroline Cosby Bagwell. Caroline was born in Franklin County, Georgia, in 1836 and married neighbor John Winkfield Bagwell in 1859. In 1860 John and Caroline lived in Franklin County next door to his parents, Albert and Rebecca Bagwell, and her parents, James and Margaret Cosby. The census described John as a farmer, though he possessed no land of his own, so he likely farmed his father's land. Caroline's parents also owned no land of their own and may have farmed Bagwell land. John Bagwell served the Confederacy but was killed in 1864 during the Atlanta Campaign. After her husband's death, thirty-five-year-old Caroline moved into her then-widowed mother's household with her two children, **Albert Gallatin "Tobe"** and **Henrietta Paralee Bagwell.** Neither Caroline nor her mother owned land, and in 1870 the household possessed a total estate worth $100. Caroline supported her children by weaving cloth and sewing, while twelve-year-old Tobe Bagwell worked as a farm laborer. They moved to Haywood Valley in about 1870. Henrietta remembered that the family attended LDS services on Sand Mountain in Alabama before joining the Haywood Valley Branch with her mother and brother. Caroline, Tobe, and Henrietta joined John Morgan's first expedition to Colorado. While still in winter quarters in Colorado, Henrietta married Georgia convert Patrick Haynie. In 1880, Patrick and Henrietta lived next door to her mother and brother, who shared a residence. Tobe was employed as a clerk in the Manassa General Store.

William H. Bagwell and Margaret (Lawrence) Bagwell. Evidence suggested, but did not confirm, a family connection to Caroline Cosby Bagwell. Although William did not appear on branch membership or baptism lists, he joined the LDS Church and relocated to the Colorado colony along with his wife, Margaret, who was Thomas Anderson Lawrence's daughter.

Gabriel Barbour and Mary Ellen (Powell) Barbour. Gabriel Barbour was born in 1818 in Georgia, and John Morgan's journal suggests that he was Thomas Barbour's brother. Although his wife, Mary Ellen, was baptized in November 1876, Gabriel was not baptized until spring of the following year. He was later set apart as second counselor to branch president Thomas A. Lawrence. The 1870 census described Gabriel as a "grocer dealer," although he owned no property and the value of his personal estate was only $200. However, county tax records for 1871 show that he possessed 160 acres of land valued at $2,000 and acted as agent for other Chattooga County landowners. The 1880 census described Gabriel Barbour as a farmer but also as "maimed, crippled, bedridden, or otherwise disabled." His wife was also described as physically ill. Neither relocated to the Colorado colony. Gabriel's sister, Mary Caroline Barbour Manning, was the wife of William P. Manning, and both were members of the Beech Creek Branch in Floyd County.

John J. Barbour and Susan (Pace) Barbour. John Joseph Barbour was the son of Thomas Barbour and was born in Georgia in 1847. He and his wife Susan were among Morgan's first converts, and John served as the first president of the

Haywood Valley Branch. He resigned after one year and was replaced by Thomas A. Lawrence. He remained active in the branch, serving as first counselor to Lawrence but expressed reservations that resulted in a letter written to Joseph Smith III of the LDS Reorganized Church in which Barbour solicited advice regarding the practice of polygamy. John J. Barbour was a Confederate, though only conditionally. He enlisted in the First Battalion, Georgia Infantry, in 1863, but when he was stationed in Murfreesboro, Tennessee, his father traveled to camp with a substitute, and John returned to Chattooga County with his father. John then traveled to the north, where he remained until after the Confederate surrender. Like his older brother, John labored on his father's farm in 1870. He possessed no land, and his personal estate was estimated at $150. Still landless in 1880, he possessed household, tools, crops, and livestock valued at $388. Although neither John nor his wife emigrated to the West, at least one of their children—daughter *Susannah*—eventually relocated to the Colorado colony with her husband, James Marlow Anderson. She later divorced him and remarried Hartzel Howland Flower in Manassa.

Thomas Barbour and Elizabeth Barbour. Thomas Barbour was born in North Carolina in about 1809. He was baptized on November 12, 1876, when he was approximately sixty-seven years old, and he was listed as John Morgan's first convert. His wife, Elizabeth, was baptized on the same day. Elizabeth was Barbour's second wife; his first wife, Martha Ann Pratt, died after 1860 but before 1870. In 1860 Barbour owned a prosperous farm in Chattooga Valley, with real estate valued at $25,000 and a personal estate estimated at $17,775, which included the value of sixteen slaves. When the war began, Barbour declared himself a Unionist and claimed to have suffered financially as a result when the Confederate government confiscated, and never returned, several hundred acres of his land. By 1870, the value of his real estate was estimated at $5,000 and his personal estate at $300. His neighbors included sons Thomas and John and brother Gabriel Barbour. In that year, Thomas Barbour's household included seven black residents, described as domestic servants or farm laborers. From 1870 to 1880, Barbour reported wages paid and debts collected, which suggests that he employed farm laborers and/or rented his land to tenants, including his two sons. In 1874, Barbour filed a claim with the Southern Claims Commission and was reimbursed $3,310 for property taken by Wilder's Brigade. In 1880, the value of his land was estimated at $5,100; the balance of his possessions totaled $517. He did not emigrate to Colorado.

Thomas J. Barbour and Joanna W. Barbour. Thomas and his wife Joanna were among Morgan's first Georgia converts. Thomas was the eldest son of Thomas Barbour. Against his father's wishes, Thomas J. enlisted in the Confederate Army (Sixth Georgia Cavalry) in August 1862, but he stayed only a few months. He deserted in early 1863 and returned home, then made his way north, where he joined the Union Army (Twelfth Tennessee Cavalry). Thomas possessed no land of his own in 1870; instead, he supported his wife and children by laboring on his father's farm, perhaps in a tenancy arrangement. By 1875, Thomas J. had obtained 160 acres of Chattooga County land valued at $500 but was listed among the county's tax defaulters. A year later, he sold 150 acres to William Marshal, leaving him with 10 acres valued at $100. He disappeared from Chattooga County records in 1877 but reappeared in 1880 in Red River, Texas. It is not clear if he relocated to the Colorado colony prior to that time.

Duncan G. Campbell. Duncan was born in Alabama in 1823 and married Georgia-born Mary Elizabeth Barbour, who was likely the daughter of Thomas Barbour. Duncan fought for the Confederacy (Fourth Tennessee Cavalry) and is likely the person described in Thomas Barbour's Southern Claims Commission document as his "Confederate son-in-law." He appeared in the Chattooga County tax records in 1875, where he was listed as possessing no land or other property. By 1880 he had relocated to the Mormon colony in Colorado. A widower, he resided with his daughter Rosalie and worked as a laborer. ***Rosalie Campbell*** was baptized on November 12, 1876, with members of the Barbour family. Her father was baptized several months later. She married George John Koch in 1883.

Caleb Jennings and Mary Jane Jennings. According to John Morgan, Caleb was born in Virginia. The 1850 census located Caleb and Mary Jane in Clarke County, Georgia. They possessed real estate valued at $600, and Caleb was described as a "music teacher." His oldest son, Robert, managed the family's small farm. By 1860, the family had relocated to Dirt Town Valley in Chattooga County, near the households of William Marshal and Thomas Lawrence. Caleb continued to work as a music teacher, and the census listed Mary Jane as a "farmer," with real estate valued at $1,000. By 1870, the census described Caleb as a farmer, with real estate and a personal estate valued at $550, while Mary Jane was described as "keeping house," but the Chattooga County tax digest suggested that Caleb served as agent for his wife. John Morgan reported that at the time of his baptism in late 1876, Caleb could no longer walk, so he was baptized sitting in a chair. He died a short time later, and his wife was baptized after his death. When William Marshal joined the first expedition, he either sold or transferred his Chattooga County property to Mary Jane, which suggests that she and Marshal were related.

John Jennings. It is not clear if John was related to Caleb and Mary Jane Jennings. The 1870 census located twenty-five-year-old John in Chattooga County. He was married to Patsy, who was not listed as a branch member. The census described John as a farmer, but he possessed no land in 1870, and his personal estate was estimated at $100.

Elizabeth Keel. In 1860 Elizabeth lived in Alabama with her husband Joseph and two-year-old James. Joseph, described as a "day laborer," possessed no real estate and no personal estate. By 1870, the Keels relocated to Gordon County in Georgia. Still landless, Joseph worked on a farm. The 1875 tax digest placed the Keels in Chattooga County. They still had not acquired land and possessed a household valued at $168. It is not clear whether Joseph joined the LDS Church. Son **James Ransom Keel** was baptized with his mother and Sinai Ann Lawrence, the daughter of Thomas Anderson Lawrence. James appeared on the 1880 Colorado census, where he lived in a boardinghouse and worked as a laborer. In 1881, he married Sinai Lawrence. Both James and Sinai were buried in the Old Manassa Cemetery.

Thomas Anderson Lawrence. Nicknamed "Jetter" or "Jetters," Thomas was born in Georgia in 1818. In 1841, he married Sinai Ann Scoggins. The 1840 census located him in Chattooga County, and the 1850 census placed him near Dirt Town, where he owned a farm valued at $1,000 and one male slave. By 1860, the value of his farm was estimated at $2,000 and his personal estate was listed as $1,000; however, the slave schedules for that year described him as the owner of twenty-one slaves and three slave houses. Thomas also owned a flour mill. By 1870, Thomas possessed real estate and a personal estate each valued at $300. At that time his household included one white male mill worker. The agricultural schedule for 1870 estimated his farm as worth $2,000. The 1871 tax digest reported a similar estimate—$2,500—and by 1880 the value of his property was estimated at $3,000. Thomas's marriage produced eight daughters. By 1880, Thomas was a widower and all of his daughters had married, except Sinai Ann Lawrence, who remained in his household. Thomas became president of the Haywood Valley Branch after John Barbour's resignation, and it was in his home that John Morgan wrote the *Plan of Salvation* in 1878. Thomas traveled to Colorado in fall 1880, transporting his mill stones by rail car. Three daughters relocated with him, including Sinai and Margaret Zillis Bagwell, the wife of William H. Bagwell. Thomas bought land on the Conejos River, where he built a flour mill that was later put out of business by the Manassa Milling Company. *Sinai Ann Lawrence* married Georgian James Keel in 1881.

William L. Marshal and Tabitha Marshal. William was born in Virginia about 1824. The 1860 census placed him in Dirt Town Valley of Chattooga County, living next door to Caleb and Mary Jane Jennings and near Thomas Anderson Lawrence. Though he was described as a farmer at that time, there was no value assigned for real estate or personal estate. Thomas Barbour's documents filed with the Southern Claims Commission included testimony from Marshal, in which he described himself as Barbour's friend and fellow Unionist. He testified that he enlisted in the Confederate Army to avoid conscription, but later deserted with the help of Thomas Barbour. In 1870 he resided in

Texas Valley, Floyd County. Although the 1870 census described him as landless, with a personal estate of only $400, Marshal also appeared on the 1870 agricultural schedule as owning 160 acres valued at $2,000. The Floyd County Tax Digest for 1872–75 suggested a more modest farm, as his 160-acre farm was consistently valued at $600 for those years. He reappeared in Chattooga County in 1876, after purchasing 150 acres of land from Thomas J. Barbour. The total value of his household, including the land, was estimated at $585. William Marshal and wife Tabitha were among John Morgan's first converts. In 1877, the Marshal family joined the first expedition to the West. Prior to leaving Georgia, William transferred his property to Mary Jane Jennings. The Marshal family resided in Manassa in 1880. Both William and Tabitha Marshal were buried in the Old Manassa Cemetery.

John R. Mooney. John appeared on the tax digest for Chattooga County in 1879. He was landless, with a household worth only $25.

Walter Smith and Lucy Jane (Barbour) Smith. Walter Smith was born in North Carolina in 1846 and married Lucy Barbour, Thomas Barbour's daughter, in 1868. In 1870, census takers described Walter as owning neither real nor personal estate.

George W. Wilson. The 1875 tax digest located George in Chattooga County, where he owned 262 acres of land valued at $700. He joined the first expedition to Colorado.

ARMUCHIE BRANCH
Floyd County

Charles David Haynie and Evergreen (Taylor) Haynie. Robert and Emily Haynie's oldest son Charles resided in his father's Georgia household in 1870, then relocated to Alabama, where he taught school and singing and was baptized into the LDS Church. He married Evergreen Taylor in 1878 and followed his brothers to Colorado.

Joseph Pinkney Haynie and Susan (Weldon) Haynie. Joseph Haynie served as president of the Armuchie Branch. He married Susan Weldon (daughter of Francis M. Weldon) in 1876 but struggled to establish a household, and in that year county tax records listed him as landless and a tax defaulter. He had not acquired land by 1878 and possessed livestock and household goods valued at only $25. Joseph's brother, Patrick Haynie, joined the first expedition to Colorado, along with Susan's father, Francis Marion Weldon. Joseph and Susan relocated to Colorado in 1879, along with the entire Haynie family, including brothers Charles, William, and Robert. The 1880 census located them in Manassa, Colorado. Younger siblings William and Fanny resided in the household, and both J. P. and William Haynie were described as laborers.

Patrick Calhoun Haynie and Henrietta Paralee (Bagwell) Haynie. "Pack" Haynie joined the first expedition to Colorado. He married Georgia convert Henrietta Bagwell at winter quarters in Pueblo, before moving to Manassa, where he worked as a blacksmith. Caroline and Tobe Bagwell resided next door. Pack later adopted plural marriage, taking Mary Elma Wilson as his second wife.

Robert Baskin Haynie and Emily Jane Haynie. The Haynies appeared on the Floyd County census in 1870. A tenant farmer, Robert was landless and owned a personal estate valued at $500. In 1875, still landless, Haynie possessed a personal estate of only $285 and could not pay his taxes. Robert died in 1876, prior to joining the church, but Emily Haynie was baptized and migrated to Colorado with her sons (Charles, Joseph, Patrick, Robert, William). She died in Manassa in 1879.

Robert Milligan Haynie. The son of Robert and Emily Haynie, Robert migrated to Colorado with his mother and brothers. He joined the church in Colorado and eventually returned to the South as a missionary. He married southern convert Lydia Belinda Stover. Their daughter married the son of Georgia convert William Marshal.

William Luke Haynie. The son of Robert and Emily Haynie, William also relocated to Colorado and was buried in Old Manassa Cemetery.

Marcus De Lafayette Reid and Nancy (Ramsey) Reid. Reid appeared in the Floyd County tax records in 1874. In that year he owned no land but possessed a household valued at $25. By 1879 he had accumulated livestock and household goods valued at $75, but no real estate. Reid assumed leadership of the Armuchie Branch when Weldon left Georgia. The Reids migrated to the West in the 1880s.

Francis Marion Weldon and Mary Jane (Trammel) Weldon. A carpenter, Weldon owned real estate valued at $300 in 1870 but no personal estate. Tax records demonstrated a steady financial decline, as he was landless by 1877, possessing household goods valued at only $15. The Weldons were baptized in 1877, as was son *Hardy Weldon*, and they joined the first expedition to Colorado. Their daughter Susan was married to Joseph Haynie.

Beech Creek Branch
Floyd County

James Allen and Libby Allen. According to the 1870 census, James Allen owned real estate valued at $300 and a personal estate worth $500. Although the agricultural schedule of that year estimated his farm at $3,000, that valuation seems excessively high. The value of his 160 acres never exceeded $500, according to county tax records for the years 1872–80. Allen may have engaged in tenancy agreements, as he consistently reported debts owed to him. The entire Allen family—including children *James Jr.*, *Rebecca*, and *Harriett Allen*—joined the church in 1877. The 1880 census described James Allen as a widower and sixteen-year-old son James Jr. as suffering from consumption. The Allens did not emigrate to the West.

John B. Daniel and Sabra Daniel. A widower in 1860, Daniel married wife Sabra prior to 1870. In 1877, John, Sabra, and daughters *Martha* and *Mary Allen* joined the LDS Church and Daniel became president of the Beech Creek Branch. Daniel owned a small farm valued at $500 in 1870, but tax records showed that by 1873, Daniel possessed 480 acres worth $1,000. His acreage and property value steadily declined. By 1880, Daniel owned only 360 acres valued at $300. The Daniels later relocated to Manassa. Frances Daniel Littlejohn, John's oldest daughter, was married to Thomas Littlejohn of Floyd County's Pleasant Hill Church Branch.

Elias and Providence Dennington. According to the 1870 census, the Denningtons owned no property and possessed a personal estate of only $200. However, the agricultural schedule for that year described him as a farmer with 28 acres valued at $500. County tax records confirmed that Dennington owned no land of his own in 1870, but he may have farmed his mother's land. By 1877, he had obtained 160 acres valued at $160. The Denningtons joined the first expedition to Colorado, but they did not remain there. The 1880 census located the family in Greene County, Arkansas.

William R. Manning and Mary Caroline (Barbour) Manning. William and Mary (related to the Barbours of Haywood Valley Branch and neighbors of the Daniel family) were baptized in 1877, along with their children, *William, Thomas,* and *Joanna Manning*. According to a local credit reporter, Manning and D. J. Sanders partnered in a dry goods and grocery in Rome, Georgia. Reports through 1856 and 1857 indicated that D. J. Sanders & Co. was "doing well" and had accumulated a value in excess of $50,000, but by January 1858 William Manning was "out of the firm," selling his share in time to avoid a February fire that completely destroyed the business. Manning appeared on the 1860 census twice. On July 9, census takers located him in Rome, with real estate valued at $4,400 and a personal estate worth $65,000 (which included seven slaves). He also appeared in the Flatwoods District of Floyd County as a "farmer" on a schedule dated July 26. The second census estimated his real estate at $2,500 and his personal estate at $16,000. This might suggest that he maintained a home in Rome and a farm in the Floyd County countryside, but that is not confirmed. By 1870 Manning owned only 283 acres of land valued at $2,000, plus a personal estate of $300. His acreage and net worth steadily deteriorated. According to county tax records for 1879, Manning possessed only 60 acres valued at $300. The Mannings did not emigrate to the Colorado colony.

Rock Springs Branch
Walker County

James Byrum and Sarah May Byrum. The Byrums were the only members of this branch. They did not appear on the 1870 census and did not emigrate to Colorado.

Cassandra Branch
Walker County

William Dixon Bailey and Martha Jane (Coxwell) Bailey. Dixon Bailey served as president of the Cassandra Branch. The Baileys were baptized in September 1877, as were daughters *Martha Queen Victoria Bailey* and *Mary Naomi Bailey*. Dixon Bailey declared himself a Unionist following the war and filed a claim with the Southern Claims Commission for property taken by Union troops. His claim was refused, perhaps because documents proved that Bailey also sold grain to the Confederate Army. In 1870 the Baileys resided next door to convert James Merett Faucett. According to the population schedule for that year, Bailey owned a small farm valued at $500 and possessed a personal estate worth $500. By 1879, Bailey's net worth was calculated at $960. Martha Coxwell Bailey was the sister of Victoria Coxwell Faucett, wife of Jesse Barlett Faucett, also a member of the Cassandra Branch. The Baileys did not emigrate to Colorado. In 1879, Martha Queen Victoria Bailey married Alphonzo Cromwell Faucett, the son of James Merett Faucett.

Nathaniel Connally. John Morgan considered Connally, although he was never baptized, to be a member of Cassandra Branch. A farmer, with property valued at $1,000, Connally was the brother of Price Connally and uncle to Elizabeth Nations Elledge of the Varnell's Station Branch.

Price Connally. Price was the brother of Nathaniel Connally and uncle to Elizabeth Nations Elledge. The 1870 census estimated the value of Connally's 160-acre farm at $3,000 in 1870; by 1881, he retained only 100 acres valued at $2,000. He did not emigrate to Colorado.

Alfonzo Cromwell Faucett and Martha Queen Victoria (Bailey) Faucett. County tax records described Alfonzo Faucett as landless, with possessions valued at $125. Alfonzo married Martha Queen Victoria Bailey, the daughter of convert William Dixon Bailey, in Georgia. But family and individual records indicated that Alfonzo married plural wife *Susannah Barbour* (the daughter of Haywood Valley convert John Joseph Barbour) in Colorado.

James Merett Faucett and Elmira (Bowers) Faucett. Though James was listed as a member of the Cassandra Branch, records indicated only that wife Emma and daughter Sarah Faucett were baptized. The 1870 census indicated that Faucett earned his living as a carpenter and owned property valued at $800 and a personal estate of $150. However, the 1870 agricultural schedule confirmed that Faucett also farmed 65 acres valued at $800. A widower by 1880, Faucett relocated to Colorado with his children. Faucett's son Alfonzo married neighbor and convert Martha Queen Victoria Bailey. Faucett's daughter, Mary Green Faucett, married Georgia convert Albion Haggard prior to emigration.

Jesse Bartlett Faucett and Victoria Coxwell Faucett. The Faucetts did not appear on the 1870 census, but Walker County tax records confirmed that Faucett owned 160 acres of land valued at $800. Jesse was the brother of James Merett Faucett and was related by marriage to branch president William Dixon Bailey.

Albion Haggard and Mary (Faucett) Haggard. Born in 1852 to Walker County parents David and Mary Haggard, Albion was orphaned at two years old. In 1860, Albion resided in the home of neighbor or relative N. B. Massey; by 1870, Albion worked as laborer for Henry Miller. According to Walker County tax records from 1874 to 1878, Albion owned no land and no other property of value. He married Mary Green Faucett, the daughter of James Merrett Faucett, and relocated to the Colorado colony by 1880.

John P. Jennings and Aquilla Melissa Jennings. Mission records indicated that Jennings also served as Cassandra Branch president. According to both census and tax records, Jennings possessed no land of his own and worked as a farm laborer. In 1879, his total net worth (household and livestock) was estimated at $23. Records suggest that Artimesia Payne was John Jennings's mother-in-law. The Jennings family did not emigrate to Colorado.

Artimesia Payne. In 1860, Artimesia Payne resided in Walker County with her husband Elijah, a farmer and Methodist preacher. Widowed by 1870, Payne possessed a farm valued at $750. In 1880, Payne resided in the home of her son-in-law, John P. Jennings.

Frank Payne and Jane Payne. Payne did not appear on the 1870 census, but Walker County tax records for 1876 described Payne as landless, with possessions valued at $20. In 1880, he resided near converts Dixon Bailey, James Faucett, John Jennings, and Artimesia Payne. There is no confirmed link to Artimesia Payne. The Paynes did not emigrate to Colorado.

McLemore's Cove Branch
Walker County

John Thomas Curry. Curry was likely related to convert Thomas Whitley. According to census records, he resided in Chattooga County in 1870 but relocated to Walker County by 1876, where he appeared in county tax records as owning nothing of value. Though he was married, his wife did not appear on baptism lists.

Andrew J. Holland. A neighbor to converts John Smalley and Tom Whitley, Holland was listed as branch member, although his wife did not appear on baptism lists. The 1870 population schedule described Holland as a farmer, with real estate valued at only $100, but a personal estate estimated at $1,250. This conflicted with the agricultural schedule, which described a much more valuable farm ($1,200). The 1875 tax digest listed him as possessing land worth $1,000.

James Patten Kilgore. According to John Morgan, Kilgore was related to W. C. Kilgore. He baptized them both on the same day and described them in his correspondence as "two of the most influential men of the community." He did not appear on the 1870 census for Walker County.

William C. Kilgore and Mary Caroline (Anderson) Kilgore. Kilgore served as president of the branch. According to census records, Kilgore owned a farm valued at $800, but also possessed a personal estate worth $1,365. Though the agricultural census estimated his farm's value at $6,000, county tax reports confirm the smaller amount. It is not clear whether or not the Kilgores relocated to Colorado, although they both resided in Utah in 1900.

A. Henry Mitchell and Matilda Mitchell. Both Henry, a Methodist minister in Walker County, and his wife were baptized in fall 1877. They did not appear on the 1870 census.

Jonathan Roach. Roach served as a private in the Confederacy. He did not appear on the 1870 census but was located on Walker County tax records for 1873–80. In 1880, he owned 80 acres valued at $40. Though he was married, Roach's wife did not appear on baptism lists.

John Smalley. The 1870 population schedule described Smalley as a "farm laborer," and his proximity to convert William C. Kilgore suggests that he may have worked Kilgore land. The 1880 population schedule also described him as a "farm laborer," and it appeared that he had relocated to convert Andrew Holland's farm. In 1870, Smalley owned absolutely nothing of value, and he remained landless. County tax records for 1873–82 confirmed that he owned nothing. Although he was married, his wife did not appear on baptism lists. He did not emigrate to Colorado.

John Thomas Whitley. In 1870, Whitley resided with his mother and aunt. Described as a "farm laborer," Whitley owned no land or personal estate and likely worked his aunt's small farm, which was valued at $200. The Whitleys' neighbors were converts John Smalley and Andrew Holland. He did not emigrate to Colorado.

William Dallas York and Tennessee (Graham) York. York appeared on the 1870 census for Dekalb County, Alabama, residing near his wife's family. Described as a "farmer," he possessed no land, with a personal estate of $150. Tax records for 1878 located York in Georgia's Walker County and described him as owning nothing of value. By 1880, York (now described as "laborer") had relocated to Lumpkin County. The 1900 census located York in Dade County, Georgia.

PLEASANT HILL CHURCH BRANCH
Floyd County

Thomas A. Littlejohn and Francis A. (Daniel) Littlejohn. The 1870 census located Thomas Littlejohn in the Walker County household of Caroline Inman, where he worked as a farm laborer. Tax records for 1873 placed him in Floyd County and described him as a tax "defaulter." By 1874, Littlejohn possessed 50 acres of land valued at $200, which he obtained from father-in-law John B. Daniel, the president of Floyd County's Beech Creek Branch. By 1879 the value of his land was estimated at only $50. The 1880 census located the Littlejohns in Floyd County, where Littlejohn earned his living hauling timber. The family later emigrated to the Colorado colony.

Felix Burnie Moyers and Cornelia (Bailey) Moyers. Felix Moyers served the Confederacy. The 1870 census described Moyers as a cabinetmaker, possessing no property and a personal estate valued at $300. Moyers, his wife Cornelia, and his children *Curtis Bailey* and *Sarah (Sallie)* all joined the LDS Church. The Moyers family joined the first expedition to Colorado, although Felix Moyers eventually joined the Reorganized Church. In Colorado, Sallie Moyers married George Washington Elledge, the son of Dillingham and Elizabeth Elledge.

JONESBOROUGH BRANCH
Clayton County

L. T. D. McKinney. McKinney appeared on branch membership lists as both sole member and branch president. McKinney was related to Elder Thomas E. Murphy who labored in Georgia and Alabama in 1875–76. According to church records,

Elder Murphy traveled to the West with the first expedition of Georgians, including nephew S. M. McKinney and niece Delila F. Murphy. Murphy and his relatives left the company to travel to Salt Lake City, where Murphy resided.

VARNELL'S STATION BRANCH
Catoosa and Whitfield Counties

John A. Dillard. "Mr. Dillard" appeared on the branch membership list, although the first name was indecipherable. It was likely John A. Dillard, who resided next door to Dillingham H. and Elizabeth Elledge in Catoosa County. According to the 1870 agricultural schedule, Dillard owned a 200-acre farm, though it was valued at only $300. Tax records for 1875 indicated that John and brothers William and Thomas Dillard owned 140 acres in Catoosa County, though John Dillard was later described as possessing no land of his own, but working as "administrator" for Thomas Dillard. The 1880 census located Dillard next door to Henry Holston, also listed as a Varnell's Station branch member. Dillard did not relocate to the Colorado colony.

Dillingham Horten Elledge and Elizabeth (Nations) Elledge. Though Dillingham Elledge appeared on the branch membership list, he was not baptized until August 1879, after the Nations family emigrated. The 1850 census located Dillingham Elledge in Murray County, Georgia. A farmer, he owned real estate valued at $1,100. In 1846, he married Elizabeth Nations Elledge, the daughter of Israel Nations and Virginia Jane Connally Nations, and in 1854 he purchased land in Catoosa County from his father-in-law. By 1860 Elledge owned real estate valued at $8,000 and a personal estate of $500. He enlisted in the Confederate Army in 1862 as captain, Company G, Thirty-Sixth (Broyles's) Georgia Infantry, but poor health forced him to resign his position in 1863. The 1870 census estimated Elledge's property at $4,000. Elizabeth's younger brother, Thomas J. Nations, and his wife Susan farmed a portion of Elledge's land. In 1871, Dillingham Elledge and son-in-law Henry Huffaker (married to Mary Frances Elledge) purchased city/town property in Varnell's

Station, where they established a business. According to Catoosa County tax and deed records, Elledge transferred his Catoosa County property to Nathaniel Connally (Elizabeth's uncle), and in 1879 Nathaniel Connally acted on behalf of Elledge and sold the property to W. L. Headrick and Company, local land speculators. On the same date, Elledge's son, James H. Elledge, also sold his 100-acre tract to W. L. Headrick and Company. In Colorado, Elledge assumed responsibility for the first post office and cooperative store. He also purchased a flour mill in partnership with Silas A. Smith, San Luis Stake president. Daughter Jane Elizabeth (Elledge) Smith married Stephen A. Smith, the son of Silas Smith.

Sarah Fullbright. A widow, Sarah lived in Catoosa County in 1870, next door to Dillingham and Elizabeth Nations Elledge. According to the 1870 census, she owned a small farm worth less than $300, but merited inclusion on the county agricultural schedule, where the farm's value was estimated at only $150. Late in 1870, she transferred her property to her daughter Elviny Hamblin, who agreed "to take care and provide for me." She left Georgia for Colorado shortly after Joseph Standing's death. She died of the measles after her arrival in Colorado and was buried in Old Manassa Cemetery.

Elizabeth "Elviny" (Fullbright) Hamblin. Elviny Hamblin was Sarah Fullbright's daughter, the mother of Mary "Molly" Hamblin and Sarah Kaneaster, and Alonzo Kaneaster's grandmother. Her husband James died in 1852, on board the *Sir Charles Napier* on his way to the California gold fields. In 1870, the census described her as widow and head of household with four children, though she owned no property and a personal estate of only $300. Later that year, her mother transferred her small farm to Elviny. After Joseph Standing's death and prior to emigration, Elviny sold the property to land speculator W. L. Headrick.

Mary "Molly" Hamblin. Elviny Hamblin's daughter and Sarah Kaneaster's sister, Mary attempted to warn Joseph Standing of the mob. After his death, she testified at the Coroner's Inquest and the trial of his accused murderers. She traveled to Colorado with her grandmother, mother, and sister.

Henry Holston. Though he appeared on the branch membership list, Holston did not join the church; instead, Elder John Morgan considered him to be a good friend to Mormon missionaries. Holston owned no land but possessed livestock and tools valued at less than $500. In 1880, Holston lived very near the Dillards and Elledges. Holston testified at both the Coroner's Inquest and trial of Standing's accused murderers.

Ignatius Henry Huffaker and Mary Frances (Elledge) Huffaker. With his brother, Isaac Asbury Huffaker, Henry enlisted in Company G, the Thirty-Sixth (Broyles's) Georgia Infantry, captained by Dillingham Elledge. The regiment was captured at Vicksburg in 1863, and Henry was imprisoned in Kentucky. After his parole, he returned to Confederate service and in 1864 was captured again in Marietta, Georgia. In 1867, he married Mary Frances Elledge, the daughter of Dillingham and Elizabeth Elledge. By 1870, he owned a mercantile in Varnell's Station, and in 1871 he and his father-in-law purchased a small farm in Catoosa County, where the Huffakers lived, and a city/town lot in Varnell's Station, where they established a business. When the Huffakers emigrated to Colorado, Henry transferred his Catoosa County property to Thomas J. Nations, who sold the land. In 1880, the Huffakers resided in Manassa, near the Hamblins and Kaneasters. Both Henry and Mary were buried in Old Manassa Cemetery.

Isaac Asbury Huffaker and Martha Ann (Foster) Huffaker. With Henry Huffaker, his brother, Isaac Asbury Huffaker joined the Confederacy, enlisting in Dillingham Elledge's Company G of the Thirty-Sixth (Broyles's) Georgia Infantry. Captured at Vicksburg, he was imprisoned with his brother in Kentucky, before returning to Confederate service. Asbury served on the coroner's jury at the inquest into Joseph Standing's death, then emigrated to Colorado. Both Asbury and Martha were buried in Old Manassa Cemetery.

Sarah Riggins Huffaker. Sarah Huffaker was the mother of Henry and Asbury Huffaker and a widow by the time she converted. She did not appear on the census for 1870, and although her sons relocated to Colorado, Sarah did not, remaining in her daughter Emily's Tunnel Hill household in Whitfield County until her death.

Sarah (Hamblin) Kaneaster. Sarah Kaneaster, the daughter of Elviny Hamblin, converted to the LDS Church, even though her husband Josiah (or Joseph) did not. In 1850, Josiah resided in his father's household, but by 1860 he and Sarah had married. The 1860 census described him as a farmer, although he owned no property of his own and farmed a portion of his father's land. Josiah Kaneaster served the Confederacy in Company B of the Thirty-Sixth (Broyles's) Georgia Infantry. He was captured at Vicksburg, paroled, and returned to service, but soon deserted. Although Josiah owned no property according to the 1870 census and subsequent tax records, he appeared on the 1870 agricultural schedule as owner of a 55-acre farm. Shortly after Joseph Standing's murder, Josiah and Sarah signed a quit claim deed, returning the land to his father, in exchange for cash to pay for travel to Colorado. Josiah later changed his mind. When Sarah left Georgia with her mother and grandmother, she left behind her husband and a son, Robert Cochran Kaneaster. Pregnant when she left Georgia, Sarah delivered a daughter in Colorado. On the day of the birth, Sarah lost an older daughter to the measles. Sarah died of the disease six days later, and her infant daughter died at the age of six months. In 1880, Josiah resided in Whitfield County with his parents and son, Robert. He later remarried.

Elizabeth Loggins. Elizabeth joined the Varnell's Station Branch, although her husband, Riley Loggins, did not. According to the 1870 census, Elizabeth and Riley Loggins owned no land and possessed an estate valued at only $100. Riley was described as working on a farm so was likely involved in a tenancy arrangement. The 1880 census located the Loggins family in Johnson County, Arkansas, where they resided near David and Jasper Nations, who participated in the murder of Joseph Standing. The decision to relocate to Arkansas with members of the mob suggests a family connection between the Loggins and Nations families, though that is not confirmed.

John S. Martin. Although Martin was married, his wife did not appear on branch membership lists. During the Civil War,

Martin served the Confederacy. In 1870, he resided in Varnell's Station of Whitfield County, where he owned a small farm. By 1878, Martin's Whitfield County farm was valued at $160. He later transferred some of that property to his son, Endymeon Martin.

John A. Nations and Mary J. (Huffaker) Nations. According to census records, in 1860 John Nations resided in the household of his father, Manley Nations, who was Elizabeth Nations Elledge's uncle. Although John and Mary expressed devotion to the Mormon elders, it is not clear if they were baptized. After Joseph Standing's death, they relocated to Arkansas with other family members who participated in Standing's murder. Interestingly, after John's death, Mary left Arkansas and moved to Manassa, Colorado.

Thomas Jefferson Nations. The younger brother of Elizabeth Nations Elledge, Thomas supported his sister's religious choice, although he was not baptized until after his emigration to Colorado. He did not serve in Dillingham Elledge's company, but did join the Confederate Army, serving with Company B, the Thirty-Sixth (Broyles's) Georgia Infantry with Josiah Kaneaster. In 1870, he and his first wife resided on the Catoosa County property of his brother-in-law. According to the census, he possessed no land of his own; instead, he farmed a portion of Elledge land. He remained in Catoosa County after the Elledge family emigrated and served as a witness to the Coroner's Inquest into Joseph Standing's death. He also rode with the posse that brought Nations family members to face trial. In 1880, the census described him as a farm laborer. After his wife's death in Georgia, he relocated to Colorado with his children, where he met and married Amanda Echols, the daughter of Polk County convert Lewis Echols.

David W. Williams and Nancy (Blair) Williams. David Williams was the son of Brittain and Elizabeth Elledge Williams, and the nephew of Dillingham H. Elledge. In 1870, David resided in the household of his father, who was a Baptist minister and established the Salem Baptist Church in Catoosa County. By 1878, Williams was married and had obtained 110 acres of land. Despite the objections of his father, Williams emigrated to the Colorado colony. The 1880 census located David and Nancy Williams in Manassa, living next door to Dillingham and Elizabeth Elledge and clerking in Elledge's cooperative store. Nancy's younger sister, Martha Blair, also resided in the Williams household. Both Nancy and Martha were related to Hugh Blair, who rode with the mob that murdered missionary Joseph Standing.

Rockmart Branch
Polk County

Benjamin Echols. The son of Lewis Echols, Benjamin emigrated with his parents to Colorado but later moved to Arizona with his sister Amanda and brother-in-law Thomas Nations. In Arizona, he married Georgiana Blair.

Lewis Barton Echols and Emily Jane (Weems) Echols. Both Lewis and Emily were born in Georgia but left for Alabama during the Civil War. They returned to postwar Georgia, where they resided on a rented farm; the 1870 census confirmed Lewis as a farmer with no real estate. By 1880, the Echols family owned 160 acres of woodland. Several members of the Echols family—*Lewis, Emily Jane,* and children *John, Ben, Sam, Martin,* and *Amanda Echols*—were baptized in 1881. Ben Echols claimed that Joseph Standing's death influenced the decision to convert. The entire Echols family emigrated to Colorado, although Lewis and Emily Jane later moved to Arizona.

Martin B. Echols and Sarah Susan (Odom) Echols. The son of Lewis Echols, Martin emigrated to Colorado with his family.

Samuel Echols and Mary Minerva (Vincent) Echols. Samuel's wife, Minerva, disapproved when he converted, and they separated for two months. They reunited when she also converted and was baptized. Minerva agreed to join the Echols family in emigrating to Colorado but was dissuaded by her parents. When she refused to leave with Samuel, he left her and his child behind. In 1882, Samuel returned to Georgia as a Southern States missionary, where he attempted, unsuccessfully, to reunite with his wife. While on his southern mission, Samuel met Arminta

Missouri Lee and persuaded her to return to Colorado with him, where they were married.

John N. Roberson. Roberson was president of the Rockmart Branch, which was established in 1879, just prior to Joseph Standing's murder. He did not appear on the census.

STOCK HILL BRANCH
Fannin County

Cornelius Jasper Stover and Palmina (McDaniel) Stover. According to family members, Cornelius served the Union Army during the Civil War (First Georgia Infantry, Fifth Tennessee Mounted Infantry), although he had two brothers in the Confederate Army. The Stovers were baptized in 1879 by Joseph Standing. In honor of Elders Standing and Clawson, the Stovers named their son (born weeks before Standing's death) Joseph Rudger Stover. Palmina Stover remembered that she had tailored the trousers Standing was wearing when he was killed. Though missionaries described Stock Hill as a Fannin County branch, and their son was born in Fannin County in 1879, the 1880 census located the Stovers in Pickens County, but they emigrated to Colorado later that year. They were buried in the Old Manassa Cemetery. Their daughter, *Lydia Belinda Stover*, married convert Robert M. Haynie.

Sources for Branches and Members: "Converts of Elder John Morgan in North Georgia during His First Mission in 1876," box 3, folder 3, John Hamilton Morgan Papers, Accn 1465, Manuscripts Division, Marriott Library, University of Utah, Salt Lake City (hereafter cited as JHM Papers); "Conferences Established by John Morgan in the Organization of the Southern States Mission," box 3, folder 5, JHM Papers; "Report of Branches of the Church in Georgia," box 1, book 1, JHM Papers. Additional information is taken from the missionary journal of Elder John Morgan: Typescript of John Morgan's Journal, November 1875–November 1892, JHM Papers. Elder James T. Lisonbee also provided information regarding Georgia's first converts: "Typescript of Diary of James T. Lisonbee, 1876–1877," box 6, folder 8, JHM Papers; Garth N. Jones, *James Thompson Lisonbee's*

Missionary Labors on the Sand Mountain of Northeastern Alabama and Northwestern Georgia: Beginning of a New Gathering in the San Luis Valley of Colorado, 1876–1878 (Provo: Brigham Young University Press, 2000). Biographical data rely on a number of primary sources, including federal, state, and county records; federal manuscript census population schedules for 1850–1900; slave schedules for 1850 and 1860; agricultural schedules for 1870; local tax digests, maintained for each of the counties under consideration in this study; and county deed books. It should be noted that the records of the 1870 census, both population and agricultural schedules, are notoriously inaccurate, so figures have been compared to county tax digests to encourage some measure of validity. Private papers available in the Church of Jesus Christ of Latter-day Saints Church History Library, Salt Lake City, are invaluable, as are family-generated genealogies collected by the LDS Church and available online at www.familysearch.org. There are significant differences among the collected genealogies, but I rely on those that most closely match census and other data. The preceding branch lists significantly underrepresent the true number of converts, as John Morgan generally recorded only the names of adult converts, even though younger family members also joined the church and the emigration to Colorado.

Sources for Haywood Valley Branch: Gary B. Mills, *Southern Loyalists in the Civil War: The Southern Claims Commission* (Baltimore: Genealogical Publishing, 1994), 31; Claim of Thomas Barbour of Chattooga County, Georgia, microfiche M1658, National Archives and Records Administration, Washington, D.C.; Robert S. Baker, *Chattooga: The Story of a Country and Its People* (privately printed, 1988), 586; "Document by a Southerner," box 3, folder 18, JHM Papers; Records of Old Manassa Cemetery, Manassa, Conejos, Colorado, available online at ftp.rootsweb.com; Individual and Family Group Records, available online at www.familysearch.org; Georgia Marriages to 1850, available online at www.ancestry.com; Index to Compiled Service Records of Confederate Soldiers Who Served from the State of Georgia, M-226, microfilm, roll 19, Georgia Department of Archives and History, Morrow, Ga. (hereafter cited as GDAH); Compiled Service Records of Confederate Soldiers Who Served in Organizations from Georgia, M-226, microfilm, roll 425, GDAH; Civil War Service Records, available online at www.ancestry.com; Chattooga County Tax Digest for 1871–80, GDAH; 1840 U.S. Federal Census, Chattooga County, Georgia, M704_38, 153; 1850 Census, Franklin County, Georgia, M432_70, 268; 1850 Census,

Clarke County, Georgia, M432_65, 54; 1850 Census, Chattooga County, M432_64, 393; 1850 Census, Slave Schedules, Chattooga County; 1860 Census, Chattooga County, M653_116, 596, 655; 1860 Census, Blount County, Alabama, M653_2, 969; 1860 Census, Franklin County, Georgia, M653_121, 600; 1860 Census, Slave Schedules, Chattooga County; 1870 Census, Chattooga County, M593_142, 116, 128, 129, 149; 1870 Census, Franklin County, Georgia, M593_150, 100; 1870 Census, Chattooga County, Agricultural Schedule, 7–8; 1870 Census, Floyd County, Agricultural Schedule, 2–3; 1880 Census, Chattooga County, Georgia, T9_139, 6, 8; 1880 Census, Red River, Texas, T9_1323, 188; 1880 Census, Conejos County, Colorado, T9_89, 164.

Sources for Armuchie Branch: "An Account by Members of the Armuchie Branch," LDS Church History Library; "Haynie Family Record," LDS Church History Library; "Document by a Southerner," JHM Papers; Records of Old Manassa Cemetery; Individual and Family Group Records; Georgia Marriages to 1850; Floyd County Tax Digest for 1872–80, GDAH; 1870 Census, Floyd County, M593_149, 144, 162; 1880 Census, Floyd County, T9_146, 208; 1880 Census, Conejos County, Colorado, T9_89, 167.

Sources for Beech Creek Branch: Georgia, volume 12, p. 176, R. G. Dun & Co. Collection, Baker Library, Harvard Business School, Boston; Floyd County Tax Digest for 1872–80, GDAH; 1860 Census, Floyd County, M653_121, 197, 327, 329; 1860 Census, Floyd County, Slave Schedule; 1870 Census, Floyd County, M593_149, 158, 229, 230, 238; 1870 Census, Floyd County, Agricultural Schedule, 5–16; 1880 Census, Floyd County, T9_146, 225, 226; 1880 Census, Greene County, Arkansas, T9_45, 262; 1900 Census, Floyd County, T623_196, 3; Individual and Family Group Records; "Document by a Southerner," JHM Papers.

Sources for Cassandra Branch: "Fausett/McKee Family History from 1630 to July 2000," LDS Church History Library; Mills, *Southern Loyalists*, 25; 1850 Census, Walker County, M432_85, 402, 472; 1860 Census, Walker County, M653_139, 847, 854; 1870 Census, Walker County, M593_180, 217, 234, 240, 252; 1870 Census, Walker County, Agricultural Schedule, 17–20; 1880 Census, Walker County, T9_169, 318; 1880 Census, Conejos, Colorado, T9_89, 173; Walker County Tax Digest for 1874–82, GDAH; Individual and Family Group Records.

Sources for McLemore's Cove Branch: John Morgan to Brigham Young, JHM Papers, box 4, folder 3; 1850 Census, Walker County, M432_85, 409; 1860 Census, Walker County, M653_139, 858; 1870 Census, Walker County, M593_180, 239, 246, 249; 1870 Census,

Chattooga County, M593_142, 164; 1870 Census, DeKalb County, Alabama, M593_15, 814; 1880 Census, Walker County, T9_169, 325, 331, 392; 1880 Census, Lumpkin County, T9_156, 337; 1900 Census, Dade County, T623_191, 1; 1900 Census, Logan, Cache, Utah, T623_1682, 12; 1870 Walker County, Agricultural Schedule, 21–22; 1873–83 Walker County Tax Digest, GDAH; Civil War Service Records; Individual and Family Group Records.

Sources for Pleasant Hill Church Branch: 1870 Census, Floyd County, M593_149, 134; 1870 Census, Walker County, M593_180, 230; 1880 Census, Floyd County, T9_146, 227; 1880 Census, Conejos County, Colorado, T9_89, 167; 1873–80 Floyd County Tax Digest, GDAH; Individual and Family Group Records.

Source for Jonesborough Branch: Journal History, December, 1877, LDS Church History Library.

Sources for Varnell's Station Branch: Civil War Service Records; List of Confederates Captured at Vicksburg, Mississippi, July 4, 1863, M2072_1, Register of Prisoners of War Received at Military Prison, Louisville, Kentucky, M598_90, Selected Records of the War Department Relating to Confederate Prisoners of War, 1861–65, M598_91, all available online at www.ancestry.com; Index to Compiled Service Records of Confederate Soldiers Who Served from the State of Georgia, M-226, microfilm, roll 19, GDAH; Compiled Service Records of Confederate Soldiers Who Served in Organizations from Georgia, M-266, microfilm, roll 425, GDAH; William Lonzo Kaneaster, "The Martyrdom of Joseph Standing," *Whitfield-Murray Historical Society Quarterly* 15, no. 2 (1996); *Whitfield-Murray Historical Society Quarterly* 21, no. 1 (2002); Catoosa County Deed Record Books (A, D, E, F), Catoosa County Courthouse, Ringgold, Georgia; Marriages, Catoosa County, Georgia, book A, 10; Georgia Marriages, 1851–1900, www.ancestry.com; Murray County, Georgia, Marriage Records, books I–VI, 1835–1905, p. 25; 1850 Census, Murray County, M432_78, 151; 1860 Census, Catoosa County, M653_114, 928, 931, 935, 941; 1860 Census, Whitfield County, M653_141, 720; 1870 Census, Catoosa County, M593_140, 304, 311, 316, 317; 1870 Census, Whitfield County, M593_183, 108, 109, 110, 114; 1870 Census, Catoosa County, Agricultural Schedule, 15–16; 1880 Census, Whitfield County, T9_171, 22, 25; 1880 Census, Catoosa County, T9_138, 229; 1880 Census, Conejos County, Colorado, T9_89, 167, 168; 1880 Census, Johnson County, Arkansas, T9_48, 289; 1900 Census, Conejos County, Colorado, T623_122, 2; 1920 Census, Conejos County, Colorado, T625_157, 1; 1872–81 Catoosa County Tax Digest, GDAH; 1878 Whitfield

County Tax Digest, GDAH; "Document by a Southerner," JHM Papers; Records of Old Manassa Cemetery.

Sources for Rockmart Branch: "Benjamin Echols, 1862–1953, Reminiscences and Journal," LDS Church History Library; "Life of Samuel Echols," LDS Church History Library; "Document by a Southerner," JHM Papers; Records of Old Manassa Cemetery; 1870 Census, Polk County, M593_170, 262; 1880 Census, Polk County, T9_161, 271; 1900 Census, Graham County, Arizona, T623_45, 23–24.

Sources for Stock Hill Branch: "Account of Lydia Belinda Stover Haynie," from Patricia Dockery, in possession of the author; Civil War Service Records; 1880 Census, Pickens County, T9_161, 512; Individual and Family Group Records.

Appendix 2

Members of Mob Accused of Elder Joseph Standing's Murder

Hugh Blair

Blair appears in Catoosa County tax records for 1878–80. He was landless, and his estate totaled only $110. He also appeared on the 1880 Catoosa County census with his wife and five children. Described as a farm laborer, he may have worked the land of William Houston Blair, to whom he was related. Two of William Blair's daughters were converted by Mormon missionaries. Nancy Blair married neighbor David W. Williams, the son of Brittain Williams and the nephew of Dillingham Elledge. They relocated to Colorado, as did a second daughter, Martha, who resided in Manassa with her sister and brother-in-law.

Andy Bradley

In 1870, Bradley resided in Catoosa County, near Hugh Blair. Although the census of that year described him as a farmer, he was landless, with a personal estate valued at $354. He was approximately forty years old at the time of Standing's murder and had moved his wife and six children to Varnell's Station in Whitfield County, where he lived near LDS converts and David Smith, who also participated in the mob. Tax records indicated that he failed to acquire land by 1880 and owned an estate valued at only $166.

BENJAMIN "BEN" CLARK

Clark was the son of William Strange Clark of Whitfield County. According to family records, he was a deacon in a Tunnel Hill Baptist church and his brother was a minister. He was approximately twenty years old at the time of Standing's murder and was related to convert John S. Martin. In 1880, he resided in his father's household, where he was described as a "farm laborer."

JAMES "JIM" FAUCETT

Although newspapers spelled his name "Fossett," Jim was a member of the Faucett family of Walker County converts. He resided in Catoosa County, where tax records for 1879 indicated that he was landless, with a total estate valued at $160.

JEFFERSON "JEFF" HUNTER

Hunter appeared on the 1880 Catoosa County census as a farm laborer in the household of John McClure, his stepfather. Hunter and mob member Mac McClure were related: Hunter married Jennie McClure, and Mac McClure married Romie Hunter.

"MAC" McCLURE

McClure did not appear on the federal census or county tax records, but according to marriage records he was linked to mob member Jefferson Hunter, who resided in the household of his stepfather, John McClure. Mac McClure married Romie Hunter, who was related to Jefferson Hunter.

DAVID DALTON "DAVE" NATIONS

Approximately thirty years old at the time of Standing's murder, Dave Nations was the son of Manley and Elizabeth Nations and a cousin to Elizabeth Nations Elledge. In 1870, he resided in his father's Catoosa County household and worked on his father's farm. In the fall of that year, he married Susan Kaneaster, the sister of Josiah Kaneaster. From 1873 to 1879, the couple resided in Varnell's Station, Whitfield County. He was landless, and county tax records for 1877 estimated his estate at $115. In 1879, he was still landless and his estate was estimated at only $80. After Standing's murder, he relocated to Johnson County, Arkansas, where he and his wife resided near other family members.

Jasper N. "Newt" Nations

Newt Nations was the son of Manley Nations and a cousin to Elizabeth Nations Elledge. He and his wife resided in Catoosa County in 1870. Though landless, he was described as "farming" and his personal estate was estimated at $183. Benjamin Clark, who also rode with the mob, was a neighbor. According to county tax digests, he had acquired no land by the time of Standing's murder in 1879. In that year, the total value of his estate was $73. He was approximately thirty-five years old at the time of Standing's murder and relocated to Johnson County, Arkansas, with other members of the family.

Joseph W. "Joe" Nations

Joe Nations was the son of Manley and Elizabeth Nations and a cousin to Elizabeth Nations Elledge. In 1870, he resided in his father's Catoosa County household and was about twenty years old at the time of Standing's murder. After the murder he relocated to Johnson County, Arkansas, where he resided in his father's household.

Manley Nations

Although Manley Nations did not participate directly in the mob, four of his sons did, and he played a prominent role in the defense of the mob. Manley Nations was the brother of Israel Nations, Elizabeth Nations Elledge's father. Manley and Israel Nations were among the first settlers to receive land Georgia claimed from the Cherokees in what became Murray County. Born in about 1815, Nations appeared on the 1850 Murray County census with real estate valued at $150 and on the Catoosa County census with real estate valued at $1,500 and a personal estate of $250. A Confederate sympathizer, he was shot and captured by federal forces in Catoosa County in 1864. He recuperated in a prison hospital in Nashville, Tennessee, where his military rank was described as "citizen." Though he refused to take an oath of loyalty, he was later paroled and returned to northwest Georgia. In 1870, his Catoosa County farm was valued at $1,700 and he possessed a total net worth of nearly $2,200. However, Catoosa County tax records indicated that by 1875 he owned no land, and from 1875 to 1879, his total estate was estimated at about $200. After Standing's murder, he and his wife Elizabeth relocated to Johnson County, Arkansas.

WILLIAM T. "BILL" NATIONS

Bill Nations was the son of Manley and Elizabeth Nations and a cousin to Elizabeth Nations Elledge. In 1870, he resided in his father's Catoosa County household. By 1878, he had established his own household but was landless, with an estate valued at only $75. He was approximately twenty-seven years old at the time of Standing's murder. He did not emigrate to Arkansas with other family members and appeared on the 1880 Catoosa County census with his wife and four children. Interestingly, census data for that year described him as blind and having "no occupation."

A. S. "JUD" SMITH

Although Jud Smith did not appear on the federal census or county tax records, he had a reputation for violence. According to locals, he killed a black man in 1876 and was subsequently tried and acquitted.

DAVID SMITH

David Smith appeared on the Varnell's Station, Whitfield County, tax records for 1871–80. He was landless in 1880, and the total value of his estate was $115. A relationship to Jud Smith was suggested in the documents but cannot be confirmed.

Sources: Marriages, Catoosa County, Georgia, book A, 1858–87, 34; Murray County, Georgia, Marriage Records, books I–VI, 1835–1905, 59; Whitfield County, Georgia, Marriages, 1852–94, 47; 1840 Census, Murray County, roll 47, p. 273; 1850 Census, Murray County, M432_78, 204; 1850 Census, Walker County, M432_85, 351; 1860 Census, Catoosa County, M653_114, 935, 941; 1870 Census, Catoosa County, M593_140, 309–15; 1880 Census, Catoosa County, T9_138, 233–34; 1880 Census, Whitfield County, T9_171, 25; 1880 Census, Johnson County, Arkansas, T9_48, 282–98; Catoosa County Tax Digest, 1872–80, GDAH; Whitfield County Tax Digest, 1870–80, GDAH; Catoosa County Historical Society, *Catoosa County Georgia Heritage*; Clark Family File, Whitfield-Murray Historical Society.

Notes

Introduction

1. The *North Georgia Citizen* advertised copies of the map for sale at a price of $3.73 each. "Here we have a complete picture of our county . . . everything of any interest is marked down, even the place where the Mormon was killed." The *Citizen* believed "every one half able should take a copy," despite the fact that at nearly four dollars, the map's cost put it well beyond the reach of the north Georgians most intimately acquainted with the recent bloodshed. Survey Map of Whitfield County, Georgia, 1879, State of Georgia, Department of Archives and History, Morrow, Ga.; *North Georgia Citizen* (Dalton, Ga.), September 4, 1879, November 27, 1879.

2. As prophet and high priest in a hierarchical priesthood organization, Joseph Smith Jr. claimed direct communication from God. In his revelations, Smith revealed that the Saints should gather together in an earthly western "Zion," which led the church first to Kirtland, Ohio, then to Independence, Missouri. In both places, Gentiles (as the Mormons referred to their non-Mormon neighbors) reviled them for their attempts to control local economic and religious practices, and in the Mormon War of 1838, the Saints were expelled from Missouri. The church found its new Zion in Nauvoo, Illinois, but soon faced controversy there, too, when Joseph Smith, who had been elected mayor of the town, ordered the destruction of an anti-Mormon newspaper. Illinois authorities arrested Smith and his brother, Hyrum, and ordered them to jail in Carthage, Illinois. On June 27, 1844, an armed mob entered the jail and shot and killed both men. The Saints left Nauvoo in 1846 under the leadership of new prophet Brigham Young, who led them to the valley of the Great Salt Lake in what would become Utah Territory after the conclusion of the Mexican War. Controversy continued to plague the Mormons, especially as their marriage practices

became public. The Mormon practice of plural marriage disturbed most nineteenth-century Americans, so much so that the 1856 platform of the Republican Party vowed to eliminate both slavery *and* polygamy, "those twin relics of barbarism." Animus toward polygamy prompted a federal invasion and military occupation of the territory in 1857–58, but the approaching Civil War soon drew the nation's attention back to the east. Still, in 1862 Abraham Lincoln signed into law the first anti-polygamy act passed by Congress, legislation largely ignored and yet inspired by the Saints, whose actions would provoke later, and more aggressive, anti-Mormon legislation. For the history of the Church of Jesus Christ of Latter-day Saints, see Leonard J. Arrington and Davis Bitton, *The Mormon Experience: A History of the Latter-day Saints* (Urbana: University of Illinois Press, 1992); Leonard J. Arrington, *Brigham Young: American Moses* (Urbana: University of Illinois Press, 1985); Fawn M. Brodie, *No Man Knows My History: The Life of Joseph Smith* (New York: Vintage, 1995); John L. Brooke, *The Refiner's Fire: The Making of Mormon Cosmology, 1644–1844* (New York: Cambridge University Press, 1996); Claudia Lauper Bushman and Richard Lyman Bushman, *Building the Kingdom: A History of Mormons in America* (New York: Oxford University Press, 1999); Richard L. Bushman, *Joseph Smith and the Beginnings of Mormonism* (Urbana: University of Illinois Press, 1984); Eric A. Eliason, ed., *Mormons and Mormonism: An Introduction to an American World Religion* (Urbana: University of Illinois Press, 2001); Jan Shipps, *Mormonism: The Story of a New Religious Tradition* (Urbana: University of Illinois Press, 1985); Kenneth H. Winn, *Exiles in a Land of Liberty: Mormons in America, 1830–1846* (Chapel Hill: University of North Carolina Press, 1989).

3. The term "elder" refers to an office in the Melchizedek Priesthood, which all male members can achieve, but the title "Elder" is generally reserved for those who labor full-time in the ministry. Leonard J. Arrington, "Mormon Beginnings in the American South" (Task Paper in LDS History no. 9; Salt Lake City: Historical Department of the Church of Jesus Christ of Latter-day Saints, 1976); LaMar C. Berrett, "History of the Southern States Mission, 1831–1861" (master's thesis, Brigham Young University, 1960); Devon H. Nish, "A Brief History of the Southern States Mission for One Hundred Years, 1830–1930," box 8677.5, Special Collections, Harold B. Lee Library, Brigham Young University, Provo, Utah; Heather M. Seferovich, "History of the LDS Southern States Mission, 1875–1898" (master's thesis, Brigham Young University, 1996); "Southern States Mission," typescript in box 5, folder 27, John Hamilton Morgan Papers, Accn 1465, Manuscript Division, Marriott Library, University of Utah, Salt Lake City (hereafter cited as JHM Papers); A. R. Mortensen, "Utah's Dixie: The Cotton Mission," *Utah Historical Quarterly* 24 (July 1961).

4. Patrick Q. Mason, *The Mormon Menace: Violence and Anti-Mormonism in the Postbellum South* (New York: Oxford University Press, 2011); Gene

A. Sessions, "Myth, Mormonism, and Murder in the South," *South Atlantic Quarterly* 75 (Spring 1976); Ken Driggs, "'There Is No Law in Georgia for Mormons': The Joseph Standing Murder Case of 1879," *Georgia Historical Quarterly* 4 (Winter 1989); William Whitridge Hatch, *There Is No Law . . . : A History of Mormon Civil Relations in the Southern States, 1865-1905* (New York: Vantage Press, 1968); David Buice, "'All Alone and None to Cheer Me': The Southern States Mission Diaries of J. Golden Kimball," *Dialogue* 24 (Spring 1991); Marshall Wingfield, "Tennessee's Mormon Massacre," *Tennessee Historical Quarterly* 17 (March 1958). See also William F. Holmes, "Moonshining and Collective Violence: Georgia, 1889-1895," *Journal of American History* 67 (December 1980); Edward L. Ayers, *Vengeance and Justice: Crime and Punishment in the 19th-Century American South* (New York: Oxford University Press, 1984), 255; W. Fitzhugh Brundage, *Lynching in the New South: Georgia and Virginia, 1880-1930* (Urbana: University of Illinois Press, 1993), 91; W. Fitzhugh Brundage, ed., *Under Sentence of Death: Lynching in the South* (Chapel Hill: University of North Carolina Press, 1997); Bertram Wyatt-Brown, *Honor and Violence in the Old South* (New York: Oxford University Press, 1986); E. Merton Coulter, *The South during Reconstruction, 1865-1877* (Baton Rouge: Louisiana State University Press, 1947), 335.

5. See Mary Ella Engel, "Gathering Georgians to Zion: John Hamilton Morgan's 1876 Mission to Georgia," in *Reconstructing Appalachia: The Civil War's Aftermath*, ed. Andrew L. Slap (Lexington: University Press of Kentucky, 2010); Mary Ella Engel, "'Deep in the Shades of Ill-Starred Georgia's Wood': The Murder of Elder Joseph Standing in Late-Nineteenth-Century Appalachian Georgia," in *Blood in the Hills: A History of Violence in Appalachia*, ed. Bruce E. Stewart (Lexington: University Press of Kentucky, 2012); Mary Ella Engel, "The Appalachian 'Granny': Testing the Boundaries of Female Power in Late-19th-Century Appalachian Georgia," *Appalachian Journal* 37 (Spring/Summer 2010): 210-25.

6. *Atlanta Constitution*, August 5, 1879, July 26, 1879.

7. *Atlanta Constitution*, August 5, 1879.

8. The debate did not end in 1890. The refusal of the House of Representatives to seat B. H. Roberts from Utah in 1898 and the attempt of the Senate to refuse a seat to Reed Smoot in the early 1900s involved more than polygamy. Sarah Barringer Gordon, *The Mormon Question: Polygamy and Constitutional Conflict in Nineteenth Century America* (Chapel Hill: University of North Carolina Press, 2002).

9. Kenneth Coleman, ed., *A History of Georgia*, 2nd ed. (Athens: University of Georgia Press, 1991), 217; Will Wallace Harney, "A Strange Land and Peculiar People," *Lippincott's Magazine* 12 (October 1873): 430-31; Henry D. Shapiro, *Appalachia on Our Mind: The Southern Mountains and Mountaineers in the American Consciousness, 1870-1920* (Chapel Hill: University of North Carolina Press, 1978), 4.

10. Orson Hyde, Salt Lake City, *Journal of Discourses* 16 (October 5, 1873): 230–31. See also J. Spencer Fluhman, *"A Peculiar People": Anti-Mormonism and the Making of Religion in Nineteenth-Century America* (Chapel Hill: University of North Carolina Press, 2012).

CHAPTER 1. "I Find My Dream Literally Fulfilled": John Morgan in Georgia

1. John Morgan to Editor, *Deseret News* (Salt Lake City), December 4, 1876, transcript in box 1, book 1, John Hamilton Morgan Papers, Accn 1465, Manuscript Division, Marriott Library, University of Utah, Salt Lake City (hereafter cited as JHM Papers); Typescript of John Morgan's Journal, November 1875–November 1892, entry dated October 5, 1876, JHM Papers; Arthur M. Richardson and Nicholas G. Morgan, *The Life and Ministry of John Morgan* (privately printed, 1965), 116–20; *Journal History of the Church*, December 4, 1876, microfilm, LDS Church History Library, Salt Lake City.

2. John Morgan to Editor, *Deseret News*, December 4, 1876, JHM Papers; Typescript of John Morgan's Journal, JHM Papers; Richardson and Morgan, *Life and Ministry of John Morgan*, 116–20; *Journal History*, LDS Church Archives.

3. John Morgan to Editor, *Deseret News*, December 4, 1876, JHM Papers; Typescript of John Morgan's Journal, JHM Papers; Richardson and Morgan, *Life and Ministry of John Morgan*, 116–20; *Journal History*, LDS Church Archives.

4. For the Morgan family, see 1840 U.S. Federal Census, Pike County, Kentucky, M704_283; 1850 Census, Decatur County, Indiana, M432_166; 1860 Census, Mattoon, Coles County, Illinois, M653_75, National Archives and Records Administration (NARA), Washington, D.C., available online, www.ancestry.com; John Morgan's Journal, January 4, 1876, JHM Papers; Andrew Jensen, *Latter-day Saint Biographical Encyclopedia: A Compilation of Biographical Sketches of Prominent Men and Women in the Church of Jesus Christ of Latter-day Saints*, vol. 1 (Salt Lake City: Publishers Press, 1971), 204; Richardson and Morgan, *Life and Ministry*, 3–8; Paul M. Angle, ed., *Created Equal? The Complete Lincoln-Douglas Debates of 1858* (Chicago: University of Chicago Press, 1958), 232–34; James M. McPherson, *Battle Cry of Freedom: The Civil War Era* (New York: Ballantine Books, 1988), 179–87, 512–19.

5. The 123rd Illinois was assigned to the Army of the Ohio from September to November 1862. From November 1862 to June 1865, it was assigned to the Army of the Cumberland. Richardson and Morgan, *Life and Ministry*, 8–9; Compiled Military Service File of John Hamilton Morgan, NARA, Washington, D.C.; Statement concerning the history of the 123rd Regiment Illinois Infantry Volunteers, Civil War, from the Adjutant General's Office,

War Department, June 15, 1926, box 5, folder 12, JHM Papers; U.S. War Department, *War of the Rebellion: A Compilation of the Official Records of the Union and Confederate Armies*, 70 vols. in 128 books and index (Washington, D.C.: Government Printing Office, 1880-91), series I, vol. 16, pt. 1, 1023-33, 1040, 1059-64; Frederick Henry Dyer, "Regimental Histories," in *A Compendium of the War of the Rebellion*, vol. 2 (Dayton: National Historical Society, 1979), 1098; Janet B. Hewett, *Supplement to the Official Records of the Union and Confederate Armies*, pt. II, vol. 14 (Wilmington, N.C.: Broadfoot, 1999), 580; McPherson, *Battle Cry*, 409, 518-22, 579-83; James M. McPherson, *Ordeal by Fire: The Civil War and Reconstruction* (New York: McGraw-Hill, 2001), 312-13, 332; Kenneth W. Noe, *Perryville: This Grand Havoc of Battle* (Lexington: University Press of Kentucky, 2001), 247-61. For eyewitness accounts, see James A. Connolly, *Three Years in the Army of the Cumberland*, ed. Paul M. Angle (Bloomington: Indiana University Press, 1959); Claire E. Swedberg, ed., *Three Years with the 92nd Illinois: The Civil War Diary of John M. King* (Mechanicsburg, Pa.: Stackpole Books, 1999); Christopher D. McManus, Thomas H. Inglis, and Otho James Hicks, eds., *Morning to Midnight in the Saddle: Civil War Letters of a Soldier in Wilder's Lightning Brigade* (Xlibris, 2012).

6. McPherson, *Battle Cry*, 558-59, 591-95; Hewett, *Supplement*, pt. II, vol. 14, 732-36; Bruce Catton, *Glory Road: The Bloody Route from Fredericksburg to Gettysburg* (Garden City, N.Y.: Doubleday, 1952), 246; Connolly, *Three Years*, 56; John Morgan to parents, January 28, 1863, transcript in box 2, folder 1, JHM Papers; Richardson and Morgan, *Life and Ministry*, 11.

7. Connolly, *Three Years*, 56, 74, 94, 97, 98fn, 101, 112-16; McManus, Inglis, and Hicks, *Morning to Midnight*, 68; Hewett, *Supplement*, pt. II, vol. 14, 563-66, 581, 732-36; *Official Records*, series I, vol. 30, pt. 1, 47-52, 445-46; *Official Records*, series I, vol. 30, pt. 3, 75, 77-78, 100-103, 113, 119, 124; John R. Elting and Michael J. McAfee, eds., *Military Uniforms in America, Volume III, Long Endure: The Civil War Period, 1852-1867* (Novato, Calif.: Presidio Press, 1982), 46; War Department Statement, JHM Papers; Robert E. Harbison, "Wilder's Brigade in the Tullahoma and Chattanooga Campaigns of the American Civil War" (master's thesis, Army Command and General Staff College, 2002), 10-20, 29-57; Samuel C. Williams, *General John T. Wilder: Commander of the Lightning Brigade* (Bloomington: Indiana University Press, 1936), 13-15; Glenn W. Sunderland, *Wilder's Lightning Brigade—And Its Spencer Repeaters* (Washington, Ill.: BookWorks, 1984); Glenn W. Sunderland, *Lightning at Hoover's Gap: Wilder's Brigade in the Civil War* (New York: Thomas Yoseloff, 1969).

8. John Morgan to Editor, *Colorado Junction*, June 8, 1878, transcript in box 1, book 1, JHM Papers; Donald E. Davis, *The Land of Ridge and Valley: A Photographic History of the Northwest Georgia Mountains* (Charleston,

S.C.: Arcadia, 2000), 7-10; Kenneth Coleman, ed., *A History of Georgia*, 2nd ed. (Athens: University of Georgia Press, 1991), 129-34; Mary Hood, "Tropic of Conscience," in *The New Georgia Guide*, a project of the Georgia Humanities Council (Athens: University of Georgia Press, 1996), 105-35; James F. Smith, *The Cherokee Land Lottery, Containing a Numerical List of the Names of the Fortunate Drawers in Said Lottery, with an Engraved Map of Each District* (Baltimore: Genealogical Publishing, 1969); Brad A. Bays, *Townsite Settlement and Dispossession in the Cherokee Nation, 1866-1907* (New York: Garland, 1998); George R. Gilmer, *Sketches of Some of the First Settlers of Upper Georgia, of the Cherokees, and the Author* (Baltimore: Genealogical Publishing, 1965); Wilson Lumpkin, *The Removal of the Cherokee Indians from Georgia* (New York: Dodd, Mead, 1907); Theda Perdue and Michael D. Green, eds., *The Cherokee Removal: A Brief History with Documents* (Boston: Bedford/St. Martin's, 1995); David Williams, *The Georgia Gold Rush: Twenty-Niners, Cherokees, and Gold Fever* (Columbia: University of South Carolina Press, 1993).

9. Susie Blaylock McDaniel, *Official History of Catoosa County, Georgia, 1853-1953* (privately published, 1953), 1-13, 194-95; Whitfield-Murray Historical Society, *An Official History of Whitfield County, Georgia, 1852-1999* (privately published, 1999), 81; William Henry Harrison Clark, *History in Catoosa County* (privately published, 1972), 126, 160; Davis, *Land of Ridge and Valley*, 39, 56, 110, 120; Robert S. Baker, *Chattooga: The Story of a County and Its People* (privately published, 1988), 431, 822; James Alfred Sartain, *History of Walker County Georgia* (privately published, 1972), 193, 260-61; Floyd Heritage Book Committee and County Heritage, Inc., *The Heritage of Floyd County Georgia, 1833-1999* (privately published, 1999), 13, 141-42; Charles O'Neill, *Wild Train: The Story of the Andrews Raiders* (New York: Random House, 1956).

10. Richardson and Morgan, *Life and Ministry*, 11; *Official Records*, series I, vol. 30, pt. 1, 40-42, 64, 171-79, 444-64; *Official Records*, series I, vol. 30, pt. 3, 267-76, 493-96, 512-13, 546, 568-69, 577-78, 609, 624, 836, 878, 999, 1001-2; Dyer, *Compendium*, vol. 2, 1098; Harbison, "Wilder's Brigade," 57-86, 100; Connolly, *Three Years*, 119-23, 175-78; McPherson, *Battle Cry*, 281, 671-74; McPherson, *Ordeal by Fire*, 362-65; Richard A. Baumgartner, *Blue Lightning: Wilder's Mounted Infantry Brigade in the Battle of Chickamauga* (Huntington, W.Va.: Blue Acorn Press, 2007); Joseph M. Brown, *The Mountain Campaigns in Georgia; or, War Scenes on the Western & Atlantic* (Buffalo: Matthews, Northrup, 1890); John Bowers, *Chickamauga and Chattanooga: The Battles That Doomed the Confederacy* (New York: HarperCollins, 1994), 74; Peter Cozzens, *This Terrible Sound: The Battle of Chickamauga* (Urbana: University of Illinois Press, 1996); Steven E. Woodworth, *Six Armies in Tennessee: The Chickamauga and Chattanooga Campaigns* (Lincoln: University of Nebraska Press, 1998); Matt Spruill, ed.,

Guide to the Battle of Chickamauga (Lawrence: University Press of Kansas, 1993).

11. When the Atlanta Campaign got under way, Sherman's Military Division of the Mississippi had been organized into three armies: James B. McPherson's Army of the Tennessee, John M. Schofield's Army of the Ohio, and Thomas's Army of the Cumberland. Wilder's Brigade, assigned to Kenner Garrard's Second Cavalry Division, took its place with the Army of the Cumberland. *Official Records*, series I, vol. 38, pt. 1, 101-2; *Official Records*, series I, vol. 38, pt. 2, 803-15; Harbison, "Wilder's Brigade," 42-49; Clark, *History in Catoosa County*, 183; McPherson, *Battle Cry*, 676-80; McPherson, *Ordeal by Fire*, 365-69.

12. In 1871, the U.S. Congress established a federal agency, the Southern Claims Commission (SCC), to investigate the claims of southern Union loyalists who had property taken for use by the Union Army. Chattooga County submitted 148 claims, of which 59 were paid. Prominent Chattooga County Unionist Wesley Shropshire collected the largest payment. Interestingly, shared political loyalties did not ameliorate discord. In Thomas Barbour's SCC file, there is a letter from Wesley Shropshire to the claims examiner. Marked "confidential," the letter challenges Thomas Barbour's claim as "exorbitant." The letter begins, "I have frequently been astonished to hear Rebels making out claims against the government for property lost during the war But never more surprised than I was the other day to hear T J Barber who has just returned from Washington say that he had reduced his father's claim down to ten thousand dollars. If the old man gets the amount he will have more money than he ever was worth before." Despite the letter, Barbour's claim was approved. Claim of Thomas Barbour of Chattooga County, Georgia, Number 3556, SCC Approved Claims, 1871-80: Georgia, Microfiche M1658, NARA; Gary B. Mills, *Southern Loyalists in the Civil War: The Southern Claims Commission* (Baltimore: Genealogical Publishing, 1994), 31; Clark, *History in Catoosa County*, 265.

13. Though slavery existed throughout the Appalachian South (and northwest Georgia planters took advantage of major slave markets in Chattanooga, Tennessee, and Rome, Georgia), Georgia's mountain counties claimed only a small percentage of the state's slaves, estimated at 13 percent in 1860. Indeed, in the state's mountain counties resided many of the yeoman and landless poor who characterized three-fourths of Georgia's white population in 1860, the landless poor often scratching a living as tenants or farm laborers. Thomas Barbour's status as a prosperous landowner and slaveholder distinguished him from other mountain residents, as, according to the 1860 population and slave schedules, Barbour owned sixteen slaves and a total estate valued at more than $42,000. SCC Claim of Thomas Barbour; Appendix 1 in this volume for Thomas Barbour; Coleman, *History of Georgia*, 187-204; McPherson, *Battle Cry*, 213-16, 223, 243;

John Inscoe, ed., *The Civil War in Georgia: A New Georgia Encyclopedia Companion* (Athens: University of Georgia Press, 2011), 24–29, 35–38; Michael P. Johnson, *Toward a Patriarchal Republic: The Secession of Georgia* (Baton Rouge: Louisiana State University Press, 1977), 18–66; William W. Freehling and Craig M. Simpson, *Secession Debated: Georgia's Showdown in 1860* (New York: Oxford University Press, 1992), 48–49, 154; James C. Cobb, *Georgia Odyssey* (Athens: University of Georgia Press, 1997), 19–20; David Williams, Teresa Crisp Williams, and David Carlson, *Plain Folk in a Rich Man's War: Class and Dissent in Confederate Georgia* (Gainesville: University Press of Florida, 2002), 13; Floyd Heritage Book Committee, *Heritage*, 372; Baker, *Chattooga*, 387–96; Clark, *History in Catoosa County*, 131; Sartain, *History of Walker County*, 264; Elizabeth B. Cooksey, "Catoosa County," "Chattooga County," "Polk County," "Walker County," in *New Georgia Encyclopedia* (*NGE*), www.georgiaencyclopedia.org; Ethelene D. Jones, "Fannin County," in *NGE*; N. M. Williamson, "Floyd County," in *NGE*; Robert E. Luckett, "Whitfield County," in *NGE*; 1860 U.S. Federal Census, Chattooga County, Slave Schedules. The 1860 census for Chattooga County reported 279 slaveholders and 2,055 slaves, the majority residing in Chattooga Valley, where Barbour lived. See also Frederick A. Bode and Donald E. Ginter, *Farm Tenancy and the Census in Antebellum Georgia* (Athens: University of Georgia Press, 1986). For slavery in Appalachia, see John C. Inscoe, *Mountain Masters: Slavery and the Sectional Crisis in Western North Carolina* (Knoxville: University of Tennessee Press, 1989); John C. Inscoe, *Race, War, and Remembrance in the Appalachian South* (Lexington: University Press of Kentucky, 2008); John C. Inscoe, ed., *Georgia in Black and White: Explorations in the Race Relations of a Southern State, 1865–1950* (Athens: University of Georgia Press, 1994); Richard B. Drake, "Slavery and Antislavery in Appalachia," in *Appalachians and Race: The Mountain South from Slavery to Segregation*, ed. John C. Inscoe (Lexington: University Press of Kentucky, 2001), 16–26; Wilma A. Dunaway, "Put in Master's Pocket: Cotton Expansion and Interstate Slave Trading in the Mountain South," in Inscoe, *Appalachians and Race*, 116–32; William H. Turner and Edward J. Cabbell, eds., *Blacks in Appalachia* (Lexington: University Press of Kentucky, 1985).

14. SCC Claim of Thomas Barbour, Appendix 1 for Thomas Barbour; Martin Crawford, *Ashe County's Civil War: Community and Society in the Appalachian South* (Charlottesville: University Press of Virginia, 2001), 13; Jonathan Dean Sarris, *A Separate Civil War: Communities in Conflict in the Mountain South* (Charlottesville: University of Virginia Press, 2006), 73–75; Gordon B. McKinney, "The Civil War and Reconstruction," in *High Mountains Rising: Appalachia in Time and Place*, ed. Richard A. Straw and H. Tyler Blethen (Urbana: University of Illinois Press, 2004), 46–58. See also Inscoe, *Mountain Masters*; John C. Inscoe and Gordon B. McKinney, *The Heart of Confederate Appalachia: Western North Carolina in the Civil*

War (Chapel Hill: University of North Carolina Press, 2000); Phillip Shaw Paludan, *Victims: A True Story of the Civil War* (Knoxville: University of Tennessee Press, 1981); Durwood Dunn, *Cades Cove: The Life and Death of a Southern Appalachian Community, 1818-1937* (Knoxville: University of Tennessee Press, 1988); Kenneth W. Noe, *Southwest Virginia's Railroad: Modernization and the Sectional Crisis* (Urbana: University of Illinois Press, 1994); Robert Tracy McKenzie, *Lincolnites and Rebels: A Divided Town in the American Civil War* (New York: Oxford University Press, 2009); Altina L. Waller, *Feud: Hatfields, McCoys, and Social Change in Appalachia, 1860-1900* (Chapel Hill: University of North Carolina Press, 1988); W. Todd Groce, *Mountain Rebels: East Tennessee Confederates and the Civil War, 1860-1870* (Knoxville: University of Tennessee Press, 2000); Gordon B. McKinney, *Southern Mountain Republicans, 1865-1900: Politics and the Appalachian Community* (Chapel Hill: University of North Carolina Press, 1978).

15. Doc Morse's pro-Union group operated out of Walker County, as did the Long-Roberts gang, who persecuted Confederates from a base in McLemore's Cove. SCC Claim of Thomas Barbour; Sartain, *History of Walker County*, 120-24; Jonathan D. Sarris, "Anatomy of an Atrocity: The Madden Branch Massacre and Guerrilla Warfare in North Georgia, 1861-1865," *Georgia Historical Quarterly* 77 (Winter 1993): 679-710; Keith S. Bohannan, "'They Had Determined to Root Us Out': Dual Memoirs by a Unionist Couple in Blue Ridge Georgia," in *Enemies of the Country: New Perspectives on Unionists in the Civil War South*, ed. John C. Inscoe and Robert C. Kenzer (Athens: University of Georgia Press, 2001); Jonathan D. Sarris, "An Execution in Lumpkin County: Localized Loyalties in North Georgia's Civil War," in *The Civil War in Appalachia*, ed. Kenneth W. Noe and Shannon H. Wilson (Knoxville: University of Tennessee Press, 1997), 131-57; Kenneth W. Noe, "Exterminating Savages: The Union Army and Mountain Guerrillas in Southern West Virginia, 1861-1862," in Noe and Wilson, *Civil War in Appalachia*; Jonathan D. Sarris, "'Shot for Being Bushwhackers': Guerrilla War and Extralegal Violence in a North Georgia Community, 1862-1865," in *Guerrillas, Unionists, and Violence on the Confederate Home Front*, ed. Daniel E. Sutherland (Fayetteville: University of Arkansas Press, 1999); Sean Michael O'Brien, *Mountain Partisans: Guerrilla Warfare in the Southern Appalachians, 1861-1865* (Westport, Conn.: Praeger, 1999); Noel C. Fisher, *War at Every Door: Partisan Politics and Guerrilla Violence in East Tennessee, 1860-1869* (Chapel Hill: University of North Carolina Press, 2001); Sarris, *Separate Civil War*; Paludan, *Victims*.

16. SCC Claim of Thomas Barbour; Compiled Military Service File of John Hamilton Morgan, NARA; John Morgan to mother, December 21, 1863, box 2, folder 1, JHM Papers.

17. *Official Records*, series I, vol. 38, pt. 2, 745-49, 803-51; *Official Records*, series I, vol. 49, pt. 1, 402-3, 452-55; Dyer, *Compendium*, vol. 2, 1098; McPherson, *Battle Cry*, 825, 848-53; Richardson and Morgan, *Life*

and Ministry, 17–18; Michael D. Hitt, *Charged with Treason: Ordeal of 400 Mill Workers during Military Operations in Roswell, Georgia, 1864–1865* (Monroe, N.Y.: Library Research Associates, 1992).

18. Compiled Military Service File of John Hamilton Morgan, NARA; Richardson and Morgan, *Life and Ministry*, 31.

19. Richardson and Morgan, *Life and Ministry*, 35–59.

20. Ibid., 90–96; John Morgan's Journal, December 27, 1875, JHM Papers; John Morgan to *Deseret News*, November 28, 1875, box 2, folder 1, JHM Papers; Rex Thomas Price, "The Mormon Missionary of the Nineteenth Century" (Ph.D. diss., University of Wisconsin–Madison, 1991), 91; Record of Elders in the Southern States Mission 1877–1898, Southern States Mission, 1832–1888, Manuscript History and Historical Reports, reel 1, Church Archives, Salt Lake City; Devon H. Nish, "A Brief History of the Southern States Mission for One Hundred Years, 1830–1930," box 8677.5, Special Collections, Harold B. Lee Library, Brigham Young University, Provo, Utah; LaMar C. Berrett, "History of the Southern States Mission, 1831–1861" (master's thesis, Brigham Young University, 1960); Heather M. Seferovich, "History of the LDS Southern States Mission, 1875–1898" (master's thesis, Brigham Young University, 1996); Leonard J. Arrington, "Mormon Beginnings in the American South" (Task Paper in LDS History no. 9; Salt Lake City: Historical Department of the Church of Jesus Christ of Latter-day Saints, 1976).

21. John Morgan to Editor, *Deseret News*, February 3, 1876, transcript in box 1, book 1, JHM Papers; John Morgan's Journal, entries dated March 5, 1876, to May 15, 1876; Price, "Mormon Missionary," 154–55, 167, 216, 223.

22. John Morgan and Joseph Standing to Editor, *Deseret News*, April 3, 1876, transcript in box 1, book 1, JHM Papers; Richardson and Morgan, *Life and Ministry*, 104; Price, "Mormon Missionary," 10, 13, 51, 128, 312–14, 340–41, 389–90, 486.

23. Joseph Standing to Editor, *Deseret News*, May 5, 1876, transcript in box 1, book 1, JHM Papers; John Morgan's Journal, entries dated February 3, 1876, February 14, 1876, April 13, 1876, August 20, 1876, JHM Papers; Richardson and Morgan, *Life and Ministry*, 92, 111–15; Typed Version of John Morgan's Journal, in Research Material, box 4, folder 1, JHM Papers; Price, "Mormon Missionary," 167, 215–16. For Joseph Standing, see Jensen, *Latter-day Saint Biographical Encyclopedia*, 719–21; Individual Record, AFN: 277V-QM; 1870 U.S. Federal Census, Salt Lake City Ward 12, Salt Lake, Utah Territory, M593_1611, 624; 1860 U.S. Census, Salt Lake City Ward 12, M653_1313, 157; 1850 U.S. Census, Great Salt Lake, Utah Territory, M432_919, 87.

24. Richardson and Morgan, *Life and Ministry*, 116; Cooksey, "Catoosa County," "Chattooga County," "Polk County," "Walker County," in *NGE*; Williamson, "Floyd County," in *NGE*; Luckett, "Whitfield County," in *NGE*.

25. Typed Version of John Morgan's Journal, box 4, folder 2, JHM Papers.

According to this source, John Morgan searched for the grave of a friend with whom he had exchanged coats. In 1894, in coverage of John Morgan's funeral, the *Deseret News* repeated the story, but described the article of clothing as a "cap." Richardson and Morgan, *Life and Ministry*, 573-74.

26. Converts of Elder John Morgan in North Georgia during his first mission of 1876, box 3, folder 3, JHM Papers; Report of Branches of the Church in Georgia, box 1, book 1, JHM Papers.

CHAPTER 2. "There Is Something Terrible Coming":
Establishment of the North Georgia Mission Field

1. Small congregations of church members are called "branches." Branches are led by a branch president and two counselors. As the number of congregants increases, branches typically become wards, then stakes. Rex Thomas Price, "The Mormon Missionary of the Nineteenth Century" (Ph.D. diss., University of Wisconsin-Madison, 1991), 304-8, 317-18, 390, 414-15; Leonard J. Arrington and Davis Bitton, *The Mormon Experience: A History of the Latter-day Saints* (Urbana: University of Illinois Press, 1992), 126; Leonard J. Arrington, Feramorz Y. Fox, and Dean L. May, *Building the City of God: Community and Cooperation among the Mormons* (Salt Lake City: Deseret Book Company, 1976), 13.

2. "Report of Branches of the Church in Georgia," box 1, book 1, John Hamilton Morgan Papers, Accn 1465, Manuscript Division, Marriott Library, University of Utah, Salt Lake City (hereafter cited as JHM Papers); John Morgan to John Taylor, January 11, 1879, transcript in "Typescript Letters from John Morgan to Church Leaders, 1878-1887," box 2, folder 3, JHM Papers; *Atlanta Constitution*, August 5, 1879; Richard E. Small, *The Post Offices of Georgia, 1764-1900* (Centerville, Va.: R. E. Small, 1998); Marion R. Hemperley, *Cities, Towns, and Communities of Georgia between 1847-1962* (Easley, S.C.: Southern Historical Press, 1980); Kenneth K. Krakow, *Georgia Place-Names: Their History and Origins* (Macon, Ga.: Winship Press, 1994).

3. John Morgan's Journal, June 20, 1877, June 28, 1877, August 27, 1877, October 23, 1877, November 10, 1877, JHM Papers; Typed Version of John Morgan's Journal, box 4, folder 2, 100-112, JHM Papers; John Morgan to Editors, *Deseret News*, September 21, 1877, JHM Papers.

4. John Morgan to Editor, *Deseret News*, January, 1877, box 1, book 1, JHM Papers; Kenneth Coleman, ed., *A History of Georgia*, 2nd ed. (Athens: University of Georgia Press, 1991), 187-224; William W. Freehling and Craig M. Simpson, *Secession Debated: Georgia's Showdown in 1860* (New York: Oxford University Press, 1992); Michael P. Johnson, *Toward a Patriarchal Republic: The Secession of Georgia* (Baton Rouge: Louisiana State University Press, 1977), 11-15, 66; James C. Cobb, *Georgia Odyssey* (Athens: University of Georgia Press, 1997), 25-28; John Inscoe, ed., *The Civil War in Georgia: A New Georgia Encyclopedia Companion* (Athens: University

of Georgia Press, 2011), 185–94; Derrell C. Roberts, *Joseph E. Brown and the Politics of Reconstruction* (University: University of Alabama Press, 1973); C. Mildred Thompson, *Reconstruction in Georgia: Economic, Social, Political, 1865–1872* (Savannah: Beehive Press, 1972); Robert Preston Brooks, *The Agrarian Revolution in Georgia, 1865–1912* (New York: AMS Press, 1971); Alan Conway, *The Reconstruction of Georgia* (Minneapolis: University of Minnesota Press, 1966); Edwin C. Woolley, *The Reconstruction of Georgia* (New York: Columbia University Press, 1901); Paul A. Cimbala, *Under the Guardianship of the Nation: The Freedmen's Bureau and the Reconstruction of Georgia, 1863–1870* (Athens: University of Georgia Press, 1997); Edmund L. Drago, *Black Politicians and Reconstruction in Georgia: A Splendid Failure* (Athens: University of Georgia Press, 1992); Elizabeth S. Nathans, *Losing the Peace: Georgia Republicans and Reconstruction, 1865–1871* (Baton Rouge: Louisiana State University Press, 1968); James M. McPherson, *Battle Cry of Freedom: The Civil War Era* (New York: Ballantine Books, 1988), 213–16, 223; Eric Foner, *Reconstruction: America's Unfinished Revolution, 1863–1877* (New York: Harper & Row, 1988); Dan T. Carter, *When the War Was Over: The Failure of Self-Reconstruction in the South, 1865–1867* (Baton Rouge: Louisiana State University Press, 1985); Gordon B. McKinney, *Southern Mountain Republicans, 1865–1900: Politics and the Appalachian Community* (Chapel Hill: University of North Carolina Press, 1978); Andrew L. Slap, ed., *Reconstructing Appalachia: The Civil War's Aftermath* (Lexington: University Press of Kentucky, 2010); Steven E. Nash, *Reconstruction's Ragged Edge: The Politics of Postwar Life in the Southern Mountains* (Chapel Hill: University of North Carolina Press, 2016).

5. *Atlanta Constitution*, January 12, 1869, February 20, 1869, August 29, 1869, January 21, 1870; Donald E. Davis, *The Land of Ridge and Valley: A Photographic History of the Northwest Georgia Mountains* (Charleston, S.C.: Arcadia, 2000), 57–58.

6. Williams, *General John T. Wilder*, 13–15; Gordon B. McKinney, "The Civil War and Reconstruction," in *High Mountains Rising: Appalachia in Time and Place*, ed. Richard A. Straw and H. Tyler Blethen (Urbana: University of Illinois Press, 2004), 54; Ronald D. Eller, *Miners, Millhands, and Mountaineers: Industrialization of the Appalachian South, 1880–1930* (Knoxville: University of Tennessee Press, 1982); Ronald L. Lewis, *Transforming the Appalachian Countryside: Railroads, Deforestation, and Social Change in West Virginia, 1880–1920* (Chapel Hill: University of North Carolina Press, 1998); Robert S. Weise, *Grasping at Independence: Debt, Male Authority, and Mineral Rights in Appalachian Kentucky, 1850–1915* (Knoxville: University of Tennessee Press, 2001). For the New South, see Edward L. Ayers, *The Promise of the New South: Life after Reconstruction* (New York: Oxford University Press, 1992); C. Vann Woodward, *Origins of*

the New South, 1877–1913 (Baton Rouge: Louisiana State University Press, 1971); George B. Tindall, *The Emergence of the New South, 1913–1945* (Baton Rouge: Louisiana State University Press, 1967); Numan V. Bartley, *The New South, 1945–1980* (Baton Rouge: Louisiana State University Press, 1995).

7. John Morgan to Church President John Taylor, January 11, 1879, box 2, folder 3, JHM Papers; *Atlanta Constitution*, June 26, 1869, June 28, 1870, August 4, 1870, July 2, 1873, September 1, 1873; Davis, *Land of Ridge and Valley*, 8; Kevin E. O'Donnell and Helen Hollingsworth, eds., *Seekers of Scenery: Travel Writing from Southern Appalachia, 1840–1900* (Knoxville: University of Tennessee Press, 2004).

8. John Morgan to Editors, *Salt Lake City Herald*, August 23, 1878, box 1, book 1, JHM Papers; John Morgan to Editors, *Deseret News*, October 3, 1878, box 1, book 1, JHM Papers; Arthur M. Richardson and Nicholas G. Morgan, *The Life and Ministry of John Morgan* (privately printed, 1965), 189–93; Price, "Mormon Missionary," 453–60; Khaled J. Bloom, *The Mississippi Valley's Great Yellow Fever Epidemic of 1878* (Baton Rouge: Louisiana State University Press, 1993).

9. Historians have long judged the 1870 census, both in its population and in its agricultural schedules, as unreliable. County tax digests provide an alternative to census reports, yet should also be viewed with suspicion. Therefore, the following information should be considered a best summary of available data, rather than incontrovertible fact. These statistical data are based upon an analysis of the 1870 U.S. Federal Census (schedule 1, population schedules), available online at www.ancestry.com. The basis unit of analysis is "household" and collection of data is restricted to those individuals considered by census takers to be heads of household. In Catoosa County: 10 percent black heads of household (83); 3 percent mulatto heads of household (27); 86 percent white heads of household (694). In Chattooga County: 18 percent black (225); 1 percent mulatto (18); 80 percent white (974). In Fannin County: 2 percent black (16); 0 percent mulatto (0); 98 percent white (975). In Floyd County: 27 percent black (848); 5 percent mulatto (168); 68 percent white (2,154). In Polk County: 27 percent black (372); 4 percent mulatto (57); 69 percent white (961). In Walker County: 14 percent black (283); 1 percent mulatto (17); 85 percent white (1,729). In Whitfield County: 12 percent black (223); 1 percent mulatto (27); 87 percent white (1,624). Overall, in the counties that are the focus of this study, the percentages are as follows: 18 percent black; 3 percent mulatto; 79 percent white. Price, "Mormon Missionary," 393, 402–4, 406, 411; Newell G. Bringhurst and Darron T. Smith, eds., *Black and Mormon* (Urbana: University of Illinois Press, 2004).

10. John Morgan to Editor, *Deseret News*, March 9, 1877, *Journal History*, LDS Church Archives. See also John C. Inscoe, ed., *Appalachians and Race: The Mountain South from Slavery to Segregation* (Lexington: University

Press of Kentucky, 2001); John C. Inscoe, ed., *Georgia in Black and White: Explorations in the Race Relations of a Southern State, 1865–1950* (Athens: University of Georgia Press, 1994).

11. John Morgan to Editor, *Deseret News*, May 30, 1878, box 1, book 1, JHM Papers.

12. See esp. Loyal Jones, *Faith and Meaning in the Southern Uplands* (Urbana: University of Illinois Press, 1999), 14, 23–28, 203–4, and Deborah Vansau McCauley, *Appalachian Mountain Religion: A History* (Urbana: University of Illinois Press, 1995). See also Bill J. Leonard, ed., *Christianity in Appalachia: Profiles in Regional Pluralism* (Knoxville: University of Tennessee Press, 1999); Elder John Sparks, *The Roots of Appalachian Christianity: The Life and Legacy of Elder Shubal Stearns* (Lexington: University Press of Kentucky, 2001); Troy D. Abell, *Better Felt Than Said: The Holiness-Pentecostal Experience in Southern Appalachia* (Waco, Tex.: Markham Press, 1982); W. D. Weatherford and Earl D. C. Brewer, *Life and Religion in Southern Appalachia* (New York: Friendship Press, 1962); Paul F. Gillespie, *Foxfire 7* (New York: Anchor Books, 1980). See also Christopher H. Owen, *The Sacred Flame of Love: Methodism and Society in Nineteenth-Century Georgia* (Athens: University of Georgia Press, 1998); Rufus B. Spain, *At Ease in Zion: A Social History of Southern Baptists, 1865–1900* (Tuscaloosa: University of Alabama Press, 2003); Daniel W. Stowell, *Rebuilding Zion: The Religious Reconstruction of the South, 1863–1877* (New York: Oxford University Press, 1998).

13. John Morgan to Editor, *Deseret News*, June 16, 1877; *Atlanta Constitution*, November 2, 1877.

14. 1870 U.S. Federal Census, Social Statistics Schedules.

15. John Morgan to Editor, *Deseret News*, May 17, 1877, box 1, book 1, JHM Papers; Benjamin Echols, "Reminiscences and Journal, 1946–1950," microfilm, Historical Department, LDS Church Archives; Price, "Mormon Missionary," 46, 242–43, 339, 481; David B. Parker, "'Quit Your Meanness': Sam Jones's Theology for the New South," *Georgia Historical Quarterly* 77 (Winter 1993): 711–27. In his article, Parker points out that much of Sam Jones's energy after 1880 was dedicated to raising funds for the Methodist Orphan Home.

16. Price, "Mormon Missionary," 318, 481.

17. John Morgan to Editor, *Deseret News*, June 16, 1877, box 1, book 1, JHM Papers.

18. *Atlanta Constitution*, July 22, 1877. Data presented are based upon an analysis of the 1870 U.S. Federal Census (schedule 1, population schedules), available online. For distribution of wealth by race in Catoosa County: black heads of household possessed 1 percent of total wealth; mulatto heads of household possessed 0 percent of total wealth; white heads of household possessed 99 percent of total wealth. In Chattooga County: black, 1 percent; mulatto,

0 percent; white, 99 percent. In Fannin County: black, 0 percent; mulatto, 0 percent; white, 100 percent. In Floyd County: black, 27 percent; mulatto, 5 percent; white, 68 percent. In Polk County: black, 27 percent; mulatto, 4 percent; white, 69 percent. In Walker County: black, 14 percent; mulatto, 1 percent; white, 85 percent. In Whitfield County: black, 12 percent; mulatto, 1 percent; white, 87 percent. Overall for these counties: black, 18 percent; mulatto, 3 percent; white, 79 percent. For concentration of wealth in hands of a few: the ten wealthiest heads of household in Catoosa County claimed 16.04 percent of the county's total wealth; in Chattooga County, 19.34 percent; in Fannin County, 12.28 percent; in Floyd County, 22.27 percent; in Polk County, 20.25 percent; in Walker County, 15.09 percent; in Whitfield County, 18.46 percent. For heads of household claiming total estates valued at greater than $500 in Catoosa County: 40.42 percent; Chattooga County, 34.51 percent; Fannin County, 28.25 percent; Floyd County, 31.64 percent; Polk County, 27.48 percent; Walker County, 39.18 percent; Whitfield County, 37.08 percent. For heads of household claiming total estates valued at $1–500 in Catoosa County: 34.83 percent; Chattooga County, 25.55 percent; Fannin County, 45.51 percent; Floyd County, 26.44 percent; Polk County, 28.78 percent; Walker County, 40.07 percent; Whitfield County, 39.43 percent. For heads of household claiming no real or personal estate in Catoosa County: 24.75 percent; Chattooga County, 39.93 percent; Fannin County, 26.24 percent; Floyd County, 41.92 percent; Polk County, 43.74 percent; Walker County, 20.75 percent; Whitfield County, 23.48 percent.

19. Data based upon 1870 U.S. Federal Census population and agricultural schedules. By county, the mean values of estates (real and personal) are as follows: Catoosa County, $1,185; Chattooga County, $957; Fannin County, $494; Floyd County, $1,681; Polk County, $1,097; Walker County, $1,054; Whitfield County, $1,234. The mean values of estates (real and personal) for 63 convert heads of household by county: Catoosa County, $813; Chattooga County, $587; Fannin County, $0; Floyd County, $577; Polk County, $100; Walker County, $688; Whitfield County, $624. For wages paid in 1870, see the 1870 U.S. Federal Census, Social Statistics Schedules, which describes a typical wage as 75 cents. For typical wages in the late 1870s, see Robert S. Baker, *Chattooga: The Story of a County and Its People* (privately printed, 1988), 431.

20. For James M. Faucett, C. Frank Payne, William C. Kilgore, John Smalley, and Andrew J. Holland, see Appendix 1.

21. For William R. Manning, see Appendix 1.

22. John Morgan to Editors, *Deseret News*, March 9, 1877, *Journal History*, LDS Church Archives; for Price Connally, see Appendix 1.

23. Both Thomas A. Littlejohn and Joseph Haynie defaulted on their taxes, in 1873 and 1876, respectively. Thomas J. Barbour of Chattooga County appeared on the county tax digest as "defaulter" in 1875, but this

seems to have been due to a misunderstanding with tax assessors who assessed the value of his land at $500, his personal estate at $400. As a result of his unpaid taxes, his assessment was doubled to $1,800. However, in the next year's tax digest, the assessed value of his land had dropped to $100. For Thomas A. Littlejohn, Joseph Haynie, and Thomas J. Barbour, see Appendix 1. Joseph Standing to Editors, *Deseret News*, October 28, 1878, box 1, book 1, JHM Papers; Steven Hahn, *The Roots of Southern Populism: Yeoman Farmers and the Transformation of the Georgia Upcountry, 1850–1890* (New York: Oxford University Press, 1983); McKinney, "Civil War and Reconstruction," 55.

24. For Thomas Littlejohn and Robert Haynie, see Appendix 1.

25. Arrington and Bitton, *Mormon Experience*, 23; *Atlanta Constitution*, July 28, 1879.

26. John Morgan to Editor, *Deseret News*, January 1877, box 1, book 1, JHM Papers; John Morgan and James T. Lisonbee to Editor, *Deseret News*, June 16, 1877, box 1, book 1, JHM Papers; *Atlanta Constitution*, November 2, 1877.

27. Data based upon 1870 U.S. Federal Census, population schedules. In Catoosa County: 15.55 percent of heads of household were females and possessed 7.16 percent of total wealth in county (real and personal estate); Chattooga County: 19.23 percent possessing 10.06 percent; Fannin County: 13.72 percent possessing 8.35 percent; Floyd County: 17.00 percent possessing 5.62 percent; Polk County: 11.22 percent possessing 4.98 percent; Walker County: 17.35 percent possessing 8.47 percent; Whitfield County: 14.30 percent possessing 6.86 percent. For Sarah Fullbright, see Appendix 1.

28. Henry D. Shapiro, *Appalachia on Our Mind: The Southern Mountains and Mountaineers in the American Consciousness, 1870–1920* (Chapel Hill: University of North Carolina Press, 1978); Allen W. Batteau, *The Invention of Appalachia* (Tucson: University of Arizona Press, 1990); Mary Beth Pudup, Dwight B. Billings, and Altina L. Waller, eds., *Appalachia in the Making: The Mountain South in the Nineteenth Century* (Chapel Hill: University of North Carolina Press, 1995), esp. Billings, Pudup, and Waller, "Taking Exception with Exceptionalism: The Emergence and Transformation of Historical Studies of Appalachia," 2; John Alexander Williams, *Appalachia: A History* (Chapel Hill: University of North Carolina Press, 2002), 201; David C. Hsiung, "Stereotypes," in Straw and Blethen, *High Mountains Rising*, 104; S. Marc Sherrod, "The Southern Mountaineer, Presbyterian Home Missions, and a Synod for Appalachia," *American Presbyterians* 71, no. 1 (1993): 35; Deborah Vansau McCauley, *Appalachian Mountain Religion: A History* (Urbana: University of Illinois Press, 1995), 339; Loyal Jones, *Faith and Meaning in the Southern Uplands* (Urbana: Unversity of Illinois Press, 1999), 4; James C. Klotter, "The Black South and White Appalachia," *Journal of American History* 66, no. 4 (1980): 841; Nina Silber, "'What Does

America Need so Much as Americans?'" Race and Northern Reconciliation with Southern Appalachia, 1870–1900," in Inscoe, *Appalachians and Race*, 245–58.

29. Shapiro, *Appalachia on Our Mind*, 146; Sherrod, "Southern Mountaineer," 31–40.

30. Price, "Mormon Missionary," 240; Wallace Stegner, *The Gathering of Zion: The Story of the Mormon Trail* (Lincoln: University of Nebraska Press, 1981); Arrington and Bitton, *Mormon Experience*, 38; William Mulder, "Mormonism's 'Gathering': An American Doctrine with a Difference," *Church History* 23, no. 3 (September 1954): 248–64.

CHAPTER 3. "One by One They Leave Us":
The First Expedition of Georgians to the West

1. *Atlanta Constitution*, February 15, 1874 to April 5, 1874. No name, real or pseudonym, is ever given for the author; instead, he or she is identified as the author of other works, including "Dreaming," "Prison Life," "The Fatal Clue," "At Sea," and "The Night March."

2. Ibid.

3. Ibid.

4. *Atlanta Constitution*, December 6, 1871.

5. *Atlanta Constitution*, January 4, January 7, 1874.

6. *Atlanta Constitution*, May 25, 1877.

7. JHM Journal, May 7, 1877; Lisonbee Diary, March 27, 1877 to April 23, 1877; Garth N. Jones, *James Thompson Lisonbee's Missionary Labors on the Sand Mountain of Northeastern Alabama and Northwestern Georgia: Beginning of a New Gathering in the San Luis Valley of Colorado, 1876–1878* (Provo, Utah: Brigham Young University Press, 2000), 45, 51–53; Typed Version of John Morgan's Journal in Third Person, box 4, folder 2, p. 11, John Hamilton Morgan Papers, Accn 1465, Manuscript Division, Marriott Library, University of Utah, Salt Lake City (hereafter cited as JHM Papers); Arthur M. Richardson and Nicholas G. Morgan, *The Life and Ministry of John Morgan* (privately printed, 1965), 124; Rex Thomas Price, "The Mormon Missionary of the Nineteenth Century" (Ph.D. diss., University of Wisconsin–Madison, 1991), 66, 419, 447–50.

8. Richardson and Morgan, *Life and Ministry*, 130–31; Jones, *James Thompson Lisonbee's Missionary Labors*, 52. For Mormon conversion of Native Americans, see Leonard J. Arrington and Davis Bitton, *The Mormon Experience: A History of the Latter-day Saints* (Urbana: University of Illinois Press, 1992), 14, 323; Steve Pavlik, "Of Saints and Lamanites: An Analysis of Navajo Mormonism," *Wicazo Sa Review* 8 (Spring 1992): 21–30. Southern States missionaries proselytized among members of the Cherokee tribe in North Carolina with very little success; however, they fared much better among the Catawba Indians of South Carolina. For the conversion of the

Catawbas, see Daniel Liestman, "'We Have Found What We Have Been Looking For!' The Creation of the Mormon Religious Enclave among the Catawba, 1883–1920," *South Carolina Historical Magazine* 103 (July 2002): 226–46; Jerry D. Lee, "A Study of the Influence of the Mormon Church on the Catawba Indians of South Carolina, 1882–1975" (master's thesis, Brigham Young University, 1976); James H. Merrell, *The Indians' New World: Catawbas and Their Neighbors from European Contact through the Era of Removal* (Chapel Hill: University of North Carolina Press, 1989); Charles M. Hudson, *The Catawba Nation* (Athens: University of Georgia Press, 1970).

9. JHM Journal, June 28, 1877, August 27, 1877, October 22, 1877, October 23, 1877, October 24, 1877; Typed Version of John Morgan's Journal, box 4, folder 3, p. 114, JHM Papers; Jones, *James Thompson Lisonbee's Missionary Labors*, 53–54. Applying pressure to transportation companies to raise fares and thus discourage emigration was not unique to Georgia. In his work on black Exodusters in the late 1870s, Robert G. Athearn writes that riverboat lines were "urged to make passenger rates so high that the migrating blacks could not afford to book passage." See Athearn, *In Search of Canaan: Black Migration to Kansas, 1879–1880* (Lawrence: Regents Press of Kansas, 1978), and Nell Irvin Painter, *Exodusters: Black Migration to Kansas after Reconstruction* (New York: Knopf, 1977).

10. Richardson and Morgan, *Life and Ministry*, 129, 138–39; Typed Version of John Morgan's Journal, box 4, folder 3, pp. 114–15, JHM Papers; Jones, *James Thompson Lisonbee's Missionary Labors*, 58–59.

11. Richardson and Morgan, *Life and Ministry*, 136; Typed Version of John Morgan's Journal, box 4, folder 3, pp. 114–15; Lisonbee Diary, October 6, 1877, October 7, 1877, JHM Papers; Arrington and Bitton, *Mormon Experience*, 180. News of Brigham Young's death, due to complications from a ruptured appendix, did not reach Morgan until September 13, 1877, more than two weeks after Young's passing. See JHM Journal, September 13, 1877.

12. Minutes of the Semi-Annual Conference of the Saints of North Georgia and Alabama at Haywood Valley, Georgia, October 6, 1877, box 1, book 1, JHM Papers; Lisonbee Diary, November 12, 1877, November 14, 1877; Jones, *James Thompson Lisonbee's Missionary Labors*, 61–65.

13. Richardson and Morgan, *Life and Ministry*, 138–39, 144; Jones, *James Thompson Lisonbee's Missionary Labors*, 58. According to Mormon historians Arrington and Bitton, after Young's death "leadership then reverted to the Quorum of the Twelve, presided over by John Taylor, senior apostle." Taylor was held in special regard by Latter-day Saints because he was visiting with Joseph Smith in the Carthage jail when Smith was attacked by a mob and murdered. Taylor was severely injured in the attack. See Arrington and Bitton, *Mormon Experience*, 81, 180, 182. Taylor was sustained as president of the church in 1880. See "General Authorities of the Church," box 3, folder 26, JHM Papers.

14. Converts of Elder John Morgan in North Georgia during His First Mission in 1876, box 3, folder 3, JHM Papers; Conferences Established by John Morgan in the Organization of the Southern States Mission, box 3, folder 5, JHM Papers; Nicholas G. Morgan, "Mormon Colonization in the San Luis Valley," *Colorado Magazine* 27 (October 1950): 269-93; Lisonbee Diary, November 9, 1877; Jones, *James Thompson Lisonbee's Missionary Labors*, 62-63, 66, 83. For Felix Burnie Moyers, Elias Dennington, Joseph Pickney Haynie, Patrick Calhoun Haynie, Francis Marion Weldon, William L. Marshal, and the Bagwell family, see Appendix 1.

15. "Latter-day Saint Settlements in San Luis Valley," Manassa Colorado Stake, Manuscript History and Historical Reports, microfilm, LDS Church Archives, Salt Lake City.

16. JHM Journal, October 18, 1877; Lisonbee Diary, October 12, 1877, October 18, 1877, October 24, 1877, October 31, 1877, November 7, 1877; Jones, *James Thompson Lisonbee's Missionary Labors*, 64.

17. Lisonbee Diary, November 15, 1877; Jones, *James Thompson Lisonbee's Missionary Labors*, 65-66.

18. Lisonbee Diary, November 16, 1877, November 17, 1877; Jones, *James Thompson Lisonbee's Missionary Labors*, 66-67.

19. JHM Journal, November 17, 1877, November 18, 1877, November 19, 1877, November 20, 1877; Richardson and Morgan, *Life and Ministry*, 140; Jones, *James Thompson Lisonbee's Missionary Labors*, 67-68.

20. JHM Journal, November 21, 1877, November 22, 1877, November 23, 1877; Richardson and Morgan, *Life and Ministry*, 140; Jones, *James Thompson Lisonbee's Missionary Labors*, 69.

21. JHM Journal, November 24, 1877, November 25, 1877; Richardson and Morgan, *Life and Ministry*, 140.

22. JHM Journal, November 26, 1877; John Morgan to Editors, *Salt Lake Herald*, March 13, 1878, box 1, book 1, JHM Papers; Richardson and Morgan, *Life and Ministry*, 143; Ione Miller, "Mormon Emigrants Spend the Winter of 1877-78 in Pueblo," Pueblo County Historical Society, September 2001, retrieved from www.pueblohistory.org.

23. John Morgan to Church President John Taylor, November 27, 1877, box 1, book 1, JHM Papers; Jones, *James Thompson Lisonbee's Missionary Labors*, 69-70. For typical wages earned in Georgia, see 1870 U.S. Federal Census, Social Statistics Schedules for Whitfield, Floyd, Walker, Chattooga, and Catoosa Counties, Georgia; Robert S. Baker, *Chattooga: The Story of a County and Its People* (privately published, 1988), 430.

24. Arrington and Bitton, *Mormon Experience*, 126; Leonard J. Arrington, Feramorz Y. Fox, and Dean L. May, *Building the City of God: Community and Cooperation among the Mormons* (Salt Lake City: Deseret Book Company, 1976); Jones, *James Thompson Lisonbee's Missionary Labors*, 13-19.

25. JHM Journal, November 26, 1877; "Latter-day Saint Settlements in San Luis Valley"; Arrington and Bitton, *Mormon Experience*, 126.

26. JHM Journal, November 28, 1877, November 29, 1877; John Morgan to John Taylor, November 27, 1877, box 1, book 1, JHM Papers; "Latter-day Saints in San Luis Valley," Manassa Colorado Stake, LDS Church Archives.

27. JHM Journal, December 1, 1877, December 3, 1877, December 4, 1877; Jones, *James Thompson Lisonbee's Missionary Labors*, 86; Morgan, "Mormon Colonization," 275–76; Richardson and Morgan, *Life and Ministry*, 144.

28. JHM Journal, December 5, 1877, December 7, 1877; John Morgan to John Taylor, November 27, 1877, box 1, book 1, JHM Papers; Miller, "Mormon Emigrants"; Jones, *James Thompson Lisonbee's Missionary Labors*, 54, 72; Richardson and Morgan, *Life and Ministry*, 147–48.

29. JHM Journal, December 17, 1877, December 19, 1877, December 26–31, 1877; "Returned Missionary," in *Deseret News*, undated, box 1, book 1, JHM Papers; Richardson and Morgan, *Life and Ministry*, 149, 151; Jones, *James Thompson Lisonbee's Missionary Labors*, 75.

30. JHM Journal, February 16, 1878; "Latter-day Saints in San Luis Valley"; Jones, *James Thompson Lisonbee's Missionary Labors*, 75.

31. "Latter-day Saints in San Luis Valley"; Jones, *James Thompson Lisonbee's Missionary Labors*, 76; Carleton Q. Anderson, Betty Shawcroft, and Robert Compton, eds., *The Mormons: 100 Years in the San Luis Valley of Colorado, 1883–1983* (La Jara Stake of the Church of Jesus Christ of Latter-day Saints, privately printed, 1982), 6; Judson Harold Flower Jr., "Mormon Colonization of the San Luis Valley, Colorado, 1878–1900" (master's thesis, Brigham Young University, 1966), 23, 25.

32. John Morgan to John Taylor, March 8, 1878, box 2, folder 2, JHM Papers; Richardson and Morgan, *Life and Ministry*, 152.

33. John Morgan to John Taylor, March 8, 1878, box 2, folder 2, JHM Papers; John Morgan to Editors, *Deseret News*, March 18, 1878, quoted in Richardson and Morgan, *Life and Ministry*, 154.

34. Jones, *James Thompson Lisonbee's Missionary Labors*, 73, 80; William Lonzo Kaneaster, "The Martyrdom of Joseph Standing—July 21, 1879," *Whitfield-Murray Historical Society Quarterly*, Winter 1996.

35. JHM Journal, March 12, 1878; John Morgan to Editors, *Salt Lake Herald*, March 13, 1878, box 1, book 1, JHM Papers; "Riding the Denver and Rio Grande Railroad in 1878; Climbing to the Clouds on the Narrow Gauge; The Veta Pass—Highest Railway Station in the World," box 2, folder 15, JHM Papers; Richardson and Morgan, *Life and Ministry*, 155–58; Jones, *James Thompson Lisonbee's Missionary Labors*, 76.

36. John Morgan to Editors, *Salt Lake Herald*, March 13, 1878, box 1, book 1, JHM Papers; "Riding the Denver and Rio Grande Railroad in 1878," box 2, folder 15, JHM Papers. Garland City, where Morgan and Sellers met with former governor Hunt, is variously referred to in documents as Garland, Garland City, and Fort Garland.

37. John Morgan to John Taylor, March 14, 1878, box 2, folder 2, JHM Papers; John Morgan to John Taylor, March 22, 1878, box 2, folder 2, JHM Papers; JHM Journal, March 13, 1878, March 22, 1878; Richardson and Morgan, *Life and Ministry*, 158–60.

38. John Morgan to John Taylor, April 2, 1878, box 2, folder 2, JHM Papers; JHM Journal, March 24, 1878, March 25, 1878; "Latter-day Saint Settlements in San Luis Valley"; Richardson and Morgan, *Life and Ministry*, 163.

39. JHM Journal, March 16, 1878, March 17, 1878, March 18, 1878, March 25, 1878, March 27, 1878; "Latter-day Saint Settlements in San Luis Valley"; Richardson and Morgan, *Life and Ministry*, 163, 166–67.

40. James Z. Stewart to John Taylor, May 24, 1878, box 1, book 1, JHM Papers; James Z. Stewart to John Taylor, August 1, 1878, box 1, book 1, JHM Papers; James Z. Stewart to John Taylor, quoted in Richardson and Morgan, *Life and Ministry*, 163; "Latter-day Saint Settlements in San Luis Valley"; Jones, *James Thompson Lisonbee's Missionary Labors*, 76–77. According to church documents, the church later paid both of Stewart's notes.

41. John Taylor to John Morgan, July 19, 1878, box 2, folder 13, JHM Papers; John Morgan to John Taylor, August 15, 1878, box 2, folder 2, JHM Papers.

42. "Reflections on Manassa," box 3, folder 18, JHM Papers; Flower, "Mormon Colonization," 34.

43. Flower, "Mormon Colonization," 34, 36–38, 41–42.

44. D. R. Sellers to James Z. Stewart, July 25, 1878, box 1, book 1, JHM Papers.

45. Flower, "Mormon Colonization," 42–43.

46. Ibid., 43.

CHAPTER 4. "Women Is the Only Subject to Be Talked On": Threats of Violence in North Georgia

1. The RLDS is now the Community of Christ, headquartered in Independence, Missouri. Typescript of John Morgan's Journal, November 1875–November 1892, entries dated January 29–31, 1878, John Hamilton Morgan Papers, Accn 1465, Manuscript Division, Marriott Library, University of Utah, Salt Lake City (hereafter cited as JHM Papers); Roger D. Launius, *Joseph Smith III: Pragmatic Prophet* (Urbana: University of Illinois Press, 1995), 201; Roger D. Launius, *Father Figure: Joseph Smith III and the Creation of the Reorganized Church* (Independence, Mo.: Herald Publishing House, 1990); Roger D. Launius, "Methods and Motives: Joseph Smith III's Opposition to Polygamy, 1860–1890," *Dialogue* 20, no. 4 (1987): 108; Lisonbee Diary, November 4, 1877, box 6, folder 8, JHM Papers.

2. John Morgan's Journal, March 20, 1878, April 14, 1878, May 1, 1878, JHM Papers.

3. Quoted in Patrick Q. Mason, *The Mormon Menace: Violence and Anti-Mormonism in the Postbellum South* (New York: Oxford University Press, 2011), 69.

4. Volume 1, Letters and Articles on the Missionary Labors of Pres. John Morgan, box 1, book 1, JHM Papers.

5. Ibid.

6. John Morgan's Journal, November 22, 1878, JHM Papers; "Southern States Mission History from October 1875 to December 1904," box 3, folders 8 and 9, JHM Papers; John Morgan to Church President John Taylor, May 8, 1878, box 2, folder 2, JHM Papers.

7. John Morgan to Church President John Taylor, May 8, 1878, box 2, folder 2, JHM Papers.

8. John Morgan's Journal, June 23, 1877, October 1, 1877, October 5, 1877, November 14, 1877, JHM Papers; Garth N. Jones, *James Thompson Lisonbee's Missionary Labors on the Sand Mountain of Northeastern Alabama and Northwestern Georgia: Beginning of a New Gathering in the San Luis Valley of Colorado, 1876–1878* (Provo: Brigham Young University Press, 2000), 61; Arthur M. Richardson and Nicholas G. Morgan, *The Life and Ministry of John Morgan* (privately printed, 1965), 132–35.

9. Robert S. Baker, *Chattooga: The Story of a County and Its People* (privately published, 1988), 365–66; James Alfred Sartain, *History of Walker County Georgia* (privately published, 1972), 120–21; Gordon B. McKinney, "The Civil War and Reconstruction," in *High Mountains Rising: Appalachia in Time and Place*, ed. Richard A. Straw and H. Tyler Blethen (Urbana: University of Illinois Press, 2004), 52; Jonathan D. Sarris, "Anatomy of an Atrocity: The Madden Branch Massacre and Guerrilla Warfare in North Georgia, 1861–1865," *Georgia Historical Quarterly* 77 (Winter 1993): 679–710; Keith S. Bohannon, "'They Had Determined to Root Us Out': Dual Memoirs by a Unionist Couple in Blue Ridge Georgia," in *Enemies of the Country: New Perspectives on Unionists in the Civil War South*, ed. John C. Inscoe and Robert C. Kenzer (Athens: University of Georgia Press, 2001), 97–120; Jonathan D. Sarris, "'Shot for Being Bushwhackers': Guerrilla War and Extralegal Violence in a North Georgia Community, 1862–1865," in *Guerrillas, Unionists, and Violence on the Confederate Home Front*, ed. Daniel E. Sutherland (Fayetteville: University of Arkansas Press, 1999); John C. Inscoe and Gordon B. McKinney, *The Heart of Confederate Appalachia: Western North Carolina in the Civil War* (Chapel Hill: University of North Carolina Press, 2000); Sean Michael O'Brien, *Mountain Partisans: Guerrilla Warfare in the Southern Appalachians, 1861–1865* (Westport, CT: Praeger, 1999).

10. Baker, *Chattooga*, 365–66; Sartain, *History of Walker County*, 120–21; U.S. Congress Joint Select Committee, *Testimony Taken by the Joint Select Committee to Inquire into the Condition of Affairs in the Late*

Insurrectionary States: Georgia (Washington, D.C.: Government Printing Office, 1872), vol. 2; Kenneth Coleman, ed., *A History of Georgia*, 2nd ed. (Athens: University of Georgia Press, 1991), 214–17; Allen W. Trelease, *White Terror: The Ku Klux Klan Conspiracy and Southern Reconstruction* (Baton Rouge: Louisiana State University Press, 1999); George C. Rable, *But There Was No Peace: The Role of Violence in the Politics of Reconstruction* (Athens: University of Georgia Press, 1984); *Atlanta Constitution*, February 13, 15, 18, 20, 21, March 11, May 6, 8, 9, 13, 19, 20, 1877; Edward L. Ayers, *The Promise of the New South: Life after Reconstruction* (New York: Oxford University Press, 1992), 155; C. Vann Woodward, *Origins of the New South, 1877–1913* (Baton Rouge: Louisiana State University Press, 1997).

11. "Returned Missionary," n.d., box 1, book 1, JHM Papers; "Leaf from an Elder's Journal," box 4, folder 3, JHM Papers; John Morgan, "Leaf from an Elder's Journal," *Juvenile Instructor* 13, no. 2 (1878): 22.

12. John Morgan's Journal, May 3, 1878, May 5, 1878, May 23, 1878, September 8, 1878, September 10, 1878, JHM Papers.

13. Cowley later became a member of the Quorum of the Twelve Apostles, second only to the First Presidency in authority. He was removed in 1905 due to his continued adherence to plural marriage. John Morgan to Church President John Taylor, May 8, 1878, box 2, folder 2, JHM Papers; John Morgan's Journal, February 18–23, April 18, May 2, 1878, JHM Papers; Richardson and Morgan, *Life and Ministry*, 150–51.

14. John Morgan to Editors, *Deseret News*, January 4, 1879, box 1, book 1, JHM Papers.

15. John Morgan to Church President John Taylor, May 8, 1878, box 2, folder 2, JHM Papers; Minutes of the Southern States Conference, held in Haywood Valley, North Georgia, August 9, 10, and 11, 1878, box 1, book 1, JHM Papers; John Morgan's Journal, June 24, 1878, JHM Papers.

16. Minutes of the Southern States Conference, JHM Papers; Jill Mulvay Derr, Janath Russell Cannon, and Maureen Ursenbach Beecher, *Women of Covenant: The Story of Relief Society* (Provo, Utah: Brigham Young University Press, 1992).

17. Historian Jean Friedman, in her study of Georgia and North Carolina church populations, described a nineteenth-century evangelical culture that linked women in neighborhood kinship groups and discouraged the formation of independent women's networks. Just as church membership reinforced kin connections, male domination also discouraged the formation of independent women's groups within the church structure, which "tended to conserve traditional racist and sexist hierarchies." Jean E. Friedman, *The Enclosed Garden: Women and Community in the Evangelical South, 1830–1900* (Chapel Hill: University of North Carolina Press, 1985), 116; Jones, *James Thompson Lisonbee's Missionary Labors*, 63; John Morgan's Journal, January 2, 1879, JHM Papers.

18. Jones, *James Thompson Lisonbee's Missionary Labors*, 50; JHM Journal, May 29, 1877, September 19–28, 1877.

19. Minutes of the Southern States Conference, JHM Papers; John Morgan to Elder Matthias Cowley, August 23, 1878, box 1, folder 17, JHM Papers.

20. John Morgan's Journal, May 28, 1878, JHM Papers; untitled document, box 1, book 1, p. 124, JHM Papers; "Death of a Genuine Gentleman," *Deseret News*, August 27, 1884, box 3, folder 20, JHM Papers; John Morgan to Editors, *Deseret News*, October 3, 1878, box 1, book 1, JHM Papers. For Nathaniel Connally, see also Appendix 1.

21. John Morgan to Editors, *Salt Lake Herald*, August 23, 1878, box 1, book 1, JHM Papers; John Morgan to Editors, *Deseret News*, October 3, 1878, box 1, book 1, JHM Papers.

22. John Morgan to Church President John Taylor, November 16, 1878, box 2, folder 3, JHM Papers.

23. John Morgan's Journal, September 13, 1878, September 15, 1878, September 17, 1878, JHM Papers; for the Elledge, Huffaker, and Williams families, see Appendix 1.

24. John Morgan's Journal, October 7, 1878, JHM Papers; for John Nations, see Appendix 1.

25. William Lonzo Kaneaster, "The Martyrdom of Joseph Standing—July 21, 1879," *Whitfield-Murray Historical Society Quarterly* 15, no. 2 (1996): 3–6; for the Fullbright, Hamblin, and Kaneaster families, see Appendix 1.

26. Kaneaster, "Martyrdom of Joseph Standing," 3–6.

27. Susie Blaylock McDaniel, *Official History of Catoosa County, Georgia, 1853–1953* (privately printed, 1953), 140.

28. Quoted in Mary Ella Engel, "The Appalachian 'Granny': Testing the Boundaries of Female Power in Late-19th-Century Appalachian Georgia," *Appalachian Journal* 37 (Spring/Summer 2010): 210.

29. Joseph Standing to Editors, *Deseret News*, January 2, 1879, box 6, folder 5, JHM Papers; *Journal History*, LDS Church Archives; "D" Deed Record Book, Catoosa County, Georgia, p. 767, Catoosa County Courthouse, Ringgold, Ga.; Ellen Keith Thompson, "At Last the Truth: Ancestor Perishes on Way to California Gold Fields," *Whitfield-Murray Historical Society Quarterly* 21, no. 1 (2002): 15; 1850 U.S. Federal Census, Murray County, Georgia, M432_78, 208; Individual Record, AFN: 3FPZ-3N.

30. John Morgan's Journal, July 24, 1877, November 15, 1877, JHM Papers; for the Faucett and Haggard families, see Appendix 1.

31. Jones, *James Thompson Lisonbee's Missionary Labors*, 57.

32. Joseph Standing to Matthias Cowley, December 22, 1878, box 6, folder 5, JHM Papers; Joseph Standing to Editors, *Deseret News*, January 2, 1879, JHM Papers; *Journal History*, LDS Church Archives; Joseph Standing to Matthias Cowley, January 7, 1879, box 1, book 1, JHM Papers.

33. Joseph Standing to Matthias Cowley, October 18, 1878, November 30, 1878, box 6, folder 5, JHM Papers; Joseph Standing to Editors, *Deseret News*, January 2, 1879, JHM Papers; *Journal History*, LDS Church Archives.

34. Joseph Standing to Matthias Cowley, November 30, 1878, box 6, folder 5, JHM Papers; Joseph Standing to Matthias Cowley, December 22, 1878, box 6, folder 5, JHM Papers; Joseph Standing to Editors, *Deseret News*, January 2, 1879, JHM Papers; *Journal History*, LDS Church Archives.

35. John Morgan to Editors, *Deseret News*, January 4, 1879, box 1, book 1, JHM Papers; John Morgan to Church President John Taylor, January 11, 1879, box 2, folder 3, JHM Papers; John Morgan's Journal, January 16, 1879, January 23-24, 1879, February 6, 1879, March 4, 1879, March 7, 1879, March 9, 1879, JHM Papers; Joseph Hyrum Parry, "Missionary Experience and Incidents in the Life of Joseph Hyrum Parry," www.welshmormonhistory.org.

36. Parry, "Missionary Experience"; John Morgan's Journal, March 11, 1879, March 15, 1879, JHM Papers; John Morgan to Editors, *Deseret News*, March 17, 1879, JHM Papers; *Journal History*, LDS Church Archives; Joseph Standing to Matthias Cowley, March 31, 1879, box 6, folder 5, JHM Papers.

37. John Morgan's Journal, March 19, 1879, JHM Papers; Parry, "Missionary Experience"; John Morgan to Church President John Taylor, March 15, 1879, box 2, folder 3, JHM Papers.

38. John Morgan's Journal, March 24, 1879; "E" Deed Record Book, Catoosa County, Georgia, p. 160, Catoosa County Courthouse, Ringgold, Ga.; 1877 and 1878 Catoosa County Tax Digest, Georgia Department of Archives and History Morrow, Ga. (hereafter cited as GDAH).

39. *Atlanta Constitution*, January 18, January 24, 1879, January 25-26, 1879, January 28-30, 1879, February 1, 1879, February 11-15, 1879, February 21, 1879, February 26, 1879, JHM Papers; *North Georgia Citizen*, February 20, 1879; Joseph Standing to Editors, *Deseret News*, March 26, 1879, *Journal History*, LDS Church Archives.

40. Joseph Standing to Editors, *Deseret News*, March 26, 1879, *Journal History*, LDS Church Archives; Joseph Standing to Matthias Cowley, March 31, 1879, box 6, folder 5, JHM Papers; for the Loggins family, see Appendix 1.

41. Joseph Standing to Editors, *Deseret News*, March 26, 1879, *Journal History*, LDS Church Archives; Joseph Standing to Matthias Cowley, March 31, 1879, box 6, folder 5, JHM Papers.

42. Joseph Standing to Editors, *Deseret News*, March 26, 1879, *Journal History*, LDS Church Archives; Joseph Standing to Editors, *Deseret News*, June 2, 1879, *Journal History*, LDS Church Archives.

43. Joseph Standing to Editors, *Deseret News*, June 2, 1879, *Journal History*, LDS Church Archives; Joseph Standing to Matthias Cowley, April 23, 1879, box 6, folder 5, JHM Papers.

44. Kaneaster, "Martyrdom of Joseph Standing," 3-6.

45. "Memoirs of the Life of Rudger Clawson, Written by Himself," box 1, folder 1, p. 32, Rudger Clawson Papers, MS 481, Manuscripts Division, Marriott Library, University of Utah, Salt Lake City.

46. "Memoirs of the Life of Rudger Clawson," 16; Andrew Jensen, *Latter-day Saint Biographical Encyclopedia: A Compilation of Biographical Sketches of Prominent Men and Women in the Church of Jesus Christ of Latter-day Saints*, vol. 1 (Salt Lake City: Publishers Press, 1971), 719–21, 174–78; for Joseph Standing, see Individual Record, AFN: 277V-QM; 1870 U.S. Federal Census, Salt Lake City Ward 12, Salt Lake, Utah Territory, M593_1611, 624; 1860 U.S. Federal Census, Salt Lake City Ward 12, Salt Lake, Utah Territory, M653_1313, 157; 1850 U.S. Federal Census, Great Salt Lake, Utah Territory, M432_919, 87; for Rudger Judd Clawson, see Individual Record, AFN: 17WN-2D; 1860 U.S. Federal Census, Salt Lake City, Ward 18, Great Salt Lake, Utah Territory, M653_1313, 270; 1870 U.S. Federal Census, Salt Lake City Ward 12, Salt Lake, Utah Territory, M593_1611, 623.

47. "Memoirs of the Life of Rudger Clawson," 33–34.

48. Ibid., 35; *Atlanta Constitution*, May 15, 1875, July 26, 1876, September 12, 1876, September 17, 1876, September 23, 1876, March 23–24, 1877, March 31, 1877, May 6, 1877, May 16, 1877, June 3, 1877, June 9, 1877, July 14, 1877, September 25, 1877, October 19, 1877, August 27, 1878, November 1, 1878, November 6, 1878, November 8, 1878, November 14, 1878, January 10, 1879, January 18, 1879, January 26, 1879, March 1, 1879, March 31, 1879, June 15, 1879; Sarah Barringer Gordon, *The Mormon Question: Polygamy and Constitutional Conflict in Nineteenth Century America* (Chapel Hill: University of North Carolina Press, 2002), 112–13, 176; Ann Eliza Young, *Wife No. 19; or, The Story of a Life in Bondage, Being a Complete Expose of Mormonism, and Revealing the Sorrows, Sacrifices and Sufferings of Women in Polygamy* (Hartford, Conn.: Dustin, Gilmore, 1875).

49. *Atlanta Constitution*, April 2, 1879.

50. *North Georgia Citizen*, May 1, 1879; *Atlanta Constitution*, May 15, 1879; *Murray County Gazette*, May 21, 1879.

51. "Memoirs of the Life of Rudger Clawson," 38–42.

52. Joseph Standing to Matthias Cowley, May 29, 1879, box 6, folder 5, JHM Papers; Joseph Standing to Matthias Cowley, June 30, 1879, box 6, folder 5, JHM Papers.

53. Joseph Standing to Editors, *Deseret News*, June 2, 1879, *Journal History*, LDS Church Archives; Kaneaster, "Martyrdom of Joseph Standing," 3–6; for the Stover family, see Appendix 1.

54. Joseph Standing to Governor Alfred Colquitt, June 12, 1879, *Journal History*, LDS Church Archives.

55. Kaneaster, "Martyrdom of Joseph Standing," 3–6.

56. Joseph Standing to Matthias Cowley, June 30, 1879, box 6, folder 5, JHM Papers; *Millennial Star*, August 25, 1879; Parry, "Missionary Experience."

57. Parry, "Missionary Experience."

58. *Millennial Star*, August 25, 1879; *Rome Tri-Weekly Courier*, July 15, 1879; *North Georgia Citizen*, July 17, 1879.

59. Joseph Standing to M. P. Rockwood, July 18, 1879, published in *Deseret News*, August 5, 1879.

60. John Nicholson, *The Martyrdom of Joseph Standing; or, The Murder of a "Mormon" Missionary* (Salt Lake City: Deseret News Company, 1886), 12–13.

CHAPTER 5. "The Day of Grace Is Gone":
The Murder of Joseph Standing

1. This account follows closely two eyewitness accounts, from Georgian William Lonzo Kaneaster and Elder Rudger Clawson. William Lonzo Kaneaster, "The Martyrdom of Joseph Standing—July 21, 1879," *Whitfield-Murray Historical Society Quarterly* 15, no. 2 (1996): 3–6; John Nicholson, *The Martyrdom of Joseph Standing; or, The Murder of a "Mormon" Missionary* (Salt Lake City: Deseret News Company, 1886), 13–14. In 1885 Rudger Clawson related the story of Standing's murder to John Nicholson, who published the eyewitness account in book form. For the most recent examination of Joseph Standing's murder, see Patrick Q. Mason, *The Mormon Menace: Violence and Anti-Mormonism in the Postbellum South* (New York: Oxford University Press, 2011).

2. Kaneaster, "Martyrdom of Joseph Standing," 3–6; Nicholson, *Martyrdom of Joseph Standing*, 13–14; "Memoirs of the Life of Rudger Clawson, Written by Himself," box 1, folder 1, p. 32, Rudger Clawson Papers, MS 481, Manuscripts Division, Marriott Library, University of Utah, Salt Lake City, 32, 44.

3. Kaneaster, "Martyrdom of Joseph Standing," 3–6; Nicholson, *Martyrdom of Joseph Standing*, 15–16.

4. Coroner's Inquest relative to the death of Joseph Standing, July 21, 1879, Whitfield County, Georgia, Superior Court Records, Record Group 255-1-13, box 11, GDAH; Kaneaster, "Martyrdom of Joseph Standing," 3–6; Nicholson, *Martyrdom of Joseph Standing*, 17.

5. Nicholson, *Martyrdom of Joseph Standing*, 17–18.

6. Coroner's Inquest, GDAH; Nicholson, *Martyrdom of Joseph Standing*, 19–21.

7. Nicholson, *Martyrdom of Joseph Standing*, 20–21.

8. *Atlanta Constitution*, August 24, 1879; Nicholson, *Martyrdom of Joseph Standing*, 62. Jasper N. "Newt" Nations, David "Dave" Nations, William "Bill" Nations, and Joseph "Joe" Nations were sons of Manley Nations, the uncle of Elizabeth Elledge. For the Nations family who participated in the mob, see Appendix 2. For John A. Nations, see Appendix 1. On the relationship between Elizabeth's father, Israel Nations, and Manley Nations, see William Henry Harrison Clark, *History in Catoosa*

County (privately printed, 1974), 44. Manley Nations's oldest son, John A. Nations of Varnell's Station—who did not take part in the mob—received Mormon missionaries hospitably and was related to the Huffaker family by marriage.

9. For William Hugh Blair, Andrew "Andy" Bradley, David Smith, and A. S. "Jud" Smith, see Appendix 2; see also Catoosa County Historical Society, *Catoosa County Georgia Heritage, 1853-1998* (privately printed, 1998), 74. William H. Blair was the son of Samuel Blair Jr. and lived near Brittain Williams and mob member Andy Bradley. David Williams, the son of Brittain Williams, married Nancy Blair. Martha Blair, Nancy's sister, also resided with David Williams. For Jefferson "Jeff" Hunter, Mac McClure, James Faucett, and Benjamin Clark, see Appendix 2. See also "Clark Family File," Whitfield-Murray Historical Society, Dalton, Ga.; Catoosa County Historical Society, *Catoosa County Georgia Heritage*, 100. See also Nicholson, *Martyrdom of Joseph Standing*, 19-20, 62; Kaneaster, "Martyrdom of Joseph Standing," 3-6.

10. Nicholson, *Martyrdom of Joseph Standing*, 22-24. For Jonathan Owenby, see Catoosa County Tax Digest, 1872-82.

11. Nicholson, *Martyrdom of Joseph Standing*, 24-25.

12. Ibid., 27-28. According to this account—and it has been repeated many times—Joseph Standing "leaped to his feet with a bound, instantly wheeled so as to face them, brought his two hands together with a sudden slap, and shouted in a loud, clear, resolute voice—'Surrender.'" But in his testimony at the Coroner's Inquest, GDAH, taken only hours after the shooting, Clawson swore that Standing grabbed a pistol belonging to one of the members of the mob. See Coroner's Inquest, GDAH.

13. Nicholson, *Martyrdom of Joseph Standing*, 28-31; *Denver Tribune*, July 31, 1879, printed in *Atlanta Constitution*, August 7, 1879; *Liverpool Mercury*, August 5, 1879.

14. Elder Rudger Clawson's Account, *Deseret News*, August 1, 1879; Nicholson, *Martyrdom of Joseph Standing*, 30-31.

15. Coroner's Inquest, GDAH; Nicholson, *Martyrdom of Joseph Standing*, 31-33, 42.

16. Kaneaster, "Martyrdom of Joseph Standing," 3-6; Nicholson, *Martyrdom of Joseph Standing*, 34-35.

17. Coroner's Inquest, GDAH; Nicholson, *Martyrdom of Joseph Standing*, 42. For coroner Amos Sutherland, see Whitfield-Murray Historical Society, *An Official History of Whitfield County, Georgia, 1852-1999* (privately printed, 1999), 601. For Endymeon H. Martin, see 1850 U.S. Federal Census, Murray County, Georgia, M432_78, 207. In 1850, fourteen-year-old E. H. Martin resided in the household of his father, John S. Martin. See also 1870 U.S. Federal Census, Catoosa County, Georgia, M593_140, 309; Whitfield

County Tax Digest, 1872–73. John S. Martin is listed as agent for Endymeon H. Martin. Interestingly, Standing and Holston sent Kaneaster for E. H. Martin prior to the murder, so he may have served as a local justice of the peace or other authority of the law. He was the son of convert John S. Martin. For Alfred W. Clark, see Civil War Service Record, www.ancestry.com; Catoosa County Historical Society, *Catoosa County, Georgia, Cemeteries and Genealogy* (privately printed, 1998), 675.

18. Nicholson, *Martyrdom of Joseph Standing*, 43–44; Kaneaster, "Martyrdom of Joseph Standing"; *Deseret News*, August 1, 1879.

19. Coroner's Inquest, GDAH; Nicholson, *Martyrdom of Joseph Standing*, 44; *Atlanta Constitution*, July 25, 1879.

20. Nicholson, *Martyrdom of Joseph Standing*, 45–46.

21. Ibid., 47–53.

22. John Morgan, "To the Elders and Saints in the Southern States Mission," *Deseret News*, July 23, 1879; "Minutes of the Georgia Conference Held at Haywood Valley, July 25, 26, 27, 1879," *Deseret News*, August 13, 1879; David Buice, "Excerpts from the Diary of Teancum William Heward, Early Mormon Missionary to Georgia," *Georgia Historical Quarterly* 64 (1980): 318.

23. *Journal History*, July 26, 1879, July 29, 1879, July 31, 1879, LDS Church Archives; John Morgan to Matthias Cowley, July 26, 1879, box 1, folder 17, John Hamilton Morgan Papers, Accn 1465, Manuscript Division, Marriott Library, University of Utah, Salt Lake City (hereafter cited as JHM Papers).

24. *Journal History*, August 3, 1879, LDS Church Archives; Nicholson, *Martyrdom of Joseph Standing*, 53–54; *Atlanta Constitution*, August 7, 1879.

25. *Chicago Times, New York Herald, New Haven Register*, reprinted in *Atlanta Constitution*, July 25, 1879; *New York Herald*, reprinted in *Atlanta Constitution*, July 27, 1879; *Journal History*, July 23, 1879, LDS Church Archives.

26. *North Georgia Citizen*, July 24, 1879; *Atlanta Constitution*, July 25–26, 1879.

27. *Atlanta Constitution*, July 23, 1879, July 26, 1879.

28. *Rome Tri-Weekly Courier*, September 4, 1879.

29. *Rome Tri-Weekly Courier*, August 9, 1879; *North Georgia Citizen*, August 14, 1879; *Journal History*, August 1, 1879, LDS Church Archives.

30. Nicholson, *Martyrdom of Joseph Standing*, 59; Kaneaster, "Martyrdom of Joseph Standing." For Thomas Nations, see Appendix 1. See also Catoosa County Historical Society, *Catoosa County Georgia Heritage*, 215.

31. Kaneaster, "Martyrdom of Joseph Standing."

32. Whitfield County, Georgia, Superior Court Minutes, book 6, 1877–80, Microfilm Library, Drawer 160, box 46, GDAH, Morrow, Ga.; *North Georgia*

Citizen, March 27, 1879; Whitfield-Murray Historical Society, *Official History of Whitfield County*, 92; John Morgan and Rudger Clawson to Editors, *Deseret News*, October 19, 1879.

33. John Morgan to Editors, *Colorado Junction*, undated; *Latter-day Saints' Millennial Star*, August 25, 1879; *Journal History*, July 26, 1879, LDS Church Archives.

34. *Marietta Journal*, August 28, 1879.

35. *Atlanta Constitution*, August 24, 1879.

36. *Gainesville Southron*, reprinted in *Atlanta Constitution*, August 28, 1879; *Atlanta Constitution*, August 5, 1879; *Chattanooga Times*, October 12, 1879.

37. John Morgan to Matthias Cowley, September 30, 1879, box 1, folder 17, JHM Papers; John Morgan to Church President John Taylor, October 2, 1879, box 2, folder 4, JHM Papers.

38. John Morgan's Journal, October 6, 1879; Nicholson, *Martyrdom of Joseph Standing*, 55–58; John Morgan to Church President John Taylor, September 17, 1879, box 2, folder 3, JHM Papers.

39. Kaneaster, "Martyrdom of Joseph Standing," 3–6.

40. John Morgan's Journal, October 8, 1879; John Morgan to Matthias Cowley, October 9, 1879, box 1, folder 17, JHM Papers; Whitfield County, Georgia, Superior Court Minutes, GDAH; Nicholson, *Martyrdom of Joseph Standing*, 62.

41. Whitfield County, Georgia, Superior Court Minutes, GDAH; Nicholson, *Martyrdom of Joseph Standing*, 63.

42. *Atlanta Constitution*, October 23, 1879; Whitfield County, Georgia, Superior Court Minutes, GDAH; *North Georgia Citizen*, January 23, 1879.

43. *Atlanta Constitution*, October 23, 1879; Whitfield County, Georgia, Superior Court Minutes, GDAH; Nicholson, *Martyrdom of Joseph Standing*, 63.

44. *Atlanta Constitution*, October 23, 1879.

45. Nicholson, *Martyrdom of Joseph Standing*, 69–70.

46. Ibid., 70.

47. Ibid., 71–72.

48. John Morgan and Rudger Clawson to Editors, *Deseret News*, October 19, 1879, *Journal History*, LDS Church Archives.

49. Nicholson, *Martyrdom of Joseph Standing*, 73; Ken Driggs, "'There Is No Law in Georgia for Mormons': The Joseph Standing Murder Case of 1879," *Georgia Historical Quarterly* 4 (Winter 1989): 768–69.

50. John Morgan to Editors, *Salt Lake City Herald*, October 19, 1879, box 1, book 1, JHM Papers; John Morgan and Rudger Clawson to Editors, *Deseret News*, October 19, 1879, *Journal History*, LDS Church Archives; Whitfield County, Georgia, Superior Court Minutes, GDAH.

51. Whitfield County, Georgia, Superior Court Minutes, GDAH; *Rome Tri-Weekly Courier*, October 23, 1879; *Atlanta Constitution*, August 3, 1880.

CHAPTER 6. "Think Not When You Gather to Zion, Your Troubles and Trials Are Through": Georgia and the Mormon Question

1. *Baltimore Gazette*, reprinted in *Atlanta Constitution*, July 25, 1879; *Denver Tribune*, reprinted in *Atlanta Constitution*, August 7, 1879.

2. "Missionary Record, 1875–1888, Southern States Mission," box 3, folder 2, John Hamilton Morgan Papers, Accn 1465, Manuscript Division, Marriott Library, University of Utah, Salt Lake City (hereafter cited as JHM Papers); "Record of Elders in the Southern States Mission," Manuscript History, microfilm, LDS Church Archives; *Atlanta Constitution*, August 5, 1879, October 31, 1879.

3. For the Kaneaster family, see Appendix 1. See also Whitfield-Murray Historical Society, *Whitfield County, Georgia Marriages, 1852–1894* (privately printed, undated), 35; Whitfield-Murray Historical Society, *An Official History of Whitfield County, Georgia, 1852–1999* (privately printed, 1999), 391–92; "J" Deed Record Book, Whitfield County, p. 149, Whitfield County Courthouse, Dalton, Ga.; "Sylvanus Kaneaster Will," in Joseph Standing Murder File, Whitfield-Murray Historical Society, Dalton, Ga.

4. John Morgan to Matthias Cowley, March 29, 1880, JHM Papers; Judson Harold Flower Jr., "Mormon Colonization of the San Luis Valley, Colorado, 1878–1900" (master's thesis, Brigham Young University, 1966), 49–57; Carleton Q. Anderson, Betty Shawcroft, and Robert Compton, *The Mormons: 100 Years in the San Luis Valley of Colorado, 1883–1983* (La Jara Stake of the Church of Jesus Christ of Latter-day Saints, privately printed, 1982), 125.

5. Flower, "Mormon Colonization," 56–68; Anderson, Shawcroft, and Compton, *Mormons: 100 Years*, 32, 95, 185–97; 1880 U.S. Federal Census, Manassa, Conejos County, Colorado, T9_89, pp. 167–69; "Records of Old Manassa Cemetery, Manassa, Conejos, Colorado," available online, https://coloradogravestones.org/cemetery.php?cemID=284 (records were originally posted at ftp.rootsweb.com, which is no longer active); "Name and Head of Families Living in Manassa, April 1888, Also Block Number on Which Each Family Lived," author unknown, box 3, folder 18, JHM Papers; "Heads of Families Who Belonged to the Manassa Colony, April 1888, and Was Living on Farms in the Manassa Vicinity," author unknown, box 3, folder 18, JHM Papers; William Lonzo Kaneaster, "The Martyrdom of Joseph Standing—July 21, 1879," *Whitfield-Murray Historical Society Quarterly* 15, no. 2 (1996): 3–6. For Sarah Fullbright, Elizabeth Hamblin, Sarah Kaneaster, Joseph Kaneaster, Isaac Asbury Huffaker, Henry Huffaker, Thomas Barbour, John J. Barbour, Susannah Barbour, Thomas

J. Barbour, and James E. Allen, see Appendix 1. Dollie Bailey to Matthias Cowley, March 28, 1882, box 6, folder 5, JHM Papers; John Morgan's Journal, August 29, 1879, JHM Papers; John Morgan and S. C. Berthelsen to Church President John Taylor, September 3, 1879, box 2, folder 3, JHM Papers; John Morgan to Matthias Cowley, December 4, 1879, box 1, folder 17, JHM Papers; John Morgan to Matthias Cowley, November 13, 1880, box 1, folder 17, JHM Papers; John Morgan to Matthias Cowley, March 4, 1881, box 1, folder 17, JHM Papers; John Morgan to Church President John Taylor, December 9, 1885, box 2, folder 9, JHM Papers; Leonard J. Arrington, "Mormon Beginnings in the American South" (Task Paper in LDS History no. 9; Salt Lake City: Historical Department of the Church of Jesus Christ of Latter-day Saints, 1976), 15; Garth N. Jones, *James Thompson Lisonbee's Missionary Labors on the Sand Mountain of Northeastern Alabama and Northwestern Georgia: Beginning a New Gathering in the San Luis Valley of Colorado, 1876–1878* (Provo: Brigham Young University Press, 2000), 78; *Cincinnati Enquirer*, February 8, 1884.

6. See Appendix 1 and Appendix 2; 1880 U.S. Federal Census, Manassa, Conejos County, Colorado, T9_89, pp. 167–69.

7. *Atlanta Constitution*, May 16, 1880, October 28, 1880.

8. *Atlanta Constitution*, July 15, 1881, July 20, 1881, July 27, 1881, July 28, 1881.

9. John Morgan to Church President John Taylor, May 12, 1881, box 2, folder 5, JHM Papers; *Atlanta Constitution*, July 27, 1881, August 12, 1881.

10. *Atlanta Constitution*, August 13, 1881, August 18, 1881; Flower, "Mormon Colonization," 53.

11. *Atlanta Constitution*, August 21, 1881, September 3, 1881.

12. John Morgan to Church President John Taylor, October 21, 1881, box 2, folder 5, JHM Papers; John Morgan to Church President John Taylor, September 30, 1881, box 2, folder 5, JHM Papers; Church President John Taylor to Matthias Cowley, September 6, 1881, JHM Papers; *St. Louis Post-Dispatch*, reprinted in *Atlanta Constitution*, September 14, 1881.

13. *Atlanta Constitution*, March 24, 1882, February 4, 1883, May 31, 1883, November 11, 1883, December 25, 1883, January 31, 1884.

14. *Atlanta Constitution*, February 28, 1884. Joaquin Miller was the pen name of Cincinnatus Heine Miller, a frontiersman and poet who earned the title Poet of the Sierras. In 1877, he wrote a popular anti-Mormon play, *The Danites; or, The Heart of the Sierras*.

15. *Atlanta Constitution*, July 30, 1881, August 13, 1881.

16. *Atlanta Constitution*, November 25, 1881, December 15, 1881, December 27, 1881, February 16, 1882, May 27, 1885; Flower, "Mormon Colonization," 53–54; David Buice, "A Stench in the Nostrils of Honest Men: Southern Democrats and the Edmunds Act of 1882," *Dialogue* 21 (1988): 104–5.

17. Speech of Hon. Joseph E. Brown of Georgia, "The Mormon Question," delivered in the Senate of the United States, February 16, 1882, Georgia Room, Hargrett Rare Book and Manuscript Library, University of Georgia, Athens.

18. Ibid.

19. Ibid.; Buice, "Stench in the Nostrils," 106-12; *Atlanta Constitution*, February 17, 1882, March 15, 1882.

20. Speech of Hon. Joseph E. Brown of Georgia, "The Mormon Question," delivered in the Senate of the United States, January 11, 1884, Georgia Room, Hargrett Rare Book and Manuscript Library, University of Georgia, Athens.

21. Speech of Hon. Joseph E. Brown of Georgia, "Polygamy in Utah and New England Contrasted," delivered in the Senate of the United States, May 27, 1884, Georgia Room, Hargrett Rare Book and Manuscript Library, University of Georgia, Athens.

22. *Savannah News*, reprinted in *Atlanta Constitution*, January 17, 1884; *Douglasville Star*, reprinted in *Atlanta Constitution*, January 24, 1884; *Atlanta Constitution*, January 20, 1884.

23. John Morgan to Church President John Taylor, April 20, 1882, box 2, folder 6, JHM Papers; John Morgan to Church President John Taylor, July 18, 1882, box 2, folder 6, JHM Papers; Brown speeches.

24. *Atlanta Constitution*, April 1, 1883, October 10, 1883, August 14, 1884, August 15, 1884, August 19, 1884, August 26, 1884; JHM Journal, June 14, 1883, August 12, 1884.

25. See Appendix 1; "Echols, Benjamin, 1862-1953, Reminiscences and Journal, 1946-1950," MS 7867, microfilm, Historical Department, LDS Church Archives ("Life of Samuel Echols" begins on p. 121); Flower, "Mormon Colonization," 74.

26. *Atlanta Constitution*, February 10, 1884, February 15, 1884.

27. Ibid.

28. *Atlanta Constitution*, March 21, 1884; *Nashville World*, reprinted in *Atlanta Constitution*, March 23, 1884.

29. Morgan would eventually take Mary Ann Linton as his third wife. John Morgan's Journal, January 9, 1884, January 12, 1884, April 6, 1884, December 21-26, 1884, November 24, 1885, December 30, 1885, JHM Papers; John Morgan to Matthias Cowley, February 9, 1888, box 1, folder 17, JHM Papers; John Morgan to Church President John Taylor, October 21, 1886, box 2, folder 10, JHM Papers; Flower, "Mormon Colonization," 123.

30. John Morgan to Church President John Taylor, September 2, 1885, box 2, folder 8, JHM Papers; Ronald Walker, "A Mormon 'Widow' in Colorado: The Exile of Emily Wells Grant," *Arizona and the West* 25 (1983): 5-22; Flower, "Mormon Colonization," 90; Rex Thomas Price, "The

Mormon Missionary of the Nineteenth Century" (Ph.D. diss., University of Wisconsin-Madison, 1991), 116.

31. Clawson received a pardon from President Grover Cleveland in 1887. He became a member of the Quorum of the Twelve Apostles in 1898 and in 1921 became president of that body, making him next in line to become president of the church. He died in 1943. John Nicholson, *The Martyrdom of Joseph Standing; or, The Murder of a "Mormon" Missionary* (Salt Lake City: Deseret News Company, 1886), 7-8; David S. Hoopes and Roy Hoopes, *The Making of a Mormon Apostle: The Story of Rudger Clawson* (Lanham, Md.: Madison Books, 1990); Rudger Clawson, *Prisoner for Polygamy: The Memoirs and Letters of Rudger Clawson at the Utah Territorial Penitentiary, 1884-87*, ed. Stan Larson (Urbana: University of Illinois Press, 1993); *Atlanta Constitution*, October 18, 1884, October 23, 1884, October 26, 1884, November 4, 1884, January 20, 1885, April 28, 1885.

32. John Morgan Journal, January 10, 1886, January 13, 1887, February 19, 1887, April 26, 1887, JHM Papers.

33. John Morgan Journal, January 13, 1892, JHM Papers.

34. John Morgan Journal, September 20, 1892, JHM Papers; Susie Blaylock McDaniel, *Official History of Catoosa County, Georgia, 1853-1953* (privately printed, 1953), 140; Arthur M. Richardson and Nicholas G. Morgan, *The Life and Ministry of John Morgan* (privately printed, 1965), 466; Samuel C. Williams, *General John T. Wilder: Commander of the Lightning Brigade* (Bloomington: Indiana University Press, 1936), 48, 83.

35. Martha B. Crowe, "'A Mission in the Mountains': E. O. Guerrant and Southern Appalachia," *American Presbyterians* 68, no. 1 (1990): 46-54; Edward O. Guerrant, *The Galax Gatherers: The Gospel among the Highlanders*, with a foreword by Mark Huddle (Knoxville: University of Tennessee Press, 2005), 119; Samuel Tyndale Wilson, *The Southern Mountaineers* (New York: Trow Press, 1906).

Conclusion

1. John Nicholson, *The Martyrdom of Joseph Standing; or, The Murder of a "Mormon" Missionary* (Salt Lake City: Deseret News Company, 1886), 25.

2. Italo Calvino, *Invisible Cities* (New York: Harvest Books, 1972), 61-62.

3. Kenneth Coleman, ed., *A History of Georgia*, 2nd ed. (Athens: University of Georgia Press, 1991), 217.

Index

123rd Illinois Infantry, 10–17

African Americans, 29–30, 34
African Methodist Episcopal Church, 32
Allen, Harriett, 163
Allen, James, 163
Allen, James, Jr., 163
Allen, Libby, 163
Allen, Rebecca, 163
Alexander, John T., 142
Andrews Raid, 13
anti-Mormonism: Ku Klux Klan and, 70–71, 74; local disruptions and, 3, 97–98, 101–2, 104–5; Protestant clergy and, 5, 31, 73–75, 85, 115–16; newspapers, national, and, 94–95, 112, 118, 128–29, 133, 144; newspapers, state, and, 95, 113–14, 116, 140–41. *See also* anti-polygamy legislation; *Atlanta Constitution*
anti-polygamy legislation: federal, 137–40, 145, 147; in Georgia, 134–35; in Mississippi, 137; in Tennessee, 137. *See also specific acts*
Appalachia: community studies of, 5, 7; discovery of, 7, 40; exceptionalism of, 5; Protestant missions to, 6–7, 41; religion in, 31–32; reputation for violence of, 2; stereotypes of, 5, 40
Arizona, 46–47, 58
Arminianism, 30
Armuchee Ridges, 12, 27
Armuchee Branch, 24, 50, 161–63, 178
Arp, Bill, 113–14, 134–35, 141
Arrington, Leonard, 2

Atchison, Topeka, and Santa Fe Railroad, 48, 53
Atlanta Campaign, 13, 16, 17, 21
Atlanta Constitution: anti-Mormonism of, 93–95, 113, 132–33, 135–36; on anti-polygamy legislation, 135, 137, 141; Bill Arp in, 113, 134–35; on Cane Creek Massacre, 142; on converts, 4, 94; on economic potential of north Georgia, 27; on emigration, 43–47; on legal proceedings, 120–21, 126; on missionaries, 94, 128–29, 143, 147; on population of north Georgia, 39; on poverty in north Georgia, 35; on religion, 31; on Sherman, 88; on Standing's murder, 112, 114, 116–17
Ayers, Edward, 71–73

Bagwell, Albert Gallatin "Tobe," 50, 56–57, 62, 155, 160
Bagwell, Caroline Cosby, 50–51, 57, 64, 155–56
Bagwell, Henrietta Paralee, 155–56; emigration of, 50, 57, 60; marriage of, 63–64, 162
Bagwell, Margaret (Lawrence), 156
Bagwell, William H., 156, 160
Bailey, Martha Jane (Coxwell), 77, 165
Bailey, Martha Queen Victoria, 165–66
Bailey, Mary Naomi, 165
Bailey, Millard, 77
Bailey, William Dixon, 70–71, 165–66
Baltimore Gazette, 128
baptism, female converts and, 84

Baptists, 30, 66, 105, 116; anti-Mormonism of, 31–32, 80; missions of, 41. *See also* Protestants
Barbour, Elizabeth, 157
Barbour, Gabriel, 23, 156–57
Barbour, Joanna W., 158
Barbour, John J., 49, 156–57, 160; Civil War and, 15; Joseph Smith III and, 66–67, 70
Barbour, Mary Ellen (Powell), 156–57
Barbour, Susan (Pace), 156
Barbour, Susannah, 166
Barbour, Thomas, 35, 50, 156–58, 160–61; baptism of, 22; Unionism of, 14–16
Barbour, Thomas J., 15, 22, 158, 161
Beech Creek Branch, 23–24, 49, 156; members of, 163–64, 169, 178
Berea College, 40
Bible: and Mormon preaching, 19; and slavery, 68
"black beast" stereotype, 117
Blair, Hugh, 181; capture of, 114–15; legal proceedings and, 115–16, 119, 122–23, 125; Standing's murder and, 104, 131
Blair, Martha, 104, 131
Bloomington Leader (Illinois), 69
Bloomington Pantagraph (Illinois), 69
Book of Mormon, 1–2, 19
Boyle, Henry G., 18, 29, 46, 58
Bradley, Andy, 181; capture of, 114–15; legal proceedings and, 115–16, 119, 122–23, 125; Standing's murder and, 104–5
Bragg, Braxton, 12, 13
Brasstown Branch, North Carolina, 86–87
Brown, Anna, 46
Brown, Joseph E., 137–41, 154
Brunswick Herald, 144
"burned-over" district, 1
Butt, William B., 133
Byrum, James, 165
Byrum, Sarah May, 165

Calvinism, 30–31
Calvino, Italo, 151
Campbell, Duncan G., 158
Campbell, John, 82
Campbell, Rosalie, 158
Cane Creek Massacre, 142
Cassandra Branch, 23, 24, 165–67, 178
Catholics, 32, 41
Catoosa County, Ga., 1, 12, 13, 21, 23, 29
Catoosa Courier, 113
Chattanooga, Tenn., 8, 12, 13, 21
Chattanooga Times, 118
Chattooga County, Ga., 12, 98; Civil War in, 14, 16, 21, 26; converts in, 22–23, 35, 75, 152, 155–61; emigration from, 46, 50; Ku Klux Klan in, 71, 74; Morgan and, 9, 70, 76
Cherokee Nation, 12
Chicago Herald, 133
Chicago Times, 112
Chickamauga, 13, 21, 26
Church of Jesus Christ of Latter-day Saints: African Americans and, 29; "first principles" and, 19, 25; founding of, 1–2; gathering and, 3, 10, 42, 46–47, 50; missionaries to antebellum Georgia, 2; Native Americans and, 47; Reorganized Church and, 66–70; restorationism and, 2
Clark, Alfred, 103, 108–9
Clark, Benjamin "Ben," 105, 109
Clawson, Rudger, 91–93; defense of polygamy by, 95–96; funeral and, 111; imprisonment of, 146–47; legal proceedings and, 118–22; Standing's murder and, 98–110, 116, 126, 128, 150
Cleaveland, Kate, 103
Colorado colony, 6, 129, 142. *See also* Manassa
Colquitt, Alfred H., 97, 108, 114
Compromise of 1877, 27
Conejos County, Colo., 62–65
Congregationalists, 32
Connally, Nathaniel, 23, 78–80, 165, 171
Connally, Price, 23, 37, 165
converts: agriculture and, 35–36; Civil War and, 14–16, 22; emigration and, 46, 49–53, 87–88; land ownership of, 35–36, 38; mobility of, 38; pessimism of, 27, 34, 37, 39; polygamy practiced by, 130, 133; poverty of, 33, 35–38, 47, 54, 79, 201n19; slaveholding and, 15, 35; social bonds and, 23, 78, 80–83, 130–31, 152; taxes and, 37–38
converts, female: baptism of, 83–84; defenders of missionaries, 90–91, 106; descriptions of, 4, 94–95, 117, 132–33, 136, 144; heads-of-households and, 39–40, 202n27; household economies and, 35; Relief Society and, 76–78, 89–90, 152; threats against, 80, 106, 118–19
"cotton missionaries," 2
Cowley, Matthias, 74; anti-polygamy legislation and, 135; letters to, 84–85, 89–90, 96, 111, 130
Curry, John Thomas, 167

Dade Coal Company, 137
Dalton, Ga., 1, 12, 14
Daniel, John B., 38, 49, 76, 163, 169
Daniel, Martha, 163
Daniel, Mary Allen, 163

Daniel, Sabra, 163
Democrats, 26, 75, 71, 139
Dennington, Elias, 49–50, 55–56, 164
Dennington, Providence, 164
Denver and Rio Grande Railroad, 58, 61–62, 64
Denver Tribune, 106
Deseret News: on converts, 78; on emigration, 58, 60; mission reports in, 6, 9–10, 27, 86; on Standing's funeral, 111; on Standing's murder, 115–16; on threats, 73
Dillard, John A., 170
Dirt Town, Ga., 9
Disciples of Christ, 32
"Dixie" in Utah, 2
Douglas, Stephen, 14
Douglasville Star, 140

Echols, Amanda, 175
Echols, Ben, 175
Echols, Benjamin, 32–33, 175
Echols, Emily Jane (Weems), 175
Echols, John, 175
Echols, Lewis Barton, 174–75
Echols, Martin B., 175
Echols, Mary Minerva (Vincent), 142–44, 175–76
Echols, Samuel, 142–44, 175–76
Echols, Sarah Susan (Odom), 175
Edlefson, Edlef, 85, 87
Edmunds, George F., 147
Edmunds Act of 1882, 137–40, 145
Edmunds-Tucker Act of 1887, 147
elders. *See specific missionaries*
Elledge, Dillingham Horten, 80, 109, 169–75; emigration of, 99, 104, 131; Standing's murder and, 117, 181; wife and, 80, 89
Elledge, Elizabeth (Nations), 169–70, 172, 174–75; conversion of, 80–81, 89–90; Standing's murder and, 104, 114, 117
Elledge, George, 88
Elledge, Jane, 117, 126, 145
Emancipation Proclamation, 11
emigration, 88; anti-polygamy legislation and, 135; arrangements for, 47, 49, 58; converts and, 46, 49, 129; gathering and, 68; warnings against, 44–45
Episcopalians, 32, 41. *See also* Protestants
Evans, Milton, 62
extralegal violence: feuding and, 3, 40; guerrillas and, 16; lynching and, 73; moonshiners and, 3, 40, 71; private mob and, 4; southern tradition of, 2–3; whitecapping and, 3

Fannin County, Ga., 23, 29, 90, 97; converts in, 96, 176, 180; proselytizing in, 86–87, 90, 93, 98
Faucett, Alfonzo Cromwell, 166
Faucett, Elmira (Bowers), 166
Faucett, James "Jim," 105–6, 131
Faucett, James Merett, 36, 165–67
Faucett, Jesse Bartlett, 70, 165–66
Faucett, Martha Queen Victoria (Bailey), 166
Faucett, Victoria Coxwell, 165–66
"first principles," 19, 25
Floyd County, Ga.: African Americans in, 30; Armuchee Branch in, 161–63; Beech Creek Branch in, 163–64; Civil War in, 21; converts in, 23, 35–38, 76, 143, 156; emigration from, 49–52; headquarters in, 76, 86; Morgan to, 8; Pleasant Hill Church Branch in, 169; threats in, 73–74
Frost, William Goodell, 40
Fullbright, Sarah, 40, 81–83, 102; baptism of, 84; death of, 130; emigration of, 88, 129; Relief Society and, 89

Gatewood Scouts, 16
gathering, the, 3, 10, 42, 46–47, 50; Bible and, 68
Georgia anti-polygamy law. *See* anti-polygamy legislation
Georgia Conference, 46, 49, 110–11
Georgia, northwest: Civil War in, 14–16, 21–22; demographics of, 34–36, 199n9, 200n18; economy in, 33–34; emigration from, 43–46; females, unmarried, in, 39–40; Native Americans and, 12; optimism of New South boosters and, 27–28, 88–89; perception of healthfulness of, 28–29; "poor man's household" in, 35; population of African Americans in, 29, 34, 199n9; poverty in, 33–34, 200n18; religious diversity in, 31–33; Unionism in, 15–16, 21–22, 26
Georgia press. *See specific newspapers*
Grant, Ulysses S., 14
Green, Henry, 85
Groesbeck, Mellie, 17
Groesbeck, Nicholas, 17
Grove Oak Branch, Ala., 25, 49. *See also* Sand Mountain, Ala.
Guerrant, Edward O., 148
Guerry, DuPont, 134

Hackett, A. T., 119–20, 123, 125
Haggard, Albion, 83–84, 166
Haggard, Mary (Faucett), 83–84, 166

Hamblin, Elizabeth "Elviny" (Fullbright): baptism of, 84; conversion of, 82; emigration of, 88, 129; Standing's murder and, 102, 106, 117; threats to, 118
Hamblin, Martha, 129
Hamblin, Mary "Molly": emigration of, 129; Standing's murder and, 102, 106; testimony of, 109, 119; threats to, 118
Hansen, John H., 67, 69
Hardy, Charles W., 86–87, 89–90, 96, 111
Harney, Will Wallace, 7
Harrison, John D., 86
Haynie, Charles David, 161
Haynie, Emily Jane, 162
Haynie, Evergreen Taylor, 161
Haynie, Henrietta Paralee (Bagwell), 57, 60, 130, 162
Haynie, Joseph Pinkney, 50–51, 56–57, 130–31, 161, 163
Haynie, Patrick Calhoun "Pack," 38, 131, 156, 162; emigration of, 50–53, 57, 64; wives of, 60, 63, 130
Haynie, Robert Baskin, 38, 162
Haynie, Robert Milligan, 131, 162
Haynie, Susan (Weldon), 161
Haynie, William Luke, 162
Haywood Valley Branch: emigration from, 46, 50; establishment of, 9–10, 23; members of, 36, 49, 66, 155–61, 177–78
Hedrick, William L., 119
Heward, Teancum William, 111
Higham, Thomas, 86–87
Holland, Andrew J., 36, 167
Holston, Henry, 170, 172; Standing's murder and, 101–3, 107, 109–10, 114; testimony of, 109, 118–19; threats to, 118
Huffaker, Ignatius Henry, 98, 109, 170, 172; conversion of, 80, 84; emigration of, 87, 89, 130
Huffaker, Isaac Asbury, 172
Huffaker, J. H., 108
Huffaker, Martha Ann (Foster), 172
Huffaker, Mary Frances (Elledge), 80, 87, 130, 172
Huffaker, Matilda, 108
Huffaker, Sarah Riggins, 172–73
Hulse, Charles W., 96
Hunt, Alexander Cameron, 61
Hunter, Jefferson "Jeff," 105, 182
Hyde, Orson, 7

Invisible Cities (Calvino), 151

Jennings, Aquilla Melissa, 166
Jennings, Caleb, 35, 159–60
Jennings, John, 159, 167
Jennings, John P., 166–67
Jennings, Mary Jane, 159–61
Jensen, Hans, 64, 65
Johnson, Andrew S., 74, 85
Johnson and McCamy, 119
Johnston, Joseph E., 16
Jones, Loyal, 41
Jones, Sam, 33
Jonesborough Branch, 23, 24, 169–70, 179
Joseph Standing Memorial Park (Georgia), 150–51
"Josephites," 66–67, 70. *See also* Reorganized Church of Jesus Christ of Latter-day Saints
Juvenile Instructor, 73–74

Kaneaster, Fanny, 130
Kaneaster, Josiah (or Joseph), 173–74, 182; coroner's inquest and, 108; marriage of, 83–84, 89, 117, 129–31; Standing's murder and, 104; threats to, 97, 101
Kaneaster, Robert Cochran, 129
Kaneaster, Sarah (Hamblin), 171, 173; baptism of, 83–84; death of, 130; emigration of, 88, 129; marriage of, 117, 129; missionaries and, 91, 103; Relief Society and, 89; threats to, 97, 102
Kaneaster, William Lonzo, 130, 171, 173; conversion of, 81–82; missionaries and, 91; Standing's murder and, 109; threats to, 97–98, 101–2, 115, 118
Keel, Elizabeth, 159
Keel, James Ransom, 159–60
Kilgore, James Patten, 167
Kilgore, Mary Caroline (Anderson), 77, 168
Kilgore, William C., 36, 49, 74, 168
Kirtland, Bird Jackson, 60, 64
Ku Klux Klan, 70, 71, 74, 78

Lamanites, 47. *See also* Church of Jesus Christ of Latter-day Saints
Lawrence, Sinai Ann, 159–60
Lawrence, Thomas Anderson, 35, 49, 156, 159–60
LDS Church. *See* Church of Jesus Christ of Latter-day Saints
Lee, Arminta Missouri, 144
Lee, John D., 93
Lincoln, Abraham, 10
Lisonbee, James Thompson, 77; baptism, of female converts, and, 84; death of, 55; emigration and, 46–49, 51–53; Grove Oak Branch and, 25; Morgan

and, 25–26; United Order and, 25. *See also* Grove Oak Branch; Sand Mountain, Ala.
Littlejohn, Francis A. (Daniel), 169
Littlejohn, Thomas A., 38, 164, 169
Liverpool Mercury, 107
Lloyd, Thomas, 96
Loggins, Elizabeth, 89, 97, 101, 131, 173
Loggins, Riley, 89, 97–98, 101, 131
Lookout Mountain, 14
"lustful lout," Standing as, 116, 154

Manassa, Colo., 3, 6, 129, 142–46. *See also* Colorado colony
Manning, Joanna "Joan," 76, 164
Manning, Mary Caroline (Barbour), 164
Manning, Thomas, 164
Manning, William R., 23, 35–37, 73, 164
Marietta Journal, 116
Marshal, Tabitha, 77, 160–61
Marshal, William L., 35, 158–62; baptism of, 22; Civil War and, 15; emigration of, 51, 55–56
Martin, Endymeon, 108
Martin, John S., 105, 173, 182
McCallister, John D. H., 18
McClure, "Mac," 105
McCutchen, Cicero D., 115, 119, 122–23, 125
McKinney, L.T.D., 169
McKinney, S. Murphy, 52
McLemore's Cove Branch, 24, 36, 74, 167–69, 178–79
Memphis Avalanche, 93
Methodists, 30–31, 66, 122; anti-Mormonism of, 116; missions of, 41. *See also* Protestants
millennialism, 42
Miller, Joaquin, 136
missionaries. *See specific missionaries*
missionaries in southern states, 18, 74, 85–87, 91, 96, 128; accusations against, 94–95, 113–14, 116–17, 126, 132–33, 154; gospel preached by, 19–20, 25, 31–33; opposition to, 10, 70–71, 73–75, 90–91, 99; polygamy practiced by, 145–47; polygamy preached by, 19–20, 25, 31–33; proselytizing of, 18–20, 25; Reorganized Church and, 66–67, 69–70; revelation regarding, 18; as threat to household, 3–4
Missionary Ridge, 14
Mississippi, 137
Mitchell, A. Henry, 168
Mitchell, Matilda, 168
Mobile, Ala., 28
Mooney, John R., 161
Moore, W. K., 119, 123, 125

Morgan, John Hamilton, 10; African Americans and, 30; anti-polygamy legislation and, 135, 141, 147; Civil War and, 10–17; death of, 148; documents of, 6; dream of, 8–9; emigration and, 46–53, 78–79, 86–87, 129–30; and establishment of Georgia mission, 9, 25–34; gathering and, 68; Haywood Valley Branch and, 23; legal proceedings and, 115, 118–20, 123, 125; Lisonbee and, 25; Morgan, Annie Mildred Smith, and, 145; Morgan, Mellie Groesbeck, and, 145; Morgan Commercial College and, 17, 86; "Plan of Salvation" and, 76; plural marriage and, 68–69; poverty and, 33–35; Protestants and, 31–33; Reorganized Church and, 66–70; and Southern States Mission, call to, 18; —, presidency of, 58, 66; ; —, release of, 86, 147; Standing and, 20, 74; Standing's funeral and, 111; Standing's murder and, 110; threats against, 70–75, 85; Varnell's Station Branch and, 79–82, 84
"Mormon Question, the," 5, 154
Mormonism. *See* Church of Jesus Christ of Latter-day Saints
Mormonism, opposition to. *See* anti-Mormonism; anti-polygamy legislation
Morrell, Joseph, 29
Mountain Meadows Massacre, 93
Moyers, Bailey, 169
Moyers, Cornelia (Bailey), 169
Moyers, Curtis, 169
Moyers, Felix Burnie, 49, 50–52, 55–56, 169
Moyers, Sarah "Sallie," 51, 169
Murphy, Delila F., 52
Murphy, Thomas E., 23, 52–53
Murray County Gazette, 95

Nashville World, 144
Nations, David Dalton "Dave," 104, 131
Nations, Jasper N. "Newt," 104, 125, 131, 173, 183; capture of, 114–15; legal proceedings and, 119–20; Standing's murder and, 104
Nations, John A., 80–81, 131, 174
Nations, Joseph W. "Joe," 104, 131
Nations, Manley, 81, 115, 131
Nations, Mary J. (Huffaker), 131, 174
Nations, Isabella (Kaneaster), 131
Nations, Thomas Jefferson, 88, 118–19, 126, 174–75; capture, of mob, 114; legal proceedings, 115
Nations, William T. "Bill," 104

newspapers, Georgian: *Brunswick Herald*, 144; *Catoosa Courier*, 113; *Douglasville Star*, 140–41; *Marietta Journal*, 116; *Murray County Gazette*, 95; *North Georgia Citizen*, 95, 113; *Rome Tri-Weekly Courier*, 113–14. See also *Atlanta Constitution*
newspapers, non-Georgian: *Baltimore Gazette*, 128; *Chattanooga Times*, 118; *Chicago Herald*, 133; *Chicago Times*, 112; *Memphis Avalanche*, 94–95; *Nashville World*, 144; *New Haven Register*, 112; *New York Herald*, 112; *St. Louis Post and Dispatch*, 129. See also *Deseret News*
New Haven Register, 112
New Mexico, 47–48, 51, 58
New Orleans, La., 28
New South, 6, 27–28, 73
New York Herald, 112
North, Charley, 114
North Georgia Citizen, 88, 95, 99, 113

Owenby, Jonathan, 103, 105, 109, 118–19

Parks, James G., 134
Parry, Joseph Hyrum, 86–87, 98
Payne, Artimesia, 167
Payne, Frank, 36, 167
Payne, Jane, 36, 167
Payne, W. H., 119
"peculiar people," 7, 40, 154
Peery, David H., 18
Peterson, Lawrence Marcus, 59
Pigeon Mountain, 14
"Plan of Salvation, The," 76
Pleasant Hill Church Branch, 24, 164, 169, 179
plural marriage, 41, 188n2. See also polygamy
Poland Act, 93
Polk County, Ga., 23, 29, 85, 142, 175–76
poll tax, 37
polygamy, 75, 85, 95, 113, 143; discontinued, 5; missionaries and, 68–69; practice of, 4, 41; Reorganized Church and, 67, 69; testimony about, 122, 146–47
polygamy, legislation opposing. See antipolygamy legislation
Presbyterians, 32, 66, 119, 138; anti-Mormonism of, 149; missions of, 41, 148. See also Protestants
Price, Rex Thomas, 33
Protestant clergy, anti-Mormonism of, 31, 73, 75, 85; defense of mob, 115; role in violence, 116

Protestants, 6, 148–49. See also specific denominations
Pueblo, Colo., 64–65; winter quarters in, 48, 53–59, 61–63
Puryear, F. M., 46

Rainey, David P., 18
Rataree, Alex, 120
Reconstruction, 6, 40, 75
Redeemers, 26, 37, 71
Reid, Marcus De Lafayette, 162
Reid, Nancy (Ramsey), 162
Relief Society, 76–78, 89, 152
"Reorganites," 66
Reorganized Church of Jesus Christ of Latter-day Saints: converts and, 157, 169; Joseph Smith III and, 66–69; missionaries of, 66–67, 69–70
Republicans, 26, 75, 139
Restorationism, 2
Reynolds v. U.S., 93
Reynolds, George, 93
Ringgold, Georgia, 12, 13, 27
Roach, Jonathan, 168
Roane Iron Company, 28
Roberson, John N., 176
Rock Springs Branch, 165
Rockmart Branch, 175–76, 180
Rome, Ga.: African Americans and, 30; converts and, 14, 36–37, 51, 86–87, 164; headquarters in, 133, 136; legal proceedings and, 118, 143; Morgan, prophetic dream, and, 8–9, 21–22
Rome Tri-Weekly Courier, 98, 113
Romney, Miles, 19
Rosecrans, William S., 11

St. Louis Post and Dispatch, 129
Salt Lake Herald, 61, 123
San Luis Valley, Colo., 59, 61, 63
Sand Mountain, Ala., 14, 25, 49, 84. See also Grove Oak Branch
Savage, C. R., 20
Schultz, William P., 1
Scottsboro, Ala., 48, 51–52
"Sealed unto Him" (Miller), 136
Second Great Awakening, 1, 30
Sellers, Daniel R., emigration of, 50, 53, 55, 64–65; Grove Oak Branch and, 49; United Order and, 55–56, 61–63
Sellers, Hugh, 60
Sellers, Samuel, 60
Shapiro, Henry D., 7, 41
Sherman, William T., 14, 21, 88–89
Shumate and Williamson, 119–21, 126
Smalley, John, 36, 167–68
Smith, A. S. "Jud," 105, 108

Smith, David, 105
Smith, Joseph, Jr.,: as church founder, 1–2; murder of, 2; presidential campaign of, 2; as prophet, 2, 187n2; Relief Society and, 76; Reorganized Church and, 66; revelations of, 18, 138; United Order and, 25
Smith, Joseph, III, 66, 67. *See also* Reorganized Church of Jesus Christ of Latter-day Saints
Smith, Lot, 46
Smith, Lucy Jane (Barbour), 161
Smith, Ralph, 85
Smith, Walter, 161
Smith's Chapel, 80–81
Southern Highlander and His Homeland, The (Campbell), 82
Southern States Mission: Boyle and, 46; establishment of, 18; in Georgia, 6; headquarters of, 76, 136; Lisonbee and, 25; missionaries of, 2, 18, 111, 128, 175; Morgan and, 18, 58, 66, 110, 135; polygamy and, 68–69; reputation for violence of, 2; Spry and, 147; Standing and, 20
Spencer, Lydia, 146
"spiritual carpetbaggers," 3, 75
Spry, William, 147
Standing, Joseph, 20, 84–85, 87; as companion, 20, 74; funeral and monument to, 124–27; monument, Georgia, to, 150; seduction, accusations of, 90, 117; and Southern States Mission, call to, 18
Standing, Joseph, murder of: account of, 103–9; arrests for, 114–15; as benefit to mission, 129, 132; coroner's inquest and, 108–9; explanations for, 1–5, 104–5, 152–54; legal proceedings and, 118–26
Stewart, James Z., 58, 62–63
Stock Hill Branch, 24, 176, 180
Stover, Cornelius Jasper, 176
Stover, Joseph Rudger, 95
Stover, Lydia Belinda, 176
Stover, Palmina (McDaniel), 176
"A Strange Land and Peculiar People," in *Lippincott's Magazine*, 7
Street, Samuel, 1
Summerville, Ga., 14
Sutherland, Amos S., 108–9

Taylor, John, 87; anti-polygamy legislation and, 135; colonization and, 49, 54, 63, 79; Standing's murder and, 111
Taylor's Ridge, 14
Teasdale, George, 18

Tennessee: anti-polygamy legislation in, 137; Cane Creek Massacre in, 142
Texas, 47
Tinsley, James, 105
Tucker, John Randolph, 147
"twin relics of barbarism," 75

Unionism, in Georgia, 15, 21, 26
United Order, 25, 55
United Order of Pueblo, 55, 65
Universalists, 32
Uptain, Sariahann, 84

Varnell's Station Branch, 117, 152; converts in, 40, 78–80, 82, 87–89; emigration of, 119, 129; members of, 170–75, 179–80; violence in, 97, 104–5, 107–8, 153

Walker County, Ga., 79; accusations from, 117; baptism in, 83; Cassandra Branch in, 23, 165–67; churches in, 32; converts in, 36–37, 77, 105, 152; debate over Reorganized Church, in, 70; emigration from, 46; Ku Klux Klan in, 70, 74, 78; McLemore's Cove Branch in, 167–69; Rock Springs Branch in, 165
Warren, J. W., 97
Wasatch Engine Company, 20
Weldon, Francis Marion, 50–51, 56, 131, 161–63
Weldon, Hardy, 163
Weldon, Mary Jane (Trammel), 163
Wells, William B., 119
Western and Atlantic Railroad, 12, 13, 137
Whitfield County, Ga., 12; accused from, 181–82, 184; Civil War in, 21; converts in, 80; legal proceedings in, 118–20; murder in, 1, 101, 105; posse from, 114–15; threats in, 96–98; Varnell's Station Branch in, 170–75, 185
Whitley, John Thomas, 168
Whitney, Orson, 126
Wife No. 19; or, The Story of a Life in Bondage, Being a Complete Expose of Mormonism, and Revealing the Sorrows, Sacrifices and Sufferings of Women in Polygamy (Young), 93
Wilder, John T., 11, 28, 148
Wilder's Lightning Brigade, 13, 22, 148
Williams, Brittain, 80, 90, 104
Williams, David, 69, 74
Williams, David W., 80, 104, 131, 174
Williams, Nancy (Blair), 104, 131, 174
Wilson, George W., 49–51, 56, 62, 161–62
Wilson, Mary Elma "Ellie," 130
Wilson, Samuel Tyndale, 148

Winder, John R., 18
Winther, Oscar Osburn, 14
Woodruff, Wilford, 147

yellow fever, 28–29, 79
York, Tennessee (Graham), 168
York, William Dallas, 168
Young, Brigham: colonization and, 46, 48; conversion and, 38–39; death of, 49; divorce and, 93; letters from, 20, 46–47; Morgan and, 8–9, 17; Reorganized Church and, 66–67; United Order and, 25, 55–56
Young Men's Improvement Association, 126

Zion, 4, 6, 38, 42, 47

www.ingramcontent.com/pod-product-compliance
Lightning Source LLC
Chambersburg PA
CBHW010926180426
43192CB00043B/2783